Praise for *Till I Die*

'A thought-provoking, funny and ultimately heartbreaking book about how football fandom can evoke our most painful emotions.'

Dr Gwen Adshead, *Sunday Times* bestselling author of *The Devil You Know*

'Whether you're a football fan or a student of human behaviour – or both – Damien Pearse is funny about his own obsession and serious about what it reveals. In *Till I Die,* he traces his quest to understand why we surrender to a game so stingy with its goals and so generous with its capacity to ruin a season, a year, a decade. A book for anyone who has ever screamed at a television and wondered, briefly, why.'

Adam Alter, *New York Times* bestselling author of *Drunk Tank Pink*

'A unique, sharply written and highly engaging exploration of why we love the game as we do. Pearse is a fine storyteller with an eye for compelling human stories and interesting characters, all of them united through this obsession of ours.'

Daniel Gray, author of *Saturday, 3pm*

'Funny and brutally honest, this is a wonderful globe-trotting journey of self-discovery and an exploration of the tribal psychology of football fandom... Rich in anecdotes, humour and introspection, this is a story that transcends clubs, countries and cultures.'

Kieron Brady, former player for Sunderland AFC

'Absolutely brilliant.'

Dan Tester, author of *Brighton & Hove Albion On This Day*

'Nothing matches the brutality and viciousness of tribal violence. If you want insight into how tribal psychology and conflict, from religions to politics to sport, can lead us to lose our humanity and compassion, this is a brilliantly observed map of the dark side of the mind. A must-read.'

Professor Paul Gilbert OBE, author of *The Compassionate Mind*

'An insightful and sometimes disturbing examination of football passion. Damien has talked candidly with the tragic victims of the game's excesses, as well as explaining its roots. A work of great depth.'

Steve Gordos, former sports editor,
Wolverhampton Express & Star

'Really fun read... It's a question I've asked myself a lot. Why do we care so much? This book is very relatable, especially as Damien talks about his own emotions and feelings.'

Harry Mansell, host of *The Wolves 77 Club* podcast

'Have you ever worried that your partner loves football more than they love you? This book will help you understand why.'

Harvey Whitehouse, author of *Inheritance* and
Chair of Social Anthropology at the University of Oxford

'Much like a great game of football, this erudite, funny and well-informed book stays with you long after the final whistle... proves that our football terraces can be every bit as intellectually stimulating as our libraries... only with better chants and worse toilets.'

Dr Jon Stewart, author of *Dylan, Lennon, Marx and God*

TILL I DIE

Why Football Means Everything (even when it shouldn't)

Dr Damien Pearse

ONEWORLD

A Oneworld Book

First published by Oneworld Publications Ltd in 2026

A CIP record for this title is available from the British Library

ISBN 978-1-83643-263-0
eISBN 978-1-83643-264-7

Typeset by Geethik technologies
Printed and bound in Great Britain by Clays Ltd, Elcograf S.p.A.

The authorised representative in the EEA is eucomply OU,
Pärnu mnt 139b–14, 11317 Tallinn, Estonia
(email: hello@eucompliancepartner.com / phone: +33757690241)

Oneworld Publications Ltd
10 Bloomsbury Street
London WC1B 3SR
England

Contents

For Harriet, Mum, Dad, Fiona, Ben, Louis and Finlay.

'Football? Aren't we fucking lucky to have it? I mean of all the stupid things which, as a post-religious secular society, we could have alighted upon to be our font of meaning in a meaningless world. Fuck – it could have been golf. Think how awful that would be! It could have been golf. My God.'

David Goldblatt

INTRODUCTION

The Unravelling of a Grown Man

It's 16 September 2023, and Wolves are playing Liverpool at Molineux. I'm streaming the game illegally in my upstairs office in Hastings. I am a psychologist, someone who spends his days preaching mindfulness to patients who are frazzled, traumatised and overwhelmed. 'Thoughts are just thoughts,' I tell them, 'like clouds – they come, they go.' It's a mantra I've recited so often at my clinic it ought to be true. 'Emotions,' I add, 'are guests at a dinner party. Welcome them all, and they'll leave when it's time.'

But not today. Today, emotions are storming the gates.

Against the odds, Wolves score first. The players explode, arms outstretched. They point skywards, then to each other – thump the badge on their chests. Some pretend they are cradling babies. These are strange, choreographed celebrations, both ridiculous and sublime.

I roar with joy, unsettling the little dog curled up on my lap. He yawns in a deeply exaggerated way. It is a yawn that I know from the puppy trainer means, 'You're making me anxious, you unstable lunatic.' My wife calls up the two flights of stairs. 'Are you OK, babe?' 'We scored!' I bellow back. 'That's brilliant,' she replies. But I barely register.

I shout the goalscorer's name – Hwang Hee-chan. Last week I hated him. He was useless and lazy; what is the actual point of him? But today, all is forgiven. His face looks familiar now – someone I might have known at school or worked with long ago.

A blurry figure from a half-remembered summer. They all seem like that – distant yet intimately known.

For a few seconds, it feels like they're playing for me – as though years of loyalty and disappointment have finally accrued enough credit for this single, perfect moment. I forget that they're at least half my age – some so alarmingly young they could conceivably be my grandsons. I also forget that none of them were born in Wolverhampton. Not even close.

Right now, none of that matters. We're bound by something deeper. The players belong to me, and I to them, as surely as if we'd grown up on the same rain-slick streets, Wolverhampton in our blood like soot in the lungs.

My sister-in-law and thirteen-year-old nephew are in the kitchen downstairs. Occasionally, I hear the pitter-patter of his feet on the stairs. Has he been sent as an emissary? A sacrificial lamb? No – he's a human barometer, dispatched to gauge the developing weather system building ominously in the loft extension. I spot his blond choirboy haircut and big brown eyes as he peeks around the door, observing me, rigid in my recently purchased away strip, vermilion red with a gold trim. He knows not to ask the score. Too risky. 'Everything OK, Uncle Dame?' he asks. 'Yes, mate,' I say, raising a thumb. 'All good here, Barney.' He's obviously very concerned. Kids feel the atmosphere even if they don't understand it.

I'm looking back at the screen now but he lingers, studying me. There's something touching and heartbreaking about his attentiveness. He knows this game means more than it should. I give him a cursory glance, a fake smile, as if to say, *do you have anything else to say?* – and, as his head recedes from the tiny crack in the door, I feel a flicker of guilt. And then relief to be able to return to the tangled web of pixels – red, old gold and black

– shifting across my screen. The only remaining interruption is my laptop's slowly buffering circle of doom.

Wolves are 1-0 up at half-time.

I know that the next forty-five or so minutes will determine my wife's birthday. My post-match mood will bleed into everything. It will flavour the family meal, the cake, the film she's picked out. It will infect how I carry myself on the errand she's asked me to do.

My wife comes up the stairs with a cup of tea for me. She asks the score. 'We're winning 1-0,' I say. 'Great,' she replies, knowing not to make the mistake of being too enthusiastic too soon. We've developed a sort of tacit understanding. I can tell she's worried about how I'll react if things unravel in the second half. There's tension in the house: unspoken, oppressive.

'You're not alone,' she says gently. 'Your sister in Wolverhampton is watching too.'

She knows I bang on about connection all the time. That I tell patients to reach out, that isolation should be avoided where possible. But there's a hint of trepidation in her voice, the kind that only develops when you've lived with someone long enough to know that yes, they may preach mindfulness for a living – but when it comes to football, their emotional stability is . . . flimsy.

And then she momentarily forgets that I'm actually really not okay. She wants to talk about picking up a clock from the DPD depot. And I want to shout, CAN'T YOU SEE I'M ABOUT TO LOSE MY FUCKING MIND OVER A GAME OF FOOTBALL?

Instead, I grunt a vague acknowledgement. If we can just hold on for the next forty-five minutes, I might have the emotional strength to pick up a clock. If Wolves lose, I won't. Simple as that.

The game ticks on. We concede a goal in the 55th minute – Cody Gakpo – but a draw is still a positive outcome. I can handle a draw. 'Thoughts are just thoughts,' I mutter to myself, staring at the ceiling. 'Like clouds . . . they come, they go.' But with fifteen minutes left, I notice my body is betraying me. I am shaking.

My dog, Crackle, a little bundle of nerves himself, is still curled up in my lap, and his tiny, fluffy head starts rattling in rhythm with my jiggling thigh. I don't even notice I'm doing it, at first. I'm locked in some sort of involuntary frenzy, and I can't stop it. I'm supposed to be the calm one.

I try to breathe. I focus on my exhale – out-breaths fractionally longer than the in-breaths.

This, I tell my patients, kick-starts the parasympathetic nervous system. Longer out-breaths should override the alarm bells going off in my amygdala.

I shift my focus to the dog and the soft rise and fall of his chest, a black and furry metronome.

There are five minutes to go before the ninety's up. Everything depends on this.

I imagine being able to watch *Match of the Day* tonight, maybe even the repeat tomorrow morning, coffee in hand, pain au raisin flaked on my dressing gown, legs crossed like a man who's got his life together. If we draw, I can listen to talkSPORT on the radio during the week. I can enjoy the Sunday game on Sky Sports. I can listen to the two lads from the local Wolverhampton paper – Liam and Nathan – dissecting the game on YouTube. The world remains open. I imagine the birthday dinner tonight with Barney and the gang – peaceful, pleasant even. The soft hum of domestic calm. It will all be okay . . . if we can just hold on to the draw.

As we tick into the final five minutes, it becomes unbearable. I'm sweating. And then there's a voice – small and desperate. It's a child I can hear inside me now, whimpering: *Please. Please. Please.*

The ball hits the net with a thud, like a kick to the stomach. Andy bastard Robertson. He wheels away, roars down the pitch, mouth agape, fists clenched, punching the air. Some bow before him, mock-serious. It's preposterous, worse because of how effortless it seems, as though this is how life's supposed to work: talent rewarded, adulation guaranteed. I sit stiffly, fists clenched in my lap. Childish idiots. Show-offs. I hate them. I hate how easy they make it look. I hate their tanned, sculpted, muscular legs, their haircuts, their proficient cardiovascular systems. I hate how much they seem to be enjoying themselves.

I storm out of the room, warning the dog: 'Don't you follow me!' I mutter something about him being a selfish scavenger as I shut the door. It's a petty, meaningless victory, but it'll do.

There's something especially undignified about sulking without an audience, and my sense of guilt deepens when I acknowledge the truth: I'm in a face-off with a Cavapoo. It's not even a proper face-off, because the gentle scratching on the door has stopped and I imagine he's moved from my office chair to the more comfortable IKEA chair, the one I reserve for patients. He's probably curled up there now, half-asleep, as if to prove his nonchalance.

I storm back in, seething. I know enough forensic psychology to understand that cruelty to animals is a red flag. So I tell myself that what happens next is an accident. I pretend I don't notice as my thigh brushes against Crackle. He squeals, a perfectly reasonable response to being nudged by a fully-grown adult. But instead of apologising like a normal person, I snarl: 'Stop being so pathetic.'

The words hang in the air. Normally, this room allows me to peel back the layers of the toxic shame felt by my patients, offering kindness where I can. Here I am now, shaming a dog, the only creature in the house too small and too loyal to fight back.

It's pitiful.

We lose 3-1. A deflected own goal from Hugo Bueno seals it. Within seconds, I've clicked off the stream – shutting it down like I'm cutting flow from a burst sewage pipe. I grumble something borderline xenophobic about the Southeast Asian commentary. There really is little point trying to sugarcoat it now. This could ruin the rest of the weekend for everyone.

I grab my phone and head straight for the Wolves lads' WhatsApp group. Now, there are certain unspoken rules in these groups. Rule number one: if we lose, don't start with any of that measured, diplomatic bunk. I'm not in the group to offer rational critiques or constructive feedback. I'm here to rant, to vent, to release my rage.

The messages are already flying in. Some are balanced and encouraging – too encouraging. 'We gave it a good go,' someone writes, which is nonsense. Others are outright angry, but it's not enough for me. I ham out furious critiques of Gary O'Neil, our poor, beleaguered manager, who has been standing haplessly on the touchline, arms folded, looking like a man watching his car slowly slide into a canal.

'Fucking clueless,' I type. 'No tactics. No fight. What was that line-up? Was he picking players at random? Blindfolded?' And it feels good – like slamming a door when you're furious. And like sharks smelling blood, the others join in. We don't just condemn; we eviscerate him – Gary, the human piñata. For some reason, I click back onto the stream. I can see Wolves fans in the stadium doing their bit too, serenading the manager with, 'You're getting sacked in the morning.' It's brutal. And I love it. I feel a slither of relief. The shame isn't on me any more. It's on Gary.

And frankly, he deserves it. 'Yes,' I think. 'This is it. This feels better.'

'Wankers,' I type. On a roll now. 'We are shit.' But then – ping. A reply.

'I don't agree,' my mate writes. He proceeds to lay out, in painstakingly measured tones, a defence of our makeshift team. Injuries, financial constraints, unfair expectations and so on. His message is so long, so unrelentingly compassionate and fair, that it makes me want to scream. I stare at the words, my jaw tightening, eyes narrowed so much I can barely see. I should say something conciliatory, perhaps. Maybe I should acknowledge his optimism. But I don't want to. This is not the time for hope or perspective. This is the time for venom. I need him to join me in hating everything – the referee, the manager, the players, the rain, the concept of football itself.

What I really want to do is to tell him to fuck off. Instead, I shove my phone on the desk and sit there, stewing. Rumination is the arch villain to mental health. It's at the root of so much that causes us distress, especially depression and rage. I indulge it with abandon.

The camera pans to Jürgen Klopp. It goes in close, like the cameraman wants to personally humiliate me – zooming in on that massive grin, the exuberant fist pump, those blinding, horse-white teeth; a Cheshire Cat in a Nike tracksuit.

I suck my teeth. I hate him. It's not dislike or irritation, it's actual, burning hatred. And yes, Klopp is, by all accounts, one of the nicest humans around, the sort of bloke who'd help push your car if it broke down in a snowstorm.

'Klopp is a cunt,' I type.

Surely, someone will validate me and voice their agreement, a thumbs up, anything?

Nothing.

I sit there, staring at the phone screen for a while, prodding it occasionally to keep the light on. I still haven't mastered the timeout settings and how these interact with battery life.

Anyway, WhatsApp is no longer meeting my needs. I need something bigger. I head to one of the Wolves Facebook forums, where tens of thousands of fans await. There must be others in there, feeling as delirious as me. I scroll through, gauging the reactions. My body starts to relax. A grin widens on my face. It's a coliseum of rage.

Fans are baying for blood; insults flying as effortlessly as forks in a prison canteen riot. Ridicule, hyperbole – the uncensored cruelty is disturbingly soothing, and each post is a balm for my emotional pain.

One fan suggests replacing Gary O'Neil with a traffic cone, and I laugh. Someone else throws Stevie Wonder's name into the mix, and I laugh harder. By the time someone suggests Phillip Schofield, I'm practically giddy.

PART I

The Man Who Punched Jack Grealish

1

Anyone Out There?

I'm on a dog walk in February and feeling the impact of another Wolves loss on my mood.

It's my usual circuit from a Saxon church, about 5 miles from Hastings; through the cemetery, past the pond, across open fields and looping back through woods where bluebells would soon stage their slow-motion resurrection.

It is one of those crisp, cloudless winter days when the blackbirds return, convincing you that spring might have arrived early. But my mind notices nothing of the beauty around me. As I crunch along the cemetery path, the dog jumps up for the ball, leaving a paw print on my jeans.

'I haven't got the fucking ball,' I snap. 'I left it in the car.' He does it again. I'm easily irritated.

Before I get to the meadow, I sit down on a bench in the graveyard under a small oak tree. I fail to register why it's there because my head is busy wrestling with an idea.

The emotional turbulence of being a football fan had been going on for years now, decades even, giving me moments of euphoria, but also ruining countless weekends. Not just for me, but for those around me too.

It was hard to justify, really.

Of course, I could understand why I might feel a little disappointed if Wolves lost or pleased if they won, but the profundity of my mood swings were disproportionate for an adult.

I didn't even live in Wolverhampton anymore and these were a bunch of young men who wouldn't recognise me if I walked into the home dressing room with their names tattooed on my forehead.

Why does a win feel like I've popped an ecstasy tablet, and a loss like I've been hurled into an emotional pit with no exit ramp? Where does all this rage come from?

And why am I compelled to watch games week after week, even when I know that the likelihood of feeling better at the end is low.

Sitting on the bench, I started to wonder if I could use some of the skills I had picked up over the course of my career to unravel this mess.

I have been a journalist for many news organisations, including the *Wolverhampton Express & Star*, the *Press Association*, the *Guardian* and *Sky News*. I have even dabbled in sports reporting and followed England football hooligans during international tournaments.

Over the last 15 years, I have learned to unpick the messy knots of the human mind as a therapist, working in the NHS and now privately as a trauma specialist.

What if I used these skills to address the question: *Why does football matter so much?*

Behind me, a blackbird starts up again, as optimistic as a pre-season football fan. The dog drops something indistinguishable and damp at my feet and looks up, expectant. I ignore him.

Where do I begin with this project?

I already had some data from the Liverpool game, where I'd made notes tracking what felt like a disturbing experience. In fact, I'd already sketched the bones of what would become the introduction to this book. But before disappearing into a

90,000-word exercise in navel-gazing, I needed to know if I was a bit of an outlier, a fringe lunatic, languishing in my away kit, many football pitches away from the normal distribution. Or was this affliction – this compulsive, all-consuming emotional chaos – something lots of *other people* were suffering with as well? I don't think asking a few mates on WhatsApp will cut it. At best, that's a biased sample, fewer than twenty men, all from the same Catholic state school in Wolverhampton, emotionally stunted in strikingly similar ways. So I decide to go wider and test my premise on the Facebook group where I'd recently been complicit in Gary O'Neil's humiliation. That might give me some proper data.

I write: 'Hi, everyone. I'm writing a book about the madness of being a football fan, from the perspective of a psychologist. I want to answer questions like "Why does this game make me so dysregulated?" I want to check I'm not some weird, maladjusted oddball. I want to explore the emotions and behaviours other fans experience. What bemuses you about being a fan?'

Then I brace myself, genuinely uncertain of what I'll get back. These forums can get toxic very quickly. I am expecting abuse, some unpleasant trolling at the very least. The child in me covers his face and prepares for digital annihilation.

I wait.

I set off into the meadow, the low sun spilling over the wood ahead. I am glued to my phone, neck in a U-bend, arms tense, breathing shallowly. Will I be ignored? Laughed at? Maybe I'll be reported to the group's admin for misusing the forum.

Five minutes pass. Nothing. I jab at my phone, refreshing the page with the frantic concentration of someone typing at high speed with one finger. The familiar weight of shame begins to stir in my stomach. I reach the edge of the woods feeling anxious.

I loop back towards the church, barely registering the snowdrops and daffodils jostling for space beneath the naked trees. Glancing up from my phone, I spot a group of walkers heading towards me, clutching poles, chatting, laughing, entirely at home in the landscape.

I suddenly feel self-conscious.

As they pass, I tuck the phone into my pocket and offer a hearty, countryside grin. I make some wholesome remark about the promise of spring.

They nod. And as soon as they are safely out of range, I pull the phone out again.

Still nothing. I begin to suspect I really am an outlier – a man whose idiosyncratic childhood attachment style has subtly but thoroughly warped his experience of fandom. It's been ten minutes since I posted the message, and the church tower reappears through the trees at the end of my circuit.

By the time I reach the cemetery, mumbling half-hearted apologies to the dog for forgetting the ball, there are signs of life. A few likes.

Just as I crunch on to the gravel path again, I get an actual comment.

'My rage,' one man admits. 'My irrational hatred of referees,' another offers.

And then – as if they'd all been waiting for permission – the dam breaks.

Dozens of replies. Then hundreds.

'The ability we have to go from one extreme emotion to the exact opposite in seconds,' writes Matthew.

'The hate of the official when they appear to cheat against us worries me,' says Dean.

'I left at half-time at Liverpool recently,' he continues. 'Because I felt sure I would run on the pitch if Simon Hooper (the referee) came near us. I'm never violent. Can't even fight, to be fair, but something about football affects my brain.'

'How can we go from several days of depression after a disappointing loss to a feeling of optimism by the following Saturday?' asks Colin. There's despair, conspiracy theories, hatred of officials, unbridled joy, arrogance, pure, unfiltered rage, schadenfreude, relationship stress. The data was pouring in.

Then, something stranger happens. Private messages begin to arrive with friend requests. My phone is pinging constantly. People wanted to confess.

There were fans who said that they loved football as much as their children and partners. There were some who had planned weddings around fixture lists and skipped funerals for cup ties. There were those that had grieved the transfer of a player they'd never met but somehow loved.

One woman messaged me in desperation:

'I'm so sorry I have hacked this group but we're on the verge of divorce. He's obsessed. It's like I don't exist.'

She gave an intimate account of their physical disconnection, finishing with a single, aching question:

'Can you help me understand?'

Some wanted to meet me in person.

'Let me buy you dinner,' one man suggested. 'I can meet you before the game. I'd like to talk about this.'

Others asked for professional help, as if, as a mental health professional, I held the antidote to whatever this unnamed affliction was. And then there was John, who describes himself as an ex-hooligan. He travels two hundred miles from Cardiff to see

Wolves play for every home game. He tells me he's moved his season ticket to the quieter upper tier of one of the stands – not for the view, but to protect himself.

'I deliberately moved up to avoid emotional extremes,' he says. 'But VAR, and the incompetent refereeing has me back in the red mist zone. Only the fact I'm high up stops me from doing something mad.'

I stare at my phone, amazed at how honest and open people are being.

'It takes me several hours to come back to normal,' John goes on. 'But the strange thing is – away from the ground, I'm seen as a really nice guy. I don't feel like a nice guy. My fiancée keeps begging me to grow up. She says I'm making myself ill. She keeps asking: why don't you just give up your season ticket?'

Making himself ill. I could relate.

I believe most people who know me would consider me relatively sane, wise, even. Friends call me when they are in crisis. Some – especially my patients – might go so far as to describe me as calm. I've spent weeks on silent retreats – in far-flung exotic places – cultivating equanimity, that quality where you retain a state of mental balance, regardless of the external circumstances. But as in John's case, football seemed to bypass all of that maturity and wisdom. It distorted my personality, as if I was being hijacked by a younger, more volatile version of myself – one less interested in reflection and more interested in screaming and sulking.

And, like John, I was genuinely unsettled by my inability to control it. My wife would say the same thing every year: *Why don't you just take a break from it? You're so much better in the summer.*

And I'd want to bite her head off, not because she was wrong, but because she was right – and because it all sounded so bloody simple, as if it was just a switch in my brain I'd forgotten to flick.

By the time I reach the church, I have 197 direct messages.

I sit down on the bench in the cemetery and try to take it in. I am alone in this quiet place. There are shiny new gravestones with laminated photos, 'I Love You, Dad' notes attached to empty bottles of craft ale propped up against stone cherubs. Clumps of daffodils, at odd angles, some upright in their grief, others already wilting. There are ancient lichen-covered headstones too, crumbling into beds of nettles and I wonder if anyone ever came to visit.

I click on a message from Andrew, a Wolves fan who'd moved to Detroit at twenty-six. He tells me he related completely to my post. He describes his fandom as an addiction.

'It's Friday evening. I've just eaten and should be relaxing . . . but I'm already feeling anxious about tomorrow's game,' he says.

He tells me how the recent sending-off of our star Brazilian player Matheus Cunha has knocked him sideways.

'Honestly, I was quite distraught,' he says. 'Waves and waves of emotion and I didn't know what to do with it. I was listening to every podcast, checking social media. I started to ask myself: why am I doing this?'

I feel the burden of isolation begin to lift.

'What would life be like if I just walked away from it all?' Andrew continues. 'I know people would call me a fair-weather fan, but I don't care.'

And then Andrew mentions something that, although I didn't realise it at the time, would become central to this book.

'The one thing that's helped this season is the Michigan Wolves supporters' group,' he writes. 'We meet at an Irish pub in Plymouth, Michigan – just a few of us – but it helps. It really helps. To share it. Good, bad or indifferent.'

He's describing connection, a mitigant for shame, the sense of being alone in your inadequacy. He tells me his mum has just died.

He reassures me he has a therapist and is coping, but it feels good, nevertheless, to tell me. And even though Andrew is 3,800 miles away, I feel strangely close to him. I imagine him in that pub, with his grief, surrounded by fellow Wolves fans, finding a way through.

Down the gravel path, I spot two girls – twelve or thirteen maybe – walking slowly, each holding a bottle of a sports drink called Prime. One red, one blue. They approach a grave and lay the bottles down, next to four others. One of the girls begins to cry. They stand for a while, arm in arm, then walk away. I wander over, curious. The grave is covered in football memorabilia; youth trophies, medals, real leather footballs, a Manchester United teddy bear. There are colourful stones, with painted-on pictures of more footballs and bright watermelons, blue and black Nike swooshes, the Hastings Athletic FC badge and CR7, a nod to the footballer Cristiano Ronaldo. The grave belongs to Harry Dennis. He died at eleven years old.

Football, it seemed, had already been a defining part of who he was. I didn't know it then, but his mum would later help me understand something important about the irrational, fragile beauty of being a fan. And she would remind me about how football has immense power for good.

Making my way back to the car, my phone was still pinging.

2

The Punch

Debbie Drew clutches her phone in both hands, her knuckles white, tears glinting in her eyes. She has the look of someone who hasn't slept. I'd seen pictures of her before; Facebook photos of a different woman – tanned and laughing somewhere far away, cocktails with little umbrellas, surrounded by family, beaming. But the woman in front of me now feels like a shell. She's showing me pictures of her son, Paul. Here he is holding his infant son, his arms wrapped around the baby. Here he is larking about in a pub, pint in hand. A boy again, on his father's shoulders, blue and white football hats all around them, a sea of Birmingham City fans. And here he is with Debbie and his sisters.

The photographs don't align with the Paul I thought I knew, the Paul from the headlines, the snarling caricature painted by tabloids and trolls.

We are in a corner of the pub she runs in Prestleigh, a once Roman settlement on the eastern edge of the Mendip Hills in Somerset, about ten miles from Glastonbury. I have travelled here to see if Debbie can shed any light on what happened to her son. It's clear from her expression that Debbie has forgotten I was coming. But she lets me in with a cautious smile and offers coffee. The pub doesn't open for another three hours.

She tells me about a particular day when everything changed: 10 March 2019.

It's derby day, and Debbie is behind the bar, pouring pints of beer for a boisterous mix of Birmingham City and Aston Villa fans. She has worked in pubs all her life and this one, in east Birmingham, is packed. The atmosphere is lively and both sets of fans are drinking amicably enough.

Debbie's ex-husband is also called Paul. He is at the game in person with his son, Paul Junior, who had started drinking early. The pair are Birmingham City season ticket holders and rarely miss a match. Their relationship is stitched together with football. Paul Jr. has been attending games with his dad since he was four years old, perched on his father's shoulders, a young mind absorbing the roaring passion of the Blues faithful. Now twenty-seven, he has a two-year-old son of his own – Frankie – and dreams of one day taking him to matches, passing on the ritual like an heirloom.

That day, Paul Jr. is standing near the pitch with his dad and it's eight minutes into the game.

'I think he was very near the front and he just . . .' Debbie's voice trails off, as if even now she can't quite believe it. What Debbie is reluctant to say outright is that her son climbed over the barriers, evading stewards, and sprinted on to the pitch. He ran straight at Aston Villa's Jack Grealish and punched him in the back of the head.

'Someone came up the bar and said, "It's your Paul."' Then she got a phone call from Paul's dad.

'He's gone, "Aw, Gawd. Paul's run on the pitch."'

'Why did he do it?' I ask.

'I don't know why,' Debbie says, looking confused. 'He didn't know the answer himself. He just said he *had a moment* . . .'

She pauses.

'And that he hated Jack Grealish.'

'Hmmm . . .' I maintain as much neutrality as I can.

'. . . with a passion,' she adds. Moments pass, the silence stretching between us.

'. . . absolutely HATED him.' Her eyes widen.

'Yeah . . .' I murmur, unnerved by the silence.

* * *

I've seen the footage of Paul running on to the pitch more times than I care to admit. At eight minutes and thirty-eight seconds into the game, he can be seen emerging from the left side of the screen, like a stick figure, in a Burberry cap, running in a stiff, puppetish way, as though his limbs are not his own. Most of the players are facing away from him, unaware. But Villa's number three, Kristian Pedersen, appears to spot Paul, as does Blues player Jota Peleteiro, who runs towards the unfolding drama without knowing what's about to happen. The action happens in front of the home fans.

The Sky Sports cameras pan in live for a close-up on Grealish, just before the punch, predicting what is about to happen. Now Grealish is chatting to one of his teammates across the pitch – the camera still tight on his head. And then you see Paul's Burberry cap creep into the frame, a flailing arm close behind, a vicious punch in the making.

A red fade with the English Football League logo slides across the shot like a censor's wipe, as if to erase what's just happened. A replay of the preceding throw-in is shown, but it's mayhem now.

The commentator can be heard, 'There's an idiot on the field. This is disgraceful.'

The camera cuts back to the chaos on the pitch. Grealish is sitting on the turf, hunched forward, holding on to his boots and stunned.

'A fan has run on and physically attacked Jack Grealish.'

The footage shows players wrestling Paul to the ground. A steward in bright orange, the towering figure of Tyrone Mings among those forming a protective circle around the intruder. Mitchell is on the turf, his cap gone, scuttling like an earwig caught in the light. Some players seem to be holding others back, guarding him. 'An utter disgrace,' the commentator bellows.

As Paul is pulled to his feet by the hooded steward, players are screaming in his face. Two Blues players – their captain Michael Morrison and Maikel Kieftenbeld – turn to see how Grealish is. They stoop, along with goalkeeper Lee Camp, speak some words, and lift him firmly to his feet, in that ungentle footballers' way. Grealish walks away, joined by teammates. He doesn't go near the circle that's formed around his attacker.

The steward is shouting at the players, trying to clear space to escort Paul off the pitch. Another orange-clad, black-hooded steward barrels on. The camera cuts to Grealish walking away, Mings and Kortney Hause flanking him, hands resting on the back of his head and shoulder.

'Well there are lines that cannot be crossed and . . .'

Another angle is shown. This one from the side. You see Paul charging from a few metres away. It's genuinely hard to watch. He's in blue jeans, black coat and white trainers. A steward appears about ten metres behind him. Paul adjusts his stride as he gets closer to Grealish, a little shimmy to time the punch. Then his right arm swings back and lands on the side of Grealish's head. When I see the punch now it is much harder than I remember. My neighbour John told me he remembered it as a soft touch 'streaker' incident. But Grealish is knocked into the air. I pause the shot. Mid-air, he somehow still has the agility to turn and look at his attacker. Even here, the difference in athleticism and composure is glaring – Paul looks clumsy, like bad animation. Grealish, even airborne, is twisted and strong.

'. . . and Jack Grealish has done extraordinarily well to stay calm there.'

Another pundit steps in: 'Words just absolutely fail me.'

'What an absolute disgrace.'

The punch is shown again – a third replay. Another angle. Grealish is walking towards the camera this time. Moments before impact, you can see the faces in the crowd. I notice three Blues fans in particular – three young women, blue and white kits, Burberry scarves – gesticulating, stern-faced, shouting. I can't tell if it's directed at Grealish or the ref. But one fan is looking the other way – towards Paul. She seems to know what's about to happen and has her arms bent, both hands clasping her forehead. She looks like she's about to witness the Shuttle explode.

From this angle, you can see the punch doesn't land clean. He catches him enough to knock him off his feet, but the blow is mistimed. The commentator praises Grealish for his lack of reaction. And now we're forty-two seconds into the clip, and the punch is shown a fourth time – slightly different angle, straight from behind. This time it's in slow motion.

And I think – are they enjoying this? The cameramen? The directors? That it's Jack Grealish being hit?

The clip moves on to later in the game. Grealish is still on the pitch and ready to get his revenge.

In the 67th minute, he's passed the ball by Neil Taylor, on the edge of the Blues' box.

He unleashes a low shot that somehow snakes through a packed penalty area – six Blues players at least – who seem to part like waves. The ball hits the net and Grealish wheels away like a man who's just devoured the full playbook on how to look absolutely fucking out of his mind with joy. He punches the air, a kid at his own birthday party, unable to contain himself. Then he jumps into the crowd and is swallowed by fans.

'A sweet, sweet moment for Jack Grealish.'

Grealish steps back on to the pitch, shorts muddied, facing the away end, pointing at his eyes.

Did you see that? Did you see how I responded?

'What an answer that is,' the commentator says, as they replay the goal.

Then the next clip: Grealish being substituted in the 84th minute. The tannoy crackles:

'Substitution for Aston Villa, replacing number 10 Jack Grealish . . .'

The Blues fans boo. You can see them, hurling abuse, gesturing. The wanker sign is everywhere. And I think – hasn't he had enough for one afternoon?

After the match, Grealish is interviewed by Sky. He is a beaming figure in front of an advertising board replete with logos: law firms, sports brands, drinks, gambling firms.

'Best day of my life,' he says, the famous nasal drawl, perfect stubble, looking the picture of health. There's no trace of the attack and his man of the match status is confirmed – first in the official stats for goals and assists, and second for passing accuracy.

When I see Grealish here, there's something innocent and sweet about him; the way he tilts his head towards the interviewer like he's really listening and trying to engage. I'm struck by how young he looks. Just a boy, with an extraordinary gift really. I think back to the Wolves giants of my childhood – John Richards, Kenny Hibbitt, George Berry, Steve Daley. They felt enormous to me. So much older than me, watching from beside my dad in the stands. But they were young too. 'You've seen the incident back with the fan. What are your thoughts?'

Grealish wipes the top of his mouth, brushes the stubble. His eyes widen, like he's connecting mentally and physically with the footage.

'Erm, yes, you know I was just unaware at the time,' he laughs, maybe a little nervously, maybe just to buy some time. 'I think we had a corner or was it a throw-in in the corner, and obviously I was walking into position,' he smiles at the interviewer, 'and then I just felt a whack around the side of the face ... But you know, I just tried to get on with my job in the end. I think I did, you know, I scored the winner, and we've come away with three points.'

He's grinning again now, leaning forward slightly. I'm intrigued by how unflustered he appears by the pitch attack. On the surface at least, there does not appear to be any anger, or resentment. I wonder whether the victory and scoring the winner is more important than anything else. But I also wonder whether the attack has left a mark – whether he is yet to process what happened.

* * *

Paul's story intrigued me from the start, but it felt anomalous. How could it possibly frame the experience of your typical football fan? Interesting, sure, but I couldn't relate to Paul's behaviour. It wasn't representative of the fans I knew, either. I was ready to file it under extreme fandom and move on.

But YouTube had other ideas. A sequence of images changed everything. It shows the aftermath when Paul is being led off the pitch by stewards. There is a close-up of him, face flushed, T-shirt riding up over his belly. He looks awkward and triumphant in equal measure. He turns to the crowd and raises a thumb. Then, he blows kisses to a section of the Blues fans. It's like he's saying *did you see what I did for you lot?*

I zoom in on the crowd. Some look shocked, but mostly it's laughter and applause. Phones are raised above grinning faces. There are women, children, elderly men in scarves and heavy coats. The camera catches a girl creasing up, as if this is the funniest thing she's seen all season.

The vibe is celebratory.

What was going on?

Why were they so happy about a 23-year-old from their own city getting punched during a game?

Debbie keeps scrolling through more pictures on her phone. The pub is quiet, just the occasional scrape of a mop bucket behind the bar.

She shows me a photo of one of her grandchildren – Paul's youngest, a little girl – in a tiny Blues shirt.

She swipes again. This time she stops. A tear rolls down her cheek. She tilts the phone towards me.

It's an urn. The Birmingham City crest is painted on the side.

Inside, Debbie tells me quietly, are Paul's ashes.

3

Face Slashed

The day after Paul Mitchell's punch, he was in the dock, his name echoing through the Gothic corridors of Birmingham Magistrates' Court. The story was everywhere, as you'd expect, and the vast, red-bricked building pulsed with press lanyards and palm-sized notebooks covered in shorthand. Debbie and Paul Sr. are there to support their son. Debbie tells me she could hardly move for press, but before her son emerged into the dock, a figure loomed up beside her. It was Grealish's dad. 'He came straight up to me and said, "I want to see the scum that reared that boy."'

'Really?' I say.

Debbie nods. 'I took it,' she replies quickly. 'I said, "I apologise for what my son's done to you."'

The court was told that Paul had been forced to flee his home amid death threats. Paul's solicitor Vaughn Whistance said Paul had no intention of actually punching Grealish. He had only wanted to whip up the crowd. After seeing the tape, it was hard to believe that.

Paul pleaded guilty to assault and illegally entering the field of play. As well as the fourteen-week jail sentence, he was ordered to pay £100 compensation to Grealish for the pain and shock of the attack. Birmingham City banned him from St Andrew's for life and he was barred from all other football grounds in the UK for ten years.

* * *

Paul's sister Hayley drifts downstairs while Debbie and I sit with our coffees. She's in her twenties, long brown hair, still in her pyjamas. Like Debbie, she looks like someone who's had the fight knocked out of her.

'You can sit with us, if you like?' I say.

'In my pyjamas?' she replies.

I nod.

'Paul thought Grealish was a knob,' Hayley says, by way of introduction. She must have been listening in.

'He just didn't like him. I don't even know why.'

'None of us do,' Debbie says, shaking her head, and then changing the subject: 'If there was trouble in the pub, he would come and say, "Mum, it's kicking off over there . . ."'

'He didn't like violence?' I ask. The brutal footage loops in my head.

'He didn't like violence. He'd never been violent,' Debbie goes on, then turns to Hayley. 'You'd never seen him be violent, had you?'

Hayley rubs at her eyes.

'Never,' she says.

Hayley says things turned stranger after Paul left prison after serving four weeks of his sentence. She said she woke up one morning and spotted a picture someone had posted with his face horrifically slashed, apparently by a Villa fan in revenge. She called Paul, but he was fine. He was at home in Rubery, south-west Birmingham, with his partner Dion and son Frankie. Someone had superimposed his head on to a hospital patient's body.

There were news stories about the slashing in the mainstream media, too. It appeared reporters had been sent out to verify it. I dug up a story, marked Exclusive, published in the *Sun,* on 18 April, just a few days after Paul had left prison.

What struck me was that Paul appeared to have *posed* for a picture for the journalists and photographers interviewing him. There he was, standing next to a wood-chipped white wall in what was presumably his flat, all clean-shaven, in a black North Face T-shirt and blue jeans, his distinctive Birmingham City tattoos evident on his forearms.

Yet the story was hardly great PR for him, his image under the headline:

> HOOLIGAN IN HIDING
> Jack Grealish thug Paul Mitchell goes to ground after sick knife attack image goes viral on Twitter – but he still 'won't say sorry'.

Why on earth would he pose for this picture?

Paul said he regretted what he had done but he also refused to apologise to Grealish, claiming it was because he didn't think the player would accept it.

Other weird stories popped up too. Like a GoFundMe page that was set up to raise money for Paul so that he could pay his fine to Grealish. The GoFundMe appeal, reported in the local *Birmingham Evening Mail,* had a bizarre depiction of Paul Mitchell's face superimposed on to an image of King Henry VIII.

People appeared to be superimposing Paul's head everywhere.

'We'd like to raise a bit of money to help Paul pay his fine to millionaire Grealish and help his pregnant partner get by whilst he's away for a bit,' the appeal read. 'Thanks in advance.'

It was clear that there had even been some donations.

I found it hard to reconcile what Debbie was saying about him being a gentle pussycat with the force of the punch. Had she not seen it? I ask her.

She ignores the question and focuses on his popularity.

'He was the class clown,' Debbie says, 'the pub idiot.' Debbie's face looks shocked at what she's just said. 'Not an idiot,' she counters. 'Because he was absolutely loved. No one ever said a bad word about him.'

And yet inevitably Paul is reduced to a cut-out. The media offer one version – grubby, thuggish and irredeemable. Debbie offers another – gentle and blameless. Both concealed the messy humanity in the middle.

4

He Gets Hit Again

This section wasn't supposed to end like this.

It was meant to take us to the next phase of Paul Mitchell's story – his dark descent into tragedy before drilling down into the deeper psychology of football fandom.

But then something happened that I really wasn't expecting.

I'm making dinner on a Monday night in early April 2025 when I get a WhatsApp from my brother-in-law, Merlin. At this stage it should be said that the working title for the book was *The Man Who Punched Jack Grealish*. Merlin sends a link and writes 'MEN who punched Jack Grealish', emphasising the plural, followed by a row of incredulous face emojis.

I tap the newspaper article and can't quite believe what I'm reading. I stand there for a moment in the kitchen, dumbfounded, holding a wooden spoon.

I'd spent hours carefully, methodically, structuring everything around the *first* Grealish attack, the one in March 2019.

And now – this. Someone *else* has assaulted Grealish.

He's been slapped after the Manchester derby, apparently by a fan who beckoned him over as he walked down the tunnel. A young man – Alfie Holt, twenty – has been charged with assault and is due to appear before magistrates in the summer. First, I try to deny it – it's not a real punch, it's a slap, maybe it will just go away. Maybe it won't gain any traction.

The next morning, I walk to the newsagent and immediately see it on the front page of the *Sun*.

'GREALISH SLAPPED IN FACE BY UTD FAN'.

For God's sake, I think. What am I supposed to do with this? Ignore it? Rewrite the whole arc? Should I plan a sequel? I barely explained the first Grealish incident yet and now they're piling up faster than I can write the actual chapters.

I can already see my lovely editor – the one who'd been pushing me to write faster so we could release *before* the World Cup – tutting, as if to say, *I told you to write quicker, you idiot.*

I jot down the court date – 14 July. I'll go. Maybe I'll even get to speak to Grealish, if he turns up to give evidence.

* * *

The truth is, I missed the whole of the Manchester derby on Sunday, despite wanting to watch it. Wolves had won the previous day against Ipswich, so I had no issues watching more football. I was walking the dog (again), and I'd planned to come back and watch the second half but got caught up in small talk with other owners. Given a dog's relatively short lifespan, it's annoying how the coincidence of matching ages still draws gasps of delight and recognition, as if you've just discovered you were identical twins separated at birth. 'No way . . . eight years old, really? Mine's eight too!'

Then there's the awkward dance when the dogs start circling each other, noses wedged in each other's rear ends, while the owners do a kind of passive-aggressive maypole routine with the leads, everyone pretending it's fine. I'm never quite sure what tone to strike – do you acknowledge the sniffing with a wry smile or do you stare stoically into the distance like you're above all this? I learned the hard way that making a joke – 'Go on, give her a good sniff' – can backfire. Especially if you've got a male dog. The wrong owner, the wrong tone, and suddenly you're the weirdo.

* * *

Anyway, that's how I missed it. There was more fan-related drama beyond the Grealish stuff. There's a photo in almost every paper: Manchester City player Phil Foden being held by Pep Guardiola on the pitch. Pep looks remarkably grave, drawing Foden close as though shielding him from shrapnel. The younger man's head is tucked beneath Pep's salt-and-pepper beard.

Foden had been taken off after fifty-eight minutes. The United fans had started chanting about his mother, Claire Rowlands – calling her a 'slag'. Phil is famously close to his mum. She got him into football at four and bought him City pencil cases, duvet covers, posters and clocks. In 2022, she defended him backstage at an Amir Khan fight when a group of men called him a 'cunt'. She ended up getting punched in the face. Two years later, Rowlands made headlines when footage emerged of her being handcuffed and thrown out of Bentley's nightclub in Towyn, Wales. She'd knocked a cap off another partygoer's head.

After the game, Pep – draped in his trademark black Stone Island – was full of sighs and shrugs.

'It's a lack of class,' he told reporters. 'I don't understand the mind of the people involving the mum of Phil (. . .) they should be ashamed.'

Even United fans agreed their own had gone too far.

'I hate Foden,' one of them said. 'But his mum should be left out of this.'

I find a TikTok clip of Foden walking off the pitch. His head held high, he turns to the United fans, mock applauds them and gives them a thumbs-up, a gesture which says, *Yes, yes, I heard you. I'm still standing. Enjoy your little moment.* But I'm guessing this hurt more than he was letting on.

* * *

That evening, we are watching *The White Lotus* and things are unravelling fast. My wife is transfixed. She's asking me questions about the plot (was it the sweet Thai security guard?), but I'm in a dark daydream. I was thinking about Paul Mitchell, and the goading crowd, and those roaring 'your mum's a slag' at Phil Foden, and my own seemingly irrational behaviour. Ordinary people – people with friends and dogs and mortgages – change so quickly because of football. It seems others had the same idea. Texts and WhatsApps have been rolling in steadily since Grealish was attacked again. What are you going to do about this, Mr 'I'm writing a book about it'?

On screen, gunfire thunders through the luxury resort in Koh Samui as the music swells.

I stare at my phone, increasingly anxious.

'Why do people keep punching Jack Grealish?' my neighbour John asks me. I narrow my eyes and ignore it. But a few seconds later, he adds more pressure by tacking on a shrugging emoji, denoting helpless confusion.

Attacking Grealish isn't a freak incident any more. It's a pattern.

PART II

Us

5

My Brother, the Liverpool Fan

16 September 2023, Hastings.

A couple of hours after the Liverpool game, it's time for my wife's birthday dinner. In attendance are my wife, her sister Alice, my nephew Barney and me.

Alice has prepared perfectly flaky salmon with asparagus and boiled potatoes.

I sit next to Barney in my football strip. I've been sweating; the shirt fits like clingfilm now, the colours are practically fluorescent and the AstroPay logo glows in the candlelight. I can't even be bothered to get changed. I bought the shirt a few weeks earlier when we beat Everton.

It's not the only strip I have either.

My wardrobe is a mausoleum of hope, piled high with brightly coloured kits. Pink, red, black, purple and, of course, various shades of orange that purport to be Old Gold. I've got enough of the damned things to open a Wolves-themed pop-up.

Each shirt is an embarrassing relic of some brief moment of euphoria – victories that made me think, *Yes! This is it! This is the dawn of a glorious era!* (Am I really that vulnerable to a well-timed notification from the Wolves store? Did I genuinely believe, even for a moment, that I could pull it off, that I could wear it with dignity? What was I thinking?)

'I'm so sorry, Dame,' Alice says, with a tilt of the head and a softness in her voice that feels like someone gently placing a hand on your shoulder at a wake. And she means it. I know she does. But still, I feel the sharp pang of humiliation. Because even as she says it, even as she tries to comfort me, I know what she's thinking: *What an idiot. What a ridiculous, overgrown child.* And she's right, obviously. I'm a polyester-clad mid-life crisis.

The salmon lands on my plate but it might as well be wet cardboard. Healthy food feels obscene. I want to disappear back into my bag of Doritos. I stew in my misery. I am not interested in cheering up. I want to sink into the emotional pain, wallow in it, soak it up like a sponge.

The world is bleak and no amount of dill sauce can change that.

I push the salmon around and begin to address the elephant in the room. I make self-deprecating jokes about how ridiculous it is to let a football match ruin an evening. They laugh politely.

It seems to work. They relax, and for a moment, I convince myself that they're appeased, that they don't secretly think I'm an emotionally stunted man sulking over a football match on his wife's birthday. Somehow, I get the salmon down and the Cookie Dough ice cream is easier.

After dinner, my wife, ever practical, ever hopeful, tries another tack to enhance my mood. 'Shall we watch a movie?' she suggests brightly. I nod and force a smile and shuffle into the lounge like a man on his way to the gallows. The fire is crackling and the room is lit by fig-scented candles.

The movie they've chosen is *Rope* by Alfred Hitchcock. This is a tense, suffocating story about inevitable, crushing failure.

I glance at my wife, searching for a trace of malice or dark humour, but she's already cocooning herself into the cushions, blissfully unaware. I sit there, stiff and bitter, watching the screen as two doomed men hoist their own metaphorical noose, and think: *Of course. Of course it's Rope.*

I ache to drink heavily. I want to grab the nearest bottle of something strong and pour myself a large glass. Either that or take some of the diazepam left over from a prescription given to my wife for her flying phobia. I want just enough to take the edge off; to blunt the melancholy and the anger. But I can't even be bothered to get up. Instead, I sit there, watching James Stewart unravel the mystery on screen, pretending that I care. My wife glances at me occasionally, her smile small and encouraging, and I smile back, counterfeit.

I decide I won't properly watch the film and start messing with my phone and working myself up again. I picture my Liverpool-supporting brother sitting with his little congregation of plastic Scousers.

In my head, they are drinking weak lager, maybe Carling Original, and dissecting the game. They are praising certain players; their voices are hoarse with songs about Klopp and Salah and Andy Robertson.

My brother has been to Liverpool fewer times than he has big toenails. He was raised in Wolverhampton, within earshot of the ring road and the Mander Centre shopping precinct. He speaks with such a Wolverhampton accent he could be hired out by the council as a Black Country heritage artefact. And yet here he is, reborn as a Scouser. He should support Wolves. But he doesn't and right now, I hate him for it.

And his mates? They are a cabal of Southerners from the Home Counties. These are men who probably think Stoke is 'the frozen North'. They've probably never been further than Watford Gap without a compass. And yet they sit there celebrating as if they were delivered directly into the Kop end, umbilical cords cut to the sound of 'You'll Never Walk Alone'. I picture them, their smug faces gleaming like boiled hams. None of them has been to a game at Anfield, I guarantee it. I'd bet they've never once stood an inch deep in piss at half-time, shoes sticking to the toilet floor, plastic pint glasses crunching underfoot as they shuffle forward.

The worst bit is *knowing* that they *think* they are better than me.

Don't you dare, I think. Don't you dare send me a WhatsApp message. Don't you dare condescend with one of those little platitudes: '*Unlucky today, mate. Wolves played well,*' or '*I think you'll be all right this season, mate, from what I've seen.*'

Ping.

There it is.

I want to send him a photo of me setting fire to a Liverpool scarf in the garden. Why would you support a club you have absolutely no connection to? To feel superior? In my head, I craft an entire argument. It is a blistering takedown, petty, vindictive and immensely satisfying.

But no, in the end, I ignore it. Passive aggression becomes my comfort blanket.

I try to refocus on the movie so that I can at least contribute to the post-movie analysis. But try as I might, I can't get their merry little scene out of my mind. I picture my brother dashing off that patronising text in a tiny lull between smug backslaps. 'Lads, lads. One sec – just texting my brother, he's a Wolves fan.'

'Of course, of course,' they reply, magnanimously. Well I don't need it, lads.

Finally, I crack. I text him. 'Why *do* you support Liverpool?' I can't help myself. It is timed to plant just the faintest seed of doubt about his authenticity as a football fan. I want him to feel some of my shame.

He comes back almost instantly: John Barnes. I stare at my screen in horror.

Of course, John Barnes, a trump card I can't touch. Suddenly it's about race and minority representation. Without me asking for an elaboration he sends me a tedious homily about how he admired him for being a player of colour in a white league. Not only was he drawn to his dazzling skills but Barnes was a pioneer, someone who represented his core psychological values.

My brother, the fake Scouser, has weaponised John Barnes and the race card against me. It's a simple tap-in.

6

Children and Chimpanzees

By Thursday, I'd just about calmed down but the question remained: how do we become such obsessive fans of a particular team? What happens in our brains so that a casual allegiance hardens into a lifelong loyalty, defying logic and capable of throwing weekends, relationships and even lives into jeopardy? Is my brother really a plastic fan, or can he justify being a Liverpool supporter from the Black Country?

To answer this question, we need to start at the beginning. We need to understand that what comes before loving a particular team, before loving football even, is a desperate need to *belong*.

One way to ensure we are accepted is to demonstrate that we are willing to follow what our tribal elders do. This is why young children will imitate almost anything an adult does, even when the thing is pointless. In one experiment, researchers compared three- and four-year-old children with wild chimpanzees. Both groups were presented with a transparent box containing a reward. The chimps' reward was a grape, while the children got a colourful sticker.

An adult demonstrated how to open the box with a stick. But along the way, they added a few pointless steps: removing a bolt that released nothing and poking the stick into a top hole where it banged uselessly against a barrier.

The children copied *every move exactly*. They unfastened the pointless bolt and they studiously poked the stick into the blocked hole. Only then did they perform the single necessary step of sliding the stick into the side slot to release the prize. The chimps, meanwhile, skipped the nonsense, jammed the stick straight into the working hole and claimed the reward in a fraction of the time.

Anthropologists believe the reason children do this is to belong.

The children are effectively saying, *I'm like you, accept me, let me into the group.*

This sort of imitation is called a *Credibility Enhancing Display (CRED)*, a term coined by the anthropologist Joseph Henrich. CREDs signal sincerity and allegiance to a group, even if they are personally costly. There are many examples: wealthy Labour politicians sending their children to state schools, religious rituals or celibacy in priests. Football fandom is rife with them and children learn them early. Going to a match with your dad when you're five and can't even see or understand the rules, wearing strips when your team is bottom of the league, or even being able to speak about the weekend's scores or particular players by studying stats for hours, are all examples.

I remember being scolded at eight years old for singing a football anthem to the tune of 'Land of Hope and Glory':

> We hate Nottingham Forest, we hate Liverpool too,
> We hate Manchest (I thought that was the name) United,
> But Wanderers we love you.

'We mustn't hate anyone, Damien,' Miss Woodhouse, my stern Catholic school teacher, told me in the playground. 'Hating is bad. I'm docking your tutor group fifty house points.' This made me unpopular among some classmates. But I didn't care. I was signalling to my fellow young Wolves fans that I was willing to be punished for the tribe. It was my first proper initiation ritual – a playground CRED.

Sometimes, of course, these displays go catastrophically wrong. Sometimes the very things you do to try to be accepted by the tribe backfire, and you become the black sheep. There's plenty of that later.

Children, then, are exposed to the football-loving behaviour of grown-ups from very early development as their brains are still forming. And their brains are primed to imitate and internalise it.

If football isn't followed in the family, a similar process applies to peers at school. Liking the game, being able to talk about it, grants you access to the members' club. It is a relatively low bar and sharing a love of the sport offers a pathway to more intimate personal relationships.

I remember a boy at my primary school called Mark. Mark was a tragic barrel of a child, perpetually wheezing, his conversational skills reduced to grunts, burps and the occasional racial slur. He was the sort of kid who'd stuff crisps into his pocket for later, then forget and sit on them. His trousers always had a faint orange dusting of Wotsits.

And yet.

Mark had the Panini stickers. Stacks upon stacks of them, bound by string and rubber bands. He carried them around all day in a massive plastic bag, huffing and puffing under their weight. He had the rare ones; the gold foil crest of Lincoln City, the elusive Bob Latchford, the glittering holy grail of a fully completed Everton page.

We were repulsed by him, and yet we orbited him like needy planets. We more than tolerated him, we indulged him, laughing at his abhorrent jokes, all with a burning hope he might trade a sticker we needed. I've no idea what home he returned to at the end of the school day, but I knew his brothers were in jail and his mum rarely turned up to fetch him. His football stickers were his access card to the tribe.

This was the unspoken truth of our childhoods in the late 1970s: status was conferred by being good at football, or, failing that, having the most comprehensive collection of football stickers. We might have laughed at Mark behind his back, but the moment he pulled out that tower of stickers, bulging and glorious, he was the bloated, triumphant playground sticker king.

I wasn't so different from Mark anyway. I was another outcast; the skinny swot. In my comprehensive school in Wolverhampton, I stuck out like a sore thumb. I spent my summers prancing around my grandparents' place in France with a giant butterfly net, blond curls bouncing. I was happy there, a world away from school where I'd been bullied for being so weird. Looking back, it's easy to see why football – playing it and using it as a conversational currency – became my way of trying to belong.

I still have dreams (and nightmares) about the school football team sheets, pinned to the board outside the sports hall. I'd feel a bolt of terror that my name might not feature one week. But there it always was in black and white, my name beneath the goalkeeper's: right-back, proof that despite my skinniness, my braces and the rumours I was into butterfly collecting, I belonged. At least for another week.

Football is a bridge to safety and belonging through family and peer relationships.

But then comes the next phase. How do we go from liking football generally to picking a particular team?

The sports psychologist Dan Wann suggests there are many different influences on team selection. Usually it's the family's team, reinforcing the bond with the parent. But sometimes the choice goes against the grain: perhaps to boost self-esteem by joining a successful side, or to deliberately separate from family, or to align with peers when friends start to matter as much as family.

Another route to choosing a team is through individual players. Children are naturally drawn to superheroes.

Across cultures, that pull has been directed towards gods, monsters, warrior heroes. Footballers fill the same niche.

For my brother, John Barnes was that superhero. Football first opened a door into our father's world – and into mine, as his older brother. Through that doorway he found Barnes, and once he loved Barnes, Liverpool came with him.

In the UK, the top reasons people give for supporting a team are parental influence, growing up near the ground and style of play. But generational shifts are already visible. Today, among eight–twelve-year-olds, a third said they chose their team because it was the one they played with in video games.

But the most crucial question is how simple identification with a team grows to become *such* an obsession. Why do I care so much about a team that when they lose or win, it feels like a personal loss or triumph? These are eleven men I've never met, after all, and yet when they lose, I lose with them. My stomach sinks, my chest tightens, and somewhere deep in the evolutionary swamp of my brain, something confirms: *YOU ARE A LOSER.*

It doesn't make sense. I haven't kicked a ball. I haven't contributed anything beyond a few cheers, screams and insults. And yet I feel exposed and humiliated, like the defeat has revealed something essential about me.

This is the next stage. Anthropologists and evolutionary psychologists have a term for this intimate connection, when you no longer distinguish between your losses and your team's.

It's something called *identity fusion*.

To understand it better, we must go to the jungle in Papua New Guinea.

7

When the Team Becomes Me

Nearly twenty years ago, an aspiring anthropologist named Harvey Whitehouse found himself in Papua New Guinea, conducting research for his PhD at Cambridge.

There, he heard accounts of boys undergoing brutal rites of passage, so extreme he later called them Rites of Terror. They were burned, mutilated, dehydrated and beaten. Objects were forced into their noses, spines, tongues and penises. Elders hurled threats and insults as the boys endured it all.

Whitehouse wanted to understand the evolutionary purpose of such ordeals.

He began making connections with other highly charged emotional experiences that appeared to bind groups together like glue.

He considered cults.

One such example unfolded in another jungle – this time in Guyana, in November 1978.

In a remote encampment hacked from the rainforest, hundreds of people followed the charismatic leader Jim Jones, a man who promised a utopia built on equality and love. The organisation was called the People's Temple.

The camp, Jonestown, was infested by mosquitoes, had poor sanitation and a type of soil incapable of growing healthy produce. Reports to the outside world suggested that abuse was rife and that children were being separated from their parents.

Jones cultivated a siege mentality among his followers, suggesting that hostile forces were closing in. He subjected them to what became known as 'White Nights'. These were all-night rituals during which Jones would have his followers chant and pray to ward off the advancing enemies. To heighten the tension, he had henchmen fire guns from the surrounding jungle, pretending to be members of a hostile militia.

Children were among those sent to the perimeter of the camp, armed with machetes, to defend against enemies Jones claimed were closing in. On at least one occasion, Jones convinced everyone to drink what he said was a fatal potion, only to reveal afterwards that it was just a drill.

By the autumn of 1978, his followers were malnourished, abused and feared imminent invasion. A US delegation of concerned officials and journalists visited the camp. But as they left, suspicious of what they had seen and ready to report back to the wider world, they were ambushed and some of them were killed.

Jones convinced his followers they must take part in what he called 'revolutionary suicide'. They drank the fruit punch again, but this time it was laced with cyanide. More than nine hundred died and Jones shot himself. One mother at the organisation's HQ in the Guyanese capital Georgetown slit the throats of her own children on Jones's instructions.

Whitehouse was intrigued by how people could be driven to such extremes. Could parallels be drawn between the Rites of Terror in Papua New Guinea and the ritualistic experiences of the White Nights in Jonestown?

Whitehouse believed it didn't make much sense for us to fight and die for people who weren't biologically related to us. It's easier to understand how we bond and sacrifice ourselves for close relatives. We share genes, blood, marrow, memories, and some believe the same spirit. There is a *visceral oneness* within a family group.

When a child, sibling or parent suffers emotionally, we often feel their pain as if it is our own. Sometimes we even sense their physical pain, almost literally, as though our nervous systems are connected. This closeness is called *psychological kinship*. It serves a clear evolutionary function; improving the odds of passing on our DNA.

Whitehouse began to wonder whether intense rituals, often involving collective suffering, could foster the same kind of identity fusion, not just with relatives, but with unrelated individuals. He and his colleagues set out to investigate, conducting a series of studies exploring the key ingredients that lead to identity fusion between unrelated individuals.

In Misrata, Libya, for example, during the uprising against Gaddafi, Whitehouse discovered that revolutionaries often felt closer to their fellow fighters than to their own families. But this wasn't true for all revolutionaries. Those who provided logistical support, away from the front lines, still felt closest to their biological kin. Those on the front lines, the ones who shared the fear, fused most strongly with their comrades. The highly charged, emotionally intense experience was the key.

For our ancestors, fusing with non-relatives, especially under threat, offered an edge in tribal warfare. In foraging societies, fusion enabled bands to stand united in the face of danger and defeat, despite the instinct to splinter and flee. In that context, anything that forged loyalty, especially shared danger or threat, would have been evolutionarily adaptive.

Whitehouse, now a professor at Oxford, came to believe that the torturous rituals in Papua New Guinea were designed to maximise cohesion by turning pain, suffering and emotional intensity up to their highest setting.

And this, of course, leads to football.

8

Flirting at a Carol Service

I'm sitting with Dr Martha Newson, a cognitive anthropologist who has worked closely with Harvey Whitehouse. She is particularly interested in how football fans have their personal identities fused with their teams, and the upending emotional and behavioural ramifications.

Martha flickers into life on Zoom. She sits at home in a burnt-orange woolly jumper, her dark hair tied in a bun. By any standards, Martha is intimidatingly clever. She has a PhD in anthropology from Oxford and is now an associate professor. The problem with talking to someone this smart is that I start walking a conversational tightrope.

My strategy alternates between excessive waffle and clipped, over-succinct replies, all in a bid to disguise my relative ignorance. The latter often shrinks my sentences to the size of a postage stamp.

'Yes.'

'Right.'

'Interesting.'

I am desperate to avoid an intellectual faux pas. This is how the conversation began with Martha. Then something shifted.

I ask her to tell me a bit about herself. To my surprise, her face lights up. She starts talking about her student days.

She'd lived in a Brighton house with nine young men while studying at Sussex. She loved free parties and sound systems. The collective joy she felt at those events inspired her to write papers on dance and psychedelic experience. She once smuggled herself into Glastonbury rolled up in a carpet in the back of a pickup truck.

Now I saw her differently. I pictured her at a rave; glitter on her face, lost in neon light, glowing as she danced. It was like the classic advice to imagine your audience naked, only far more appropriate.

I later discover that her clothing covers several tattoos (I noticed when she was giving a talk about her new book). She has armband tattoos and patterns of dots and circles across her chest. A butterfly spreads its wings on her shoulder. I recognise the butterfly instantly – the exceptionally elegant red admiral. As we'll see, tattoos are one of the most visible signals of fusion with a group. For Paul Mitchell, they came with catastrophic consequences.

Martha hadn't been a big football fan growing up, but she couldn't avoid it. Living with nine football-mad men and dating a diehard Crystal Palace supporter, she got dragged to Selhurst Park at nineteen. She was blown away – not by the football, but by the fans.

She took along her Moleskine notebook and wore glasses. She was teased relentlessly. But she loved the banter and felt accepted. She was amazed at seeing grown men hugging and kissing and crying all within half an hour.

I tell Martha how profoundly wins and losses affect me.

'I can be properly depressed for days when we lose,' I say, ruefully.

'But when we win,' I throw my fist in the air. 'I just feel on top of the world; there's no stopping me.'

Martha stops me dead.

'What do you mean when *we* win?'

I'm caught off guard. I stare at her blankly. She's leaning in, as if interrogating, head tilted, eyes a little sharper.

'I've always found that interesting,' she continues, voice softening again. 'That feeling when *WE* win. Why do you feel that when *THEY* – the team – win?'

I open my mouth, then close it.

'I understand that you feel like you're also winning,' she goes on, 'but what are *YOU* winning as an individual?'

My body reacts as if she's scolding me, even though her voice is gentle.

'Reputational honour?' she suggests.

'You don't gain resources. The players do. They gain women, money, territory, bigger stadiums. But what do *fans* like *you* gain?'

I don't have an answer. To avoid looking too stupid, I overshare. I give her an example of exactly how overinflated I get when Wolves win.

We had just beaten Leicester 3-0 at the King Power three days before Christmas, 2024. Gary O'Neil had been sacked after losing at home to Ipswich, replaced by Vitor Pereira. The victory felt like a Christmas miracle after weeks of misery. The weekend was now mine to bask in.

That evening, I went to a carol service in the little Saxon church I pass on my dog walks, the one where Harry Dennis is buried.

I swaggered in through the arched stone entrance carrying the dog like the baby Jesus, radiating smugness. In my mind, I was the youngest man there by some years, a welcome injection of youthful vigour among the tattered hymnals and grey hair.

These older women must be quietly delighted to see someone like me, I thought. I nodded at everyone with a cheeky grin, as if to say, yes, I am that rare thing, a man under sixty who knows the words to 'In the Bleak Midwinter'. I was unstoppable.

I imagined older couples whispering, husbands teasing, 'Oh, stop it, dear, he could be your son.' Wives fanning themselves with the order of service.

And then – God help me – I was smiling far too brightly at the elderly woman sitting beside us. I leant in like we were lifelong friends, reunited by candlelight.

I whipped out my phone to light her carol sheet. It felt gallant and knightly, as if I were guiding her through an Angolan minefield.

What was I doing? Was I flirting?

'It felt like I was *pumping* with testosterone,' I explain to Martha, clenching my fist, while simultaneously grimacing at the thought of me pumping with testosterone.

Martha studies me like an animal in the wild.

But then she nods.

'I mean, yeah – that attractiveness thing is spot on, isn't it?' she says. 'Because when you win in something tribal, you gain access to mates, right?'

'Yes, yes, yes,' I reply, relieved, but sounding disturbingly excited.

* * *

After her Saturdays at Selhurst Park and witnessing the unhinged behaviour of the nine lads she lived with in Brighton, Martha hypothesised that *identity fusion* might apply to football fans.

At Oxford, she sent out questionnaires to fans and the responses she got aligned with her hypothesis.

'We had people saying, *I missed my wedding for a match, I got my balls tattooed,* and it went on and on,' Martha says.

She started to distinguish between football fans who were *fused* with their team and those who simply *identified* with a club.

These two things – fusion and identification – are distinct, and this is critically important. The distinction helps to explain why some fans feel so devastated by their team's performance while, for others, it's water off a duck's back.

We can identify with many different groups without feeling a visceral connection to them.

For example, you might identify with a profession. I was a journalist before I became a psychologist, and while I felt some loss during that transition, it wasn't unbearable. It was more like changing hats. I took off my journalist hat and put on a psychologist one. I would miss the old hat but I could take it off, no problem. It wasn't glued to my head.

I also identify as an England football fan, but I can take that hat off too. When the national team plays, it's usually a pleasant experience. I care enough to enjoy the match, but my whole sense of self isn't on the line.

The same can't be said for Wolves. It is inconceivable that I might support another team, even if I tried.

I remember when Wolves were teetering on the edge of extinction in the 1980s, and I started rehearsing for the role of supporting another team. For some reason, I landed on Everton, maybe just to annoy my brother, or maybe I liked the fact they were the Merseyside underdogs.

I tuned in to a few games. But I felt nothing. I tried cheering but it was fake. It was like going on a date where there's no chemistry. Sure, the other person's attractive, good company, but you may as well be sitting opposite a potted plant.

That was my relationship with Everton. I really did try, even buying a strip. I was properly anxious about the possibility of not having a team. Like buying a new dog when the old one is on his way out. I wanted something to bond with, to take the edge off losing Wolves. But it never worked. I could never be an Everton fan.

I recall in Nick Hornby's classic football book *Fever Pitch*, he describes being unable to get a divorce from Arsenal even if he wanted one. It was not possible, he said, to go for a 'bit of slap and tickle' with Tottenham.

There are different ways to see whether someone is fused or merely identified with their team. These range from simple questionnaires – to neural correlates in brain scans, to saliva samples measuring levels of hormones in the blood.

Fused fans tend to agree with statements like: 'I am one with [my club],' 'I have a deep emotional bond with [my club],' 'I'd do more for [my club] than any other fan would' and '[My club] makes me strong.' There's also the circles test: one small circle for the self, one large circle for the team. Non-fused fans might choose two separate or loosely overlapping circles. Fused fans point to the option where the small circle is swallowed whole. Martha sees fusion in football fans as a sliding scale rather than as a binary.

Martha sought to replicate Whitehouse's work on Libyan revolutionaries and other highly fused groups with football fans. She wanted to prove her hypothesis that what shifted fans from mere identification to complete fusion were highly charged, collective, ritualistic experiences that often featured *shared suffering*.

In one study, she surveyed hundreds of Premier League and Championship fans, asking them about their most emotional experiences as fans. She confirmed that when fans had stronger emotional memories of defeats and victories, they became more fused to the team.

Then she discovered that fans of 'unsuccessful' teams who had been through lots of collective emotional suffering were especially bonded to each other and fused to the team identity. For example, she looked at the Premier League in 2013 and, using statistics from the previous decade, ranked the teams in order of success. The top five were Manchester United, Arsenal, Chelsea, Liverpool and Manchester City. The bottom five were Crystal Palace, Hull, Norwich, Sunderland and West Bromwich Albion.

Fans were asked a series of questions about how much they had *suffered* following their club. For example: 'How emotionally difficult is it to be a fan of your team?' They were also asked to write about meaningful memories about being a fan.

They were then asked about kinship with fellow fans; did they believe statements like 'My club is like family to me' and 'I see fellow members of my club as brothers and sisters.'

Finally, they were asked to imagine sacrificing their life to save five fellow fans tied to a railway track.

Would fans jump to their deaths in front of a train hurtling down the track to save fellow supporters? They had to rate their willingness on a scale of one to seven.

Martha found that fans of the *least successful* clubs were the most bonded to their fellow supporters – the ones who described them as 'brothers and sisters'. Hull City came out on top. These were also the fans who reported they had suffered the most.

By contrast, fans of Arsenal and Chelsea, who reported fewer distressing experiences, were the least bonded to fellow fans and the least likely to sacrifice themselves (hypothetically). Martha concluded that collective memories of suffering, humiliation and siege can be the most powerful binding force, far more than joy.

From an evolutionary point of view, it stands to reason. Fans of struggling clubs are like vulnerable tribes going into battle. Those tribes needed the cohesive power of fusion even more – the drive to regroup and fight again. Without it, the group would splinter and scatter.

Anthropologists believe harrowing experiences may be processed more deeply than positive ones, etching themselves into memory and forging a more radical merging of personal and social identity.

Of course, that's not to say fans of the big clubs aren't fused to their teams. Most fans of successful clubs reading this book will be fused, and those clubs have had their fair share of shared heartache and stress too.

Football is designed to create siege mentalities. This can be at the macro level, a season-long fight against relegation, and at the micro level, defending a narrow lead in a particular match.

The low-scoring nature of the game means matches are often on a knife-edge. Fans of every club spend long stretches under fire from the opposition. Defending a 1-0 lead can be one of the most agonising experiences for any fan.

The fear of losing such a treasured resource – three points and a week's worth of contentment – can be unbearable. You see it on the terraces all the time; fans in visible anguish as their team sits deep, clinging to a slender lead with thirty-five minutes still to play.

That's why going 1-0 *down* can sometimes feel like an immense relief. The anticipation of losing a victory evaporates. It's the hope that kills you, as they say.

Sir Alex Ferguson was a master at stoking that sense of siege.

Like Jim Jones, Ferguson deliberately cultivated the idea that his team were constantly under attack from hostile forces

– referees, the FA, the media, rival clubs. Gary Neville remembers it vividly: 'He created a siege mentality, like we hate everybody. It could be referees, it could be . . . anything.' Maybe that's what the others have lacked.

When I mentioned what I had learned about identity fusion to a friend who supported Brighton and Hove Albion, a few miles down the coast, he smiled.

'You should call Guy Butters,' he said.

9

The Man in the Stetson

An old man in a Stetson tentatively enters the North Stand of Brighton and Hove Albion's Amex stadium. It's clear he isn't quite sure why he's here. I'm standing just inside the entrance, in a corridor leading to a meeting room where tables and chairs have been laid out before a large television.

The man in the Stetson hesitates, slightly lost, until he's greeted by Guy Butters, centre-half for Brighton between 2002 and 2008.

Guy is six foot three. The man in the hat, hunched and frail, can't be much more than five foot.

He cranes his neck to look up at Guy, offering a nervous nod. I don't think he recognises him, but Guy's friendly grin puts him at ease.

He's guided gently into the meeting room, where he sits by himself in the corner, fiddling with his hands. Others file past me in the corridor, most of them older men, some steered by their wives.

'Come on, it's going to be all right,' one wife whispers to her husband, who looks terrified. His Brighton T-shirt shows the old Goldstone Ground.

I follow them into the room. There are about thirty men and a handful of women. The atmosphere is tense and uncertain. People tinker with old flyers and match programmes left on the tables. One man sits with his head in his hands. Someone comes over to check he is OK. He looks baffled and frightened.

Now and again a pair of eyes catches mine, searching and quizzical.

All the men are Brighton fans and all of them, carers notwithstanding, have dementia.

* * *

A booming Lancashire voice bursts through the nervous muttering like a foghorn.

It's Chris Cattlin, who played for Brighton in the 1970s. He was a full-back and also managed the team from 1983 to 1986. He's seventy-nine now; white-haired and tanned, with the raffish look of the train robber Ronnie Biggs, at the height of his notoriety.

He's been invited by Guy Butters as today's guest speaker, and he launches straight into a tirade against defenders and goalkeepers who piss around with the ball at the back.

'Does everyone agree with this tippy-tappy crap?' he bellows.

Heads turn. Most of the men look bemused, glancing at each other, shrugging, unsure whether they've heard him right.

Chris, who doesn't have dementia, is itching to tell his stories, but first Guy wants to show highlights of Brighton's recent cup tie against Oxford, a game Brighton won 6-0.

Guy pauses the footage a few seconds before the first goal.

'Right, hands up,' Guy calls. 'Was the first goal scored from outside the box or inside the eighteen-yard box?'

Silence. The men stare at the frozen frame.

'Inside the box!' one of the volunteers eventually blurts out, to my relief. As I said, I'm uncomfortable with silences.

Guy rolls the tape. Olivier Boscagli side-foots it home from inside the area. Nearly everyone looks depressed and confused.

I glance at the man in the Stetson. His face is drawn, troubled, bewildered.

Chris seizes the moment. He returns to his gripe about 'tippy-tappy' football. He lays into the former Southampton manager, Russell Martin, who was born in Brighton, and is now at Rangers, in Scotland.

'If you haven't got the players, don't do it,' he growls. 'Bloody nice bloke, but what is he doing?'

One of the wives asks her husband a question but he just shakes his head. I suspect he doesn't know who Russell Martin is. Chris barrels on.

He describes contemplating football as a career when he was a teenager, kicking a ball about on the moors.

'I watched the '66 World Cup. I saw Nobby Stiles running around the pitch, no teeth, blind as a bat, knocking lumps out of people. And I thought – I'm six foot one and a half; I can do that.'

Chris tells of his trial at Huddersfield back in the 1960s when Ian Greaves was in charge.

'There were two other lads I mated up with straight away – you'll know the names. Frank Worthington and Trevor Cherry?'

Still nothing.

'So, this is a true story – and I'll stand up for this – because what happened then is why I'm barmy like I am today.'

'The manager tells me, "Your heading isn't good enough, Chris. You're like . . . a big poof or something."'

Guy shuffles nervously.

'"Improve your heading,"' Chris presses on, volume rising.

'So Tuesday afternoon, I go in. There are three springs with medicine balls attached. Medicine balls – not footballs.'

Guy and the volunteers draw breath. What is Chris going to say next?

'And what he had us doing was leaping over these wooden boxes, like in some black-and-white war film, and slamming our heads into those bloody medicine balls. Every Tuesday. Every Thursday. Week after week.'

'Oh Christ,' a volunteer groans.

'Frank succumbed to Alzheimer's,' Chris adds ruefully.

For a moment I wonder if Chris has missed the memo. A dementia group, at the ground of football's most proudly LGBTQ-inclusive club, and Chris has managed to land a homophobic slur into a breezy tale about someone dying of Alzheimer's.

But something is stirring in the room. A few of the men are leaning forward now. Some are acknowledging each other with nods. As the day goes on, I realise it's me who is uptight about dementia jokes. Everyone else – patients, carers, volunteers – are at ease.

Chris presses on with more stories. After six months at Huddersfield he was told he'd be in the team because Bob McNab was being sold to Arsenal. But he needs a suit for the pre-match meet at the George pub. Fellow player Mick Meagan tells him there's someone who sells suits from the boot of his car at the Leeds ground, Elland Road. He goes along to Leeds with Mick.

'There's this lad and his missus in a big Zephyr,' Chris says. 'Remember them?' More nods. 'Zephyrs, red cushions in the back, dice dangling at the front.'

'He opens the boot. There are rows of suits, so shiny you could comb your hair in them.'

Chris picks one and hands over a fiver. Back in the car, on the way back to Huddersfield, Mick asks if he knows who the bloke with the suits was. Chris shrugs.

'That was Jack Charlton.' There's an audible gasp from the men.

'England centre-half, Leeds United,' Chris continues.

'What's he doing flogging suits out of the back of a car?' Chris had asked.

'To pay the mortgage,' came the reply.

The men look around at each other, shrugging, eyebrows raised, sharing their amusement. Someone is clapping.

* * *

The stories skid cheerfully down the scale of political correctness, and no one seems bothered, apart from Guy, perhaps, who narrows his eyes from time to time and glances at what I'm scribbling in my notebook.

'. . . and as you can imagine, that almost made me go blind,' Chris motors on.

By the time he gets to the tale of the player who met a barmaid at Brighton's Pink Coconut nightclub, marrying her ten days later, the mood has changed. Most of the men are locked in.

Far from missing the memo, it struck me that Chris was skilful, whether he knew it or not. His stories were studded with Brighton landmarks, familiar players and games from the 1960s and '70s, when these men were first going to matches.

Out of nowhere, one man asks Chris about a famous free kick from 3 October 1970. The TV technician finds the goal on a stream and plays it.

It's Coventry against Everton. Coventry's Willie Carr crouches, grips the ball between his heels, and flicks it up into the air behind him. Striker Ernie Hunt charges forward and volleys it over the wall into the net, past the flailing keeper Andy Rankin.

It was voted 'Goal of the Season' on *Match of the Day*. A few months later the donkey-kick trick was outlawed, and players were no longer allowed to propel the ball with two feet.

A man at the back of the room who had started the day with his head in his hands begins to stir. He gets up from his seat, clears the chairs and leaps up. He flicks his legs up behind him, mimicking the red-haired Scot.

His wife pulls him down and gives him a stern look, as if to say, don't you know you're nearly eighty? She looks over at me and rolls her eyes, fondly. There's a lot of fond eye-rolling today.

The man in the Stetson remains glum and terrified.

* * *

What happens at the Amex is a version of what psychologists call reminiscence therapy.

It works on the idea that dementia wipes away recent memories and can even erase whole decades of middle life; marriages, the births of children, entire careers gone.

But some identity-defining memories from childhood and early adulthood remain stubbornly intact. These memories are called flashbulb memories. They are the vivid, snapshot-like recollections formed during emotionally charged events, seared in our minds with cinematic clarity.

Biologically, they're driven by activation of the amygdala, our internal threat detector. Heightened emotion releases hormones that enhance memory consolidation in the hippocampus. In essence, flashbulb memories are emotionally supercharged memories.

They often cluster into 'reminiscence bumps': a window from around age ten through early adulthood, when many of these emotionally intense, new and identity-forming experiences happen. And for many people, those years coincide with their first football matches – the early, transformative moments of fandom.

When memories are charged enough – celebrating a goal with your dad in the middle of a heaving crowd, or trudging home with weeping, screaming adults after a brutal defeat – they burn themselves into the very core of autobiographical identity.

These are the kinds of memories that anthropologists like Harvey and Martha believe can spark identity fusion. Your story knots itself into the club's story, until the two can no longer be pulled apart, not even by dementia.

* * *

Guy declares we're all going on a tour, and Jenny, the elderly stadium guide, leads on, proud as a drum major. We head to the home team dressing room.

Inside, we slide into red reclining leather seats where the players sit for their half-time team talks. Above each seat is a player's name and photograph.

'What does everyone think about ladies' football?' Chris asks, a glint of mischief in his eyes.

The room goes quiet.

Guy narrows his eyes.

A man sitting beneath Carlos Baleba's nameplate clears his throat. 'Well, I used to be a referee in Sussex, and I was asked lots of times to referee ladies' football.'

A moment passes.

'I REFUSED.'

A few people gasp. John, the man sitting next to me – who used to play semi-professional – turns and shrugs.

But the man under Baleba's nameplate isn't done.

'That was then', he says. 'But now I go down and watch the ladies at Crawley.'

Guy exhales, shoulders sinking.

'I really like it,' the man continues. 'The girls don't roll around on the grass when they get fouled.'

'HEAR, HEAR,' someone calls.

'They don't lie on the floor waiting for the trainers to come on with a wet sponge,' the former ref keeps going.

'In my day you wouldn't want that wet sponge down your shorts,' another man says. 'It was ice cold. Ice cold.' He chatters his teeth.

Others wince in unison, their hands hovering protectively over their groins.

It seems that Chris is a convert, too. He says he loves how women's football is drawing in young girls and raising a new generation of female fans.

* * *

Chris is asked where they used to train when he was a player at Brighton. He says Hove Park, a public park opposite the old Goldstone Ground.

The Goldstone saw some wild swings of fortune for Brighton; relegation to the old Fourth Division in 1962/63, and then, in 1997, a final home game against Doncaster with Brighton staring down relegation to the Conference. They survived by a whisker.

As he mentions the Goldstone, something stirs in the person sitting in Kaoru Mitoma's seat.

It's the man in the Stetson. A pilot light catches in his eyes. A moment ago, he was hunched and haunted; now he leans forward and nods, as if he recognises himself again.

He straightens his Stetson.

* * *

Jenny bolts up. It's her turn to speak. Her husband was a referee, but now he has Parkinson's and dementia. He's at home in bed.

She tells a story about how, back when he was an official, he'd ask her to clean his leather boots and to dry them, so she'd stick them in the oven. That's not possible any more, she says, because players wear plastic boots. Now there's even a machine in the dressing room that warms them gently, so the players never have cold feet. Jenny introduces it with a little flourish of her hands.

The men mutter disapprovingly.

'It's bloody pathetic,' someone sitting beneath Lewis Dunk yells.

'Where's the hairdryer?' another yells.

Chris can't hold back. 'For Christ's sake – warmed-up boots? What's next, a bloody hot-water bottle down their shorts?' People are howling with laughter. One man squeezes his wife's hand and she smiles.

Chris says that when he was playing, they'd attach actual nails to the metal studs to improve the grip on boots.

The room bursts into laughter again. Pilot lights are on everywhere now.

'So they really, really are spoiled,' Jenny says, cutting through the heckles.

She starts talking about the chairman, Tony Bloom, the man who transformed the club and fought tooth and nail to get the Amex built.

Bloom is a lifelong Brighton season ticket holder, a sports bettor, and a professional poker player known as The Lizard. He's won more than £3 million in tournaments and sunk £93 million into the Amex.

'You know, we've got this guy who loves us,' Jenny declares. 'He loves you lot.'

'Do we get hairdryers?' a bloke heckles from beneath Pascal Groß.

Jenny points at him, mock-menacing. 'If you're not careful, I'll take you up to the boardroom.'

Someone wolf whistles.

Jenny grins, and you can tell she's in her element now, sparring like a stand-up. The changing room is thick with camaraderie.

Chris takes over. 'You lot should be bloody proud of yourselves.' A man who must be pushing ninety rises from beneath Bart Verbruggen's looming picture. He bows, deadpan, as if accepting an award. Everyone applauds. He sinks back down and the man beside him slips an arm around his shoulders.

'OK, everybody,' Jenny cuts in, 'we're going to take you out where the players go and show you the Tunnel Club.' She explains it's a members' restaurant for sixty-five people who pay £12,500 a year.

Chris scowls. 'Look at Chris's face,' someone chuckles.

'We loop back to where we started, but one man has broken rank. He's straying on to the pitch, clutching a programme.

'This way,' his wife orders. He ignores her. 'IAN. THIS. WAY.'

She turns to me with a weary smile, as if to say, *see how hard this is?*

He swivels, still gripping the programme. 'Does anyone want a programme?' he asks. Another man chuckles. The procession trudges on.

Back in the first meeting room, everyone gives Chris a hearty round of applause. Guy announces the next meeting and people scribble down the date.

Jenny wanders over to me, beaming. 'I bet you're pleased you came today?' she says.

'I am – it's amazing.'

'It's a real eye-opener, isn't it?' she says, draping an arm around me like we're old mates.

'My husband's in bed at home,' she says. 'I've taken a chance and left him on his own, so I'll probably find him on the floor.'

She's only half joking.

'The one thing everyone has,' Jenny says, 'is that we all love Brighton. You can tell, can't you?'

'Yes,' I say.

* * *

Jenny leaves and I'm sitting with my notes across the table from a man in his sixties who is with his father.

Chris thunders on in the background: '. . . I mean, what does Frank Worthington know about women?' He's still got a receptive audience.

I start talking to the younger man opposite me. His name is Andy Gadd. He's sixty-one, a Brighton season ticket holder, and he's here with his father David, who is eighty-seven.

David's wife, Jeanette, is back at home; father and son are having a boys' day out to give her some peace.

They've lived in the Woodingdean area of Brighton all their lives, and David first took Andy to a game when he was ten. He's seen dozens of Brighton managers and players come and go, including Chris and Guy. He was diagnosed with dementia three years ago.

'We've loved football, haven't we, Dad,' Andy reflects, glancing over. 'You got me playing as a kid as well.' His dad nods. 'And you'd come along and run the line when I was little, when I was playing?'

'I did, yeah,' David says.

'It was good fun going to the Goldstone, wasn't it, Dad?'

'It was good fun, yeah,' David smiles.

'The Goldstone, yes, the Goldstone,' he repeats, eyes slightly brighter. 'Long time ago now,' he adds, voice falling to a murmur.

I ask Andy what it's been like to watch his father's dementia develop.

'It's a horrible disease,' Andy says. 'There doesn't seem to be a cure, but football helps. You can see people when they remember, when they get engaged, they're there, in the moment. They light up.' He pats his father gently on the shoulder, grounding him with his gaze.

I say goodbye and head back to the entrance to wait for Guy and Jenny. The men are filing out.

At the end of the line is the man in the Stetson. He's still slightly hunched, but his face has opened. He reaches out a hand.

'My name is Steve,' he says.

'Damien,' I reply.

He tips his Stetson as if to say, 'So long, stranger,' and disappears into the grey light towards the bus stop on the A27.

10

Back in the Dock

Days after being released from jail, Paul Mitchell breezed back through the turnstiles at St Andrew's again.

Although he'd been banned for life, he was undeterred and no one seemed to be stopping him.

'He went in disguise,' Debbie tells me from the pub near Glastonbury.

'Disguise?'

'Cap and glasses,' Paul's sister Hayley clarifies.

'No fake moustache or beard?' I ask, genuinely intrigued. It struck me that Birmingham City weren't policing Paul's ban too tightly.

Debbie frowns.

'Well,' she says, 'they've got facial recognition. Glasses probably block it.'

Debbie explains that up until the last few months of his life, Paul had not stopped going. And even though there must've been people in the crowd who recognised him, no one said a word.

By the time Blues faced Albion on 3 April 2022, Paul had been slipping into games for three years.

He was there in the Main Stand, watching a scrappy derby. Blues hadn't beaten Albion in nine attempts. Albion were chasing the play-offs and Blues were nineteenth – safe but irrelevant.

In the sixty-seventh minute, still goalless, Blues are awarded a penalty after Albion's Conor Townsend handles in the box. Lyle Taylor, on loan from Forest, does his trademark stutter-step walk-up and strikes it past Sam Johnstone.

A surge of bodies spills from the Main Stand on to the side of the pitch in chaotic joy. No one clocked Paul in the melee at the time. But later, the stewards combed through the CCTV and recognised his Blues tattoos.

I let out a sympathetic tut.

Debbie cradles her head in her hands, pressing on her forehead. 'Another bloody nightmare.'

Paul was arrested once more and charged with breaching his football ban.

On Tuesday, 6 September 2022, Debbie and Paul's stepdad accompanied him back to Birmingham Magistrates' Court. This time Paul was wearing a smart blue suit. His hair was cropped short.

The national press hadn't been tipped off. Birmingham City stayed quiet. Perhaps they were embarrassed that Paul had slipped in so easily for years.

Paul's solicitor, Shabeer Qureshi, told the court Paul had enrolled on a construction management course at university, and was due to start that month.

Mr Qureshi argued he had 'turned his life around' and pleaded for a chance to keep going with the 'positive things' he'd begun. He asked the court not to send Paul back to jail. He had two young children now.

The courtroom doors creaked open. Two white-shirted guards entered and stood beside Paul.

The judge sentenced him to another twelve weeks.

Debbie sobbed in the public gallery. Paul blew her a kiss as he was led away.

'It's six weeks,' he said defiantly, suggesting he'd only serve half his sentence. But Paul's life was spiralling out of control.

* * *

Why had Paul risked so much to run on to the pitch again?

He had two boys now – Frankie and Freddie – and he adored them. He was missing out on precious weeks in their lives. Apart from a drink-driving conviction in his teens, Paul had no other criminal record.

I wondered if there were any clues in his childhood, something that might explain his impulsive, extreme behaviour. Debbie leans back for a moment, then starts talking about when Paul was small.

He was born in Solihull Hospital, the youngest of three. His sisters, Hayley and Jodie, were eighteen months and eight years older, respectively.

Debbie and his father, Paul senior, were publicans, moving around venues across the Midlands. By the time Paul was born, their marriage was strained. Debbie tried to hold it together for the sake of her son.

She tightens the cord of her dressing gown, like a seat belt, and plays 'My Boy' by Elvis on her phone. The sound is thin and crackly. She mouths along, her expression fixed. It's a song about staying in an unhappy, unstable marriage for the sake of a child. She would rock Paul in her arms and sing him the lyrics, as the marriage fell apart.

Debbie insists her husband wasn't violent, but it's clear that even with all she did, Paul's early years were turbulent. Those first years, from birth to two, are critical for learning how to regulate emotion, and Paul's were anything but settled. He was still an infant when his parents separated for good and he divided his time between his mum and dad.

Paul's attachment to Birmingham City followed the usual path. At first, it was about the adults, the tribal onboarding. By the age of four, he was going to Blues games every weekend with his dad. Football became a sure-fire way to stay close to him after the separation.

On some level, I figured his dad leaving must have felt like abandonment. Children often blame themselves when things go wrong between their parents. It's safer to believe you're a bad child with good parents than a good child with bad ones.

The latter is too destabilising. If your parents can't be trusted, you're not safe. So, the young mind bends the story, preserves parents as protectors, and internalises the shortcomings instead.

Our core beliefs form early on, particularly negative ones – 'I'm not good enough,' 'There's something wrong with me' – are adaptive at first. They keep the vision of parents intact and allow the child to feel protected. But they calcify and often turn into shame, an emotion that is very hard to alleviate.

From the age of four, Paul and his dad were travelling on coaches to away matches, sometimes alongside members of Birmingham's hooligan firm, the Zulu Warriors.

Like for so many fans, the match was a ticket to attention, to love. It was a way of bridging a relationship fractured too early. It was also his induction into a wider tribe.

Debbie says Paul senior wasn't a Zulu himself but knew and respected them. I picture the young Paul on those coaches, knees tucked under his chin, watching closely – how men carried themselves, how status was measured, what masculinity looked like.

I imagined him absorbing football-related banter – an effortless conversational currency that bonded everyone together, no matter their age or background. Like core beliefs, these lessons about masculinity imprint young and are absorbed without awareness. He admired the Zulus, but Debbie says Paul never became one because he was 'too soft'.

There were flashes of impulsivity when he was a kid, like when he set fire to a bush in the family garden and the fire brigade were called. But Hayley remembers his childhood for different reasons; she says she was Paul's protector against the playground bullies who tormented him. Paul got his GCSEs then went into the pub trade like his parents, first as a glass collector, then managing his own venues and also training as a chef.

Behind the bar, Paul thrived as the 'class clown'. Punters liked him. He wore Burberry, the brand adopted by the Zulus.

In his early twenties, he met Dion. Their first son, Frankie, came soon after.

Debbie scrolls through her phone, pausing on a gallery of pictures. 'This is him with Frankie,' Debbie says, 'Frankie is a Blues fan too.'

She presses play on a video.

The screen lights up. It's Paul at home, with a toddler. There is Blues memorabilia all around.

'Say hello,' Paul says, grinning.

'Hello,' Frankie giggles.

'Hello,' Paul echoes.

'Hello,' Frankie repeats, creasing into hysterics.

'Hello, Frankie.'

'Hello, Dad.'

'My Frankie.'

'My dad.'

It continues until both collapse into helpless laughter, Paul clutching his son to his chest like he's holding the whole world.

Debbie keeps scrolling through the tender family moments. Nestled among them is the infamous photo: Paul mid-swing, his fist connecting with Grealish's jaw.

11

The Blue Girl

Just two days after Paul ran on to the pitch for the first time, another football fan was preparing an audacious disguise.

The date was 12 March 2019. The place: Tehran, Iran's capital, more than 2,700 miles from St Andrew's.

Sahar Khodayari was a 29-year-old supporter of Esteghlal FC, one half of the city's great rivalry with Persepolis. That day, Esteghlal FC were playing Al Ain FC, from the United Arab Emirates, in the Asian Champions' League.

Sahar's story reveals, perhaps more clearly than any in this book, the extraordinary lengths people will go to in order to belong – and the price they pay.

She was born in 1990, eleven years after the 1979 revolution that transformed Iran into an Islamic Republic presided over by Ayatollah Khomeini.

Before the revolution, the streets of Tehran appeared fairly modern. Women wore jeans, miniskirts and short-sleeved tops, and styled their hair according to the latest trends. They had been free to watch football in stadiums, including Tehran's Azadi Stadium, one of the largest in the world.

Esteghlal and Persepolis both boasted huge female fan bases.

But after the Shah fell in 1979, everything changed. Khomeini decreed that all women must cover their hair. Women were banned from entering stadiums, and strict gender segregation became the law of the land.

On the morning of the match against Al Ain, Sahar did what other young women, desperate to see football, had learned to do in Iran. She sat in front of a mirror, took off her hijab and started to assemble her male disguise.

She replaced her headscarf with a blue wig, stuck on a fake beard and pulled on a long men's overcoat over her normal clothes. She topped her outfit with a baseball cap and headed to the stadium.

More than 65,000 were attending the game that day. Sahar was absorbed into the moving crowd of men outside the stadium, a river of deep royal blue flowing slowly towards the gates.

Uniformed guards stood at the barriers, pulling people out of the flow at random, patting them down, waving others through. Sahar kept her head down beneath the baseball cap, the fake beard itching against her skin. The long coat hid the outline of her body.

She had rehearsed the walk and knew to keep silent if possible.

But at the final checkpoint, a guard stopped her and gestured for her to step aside.

He reached out to search her.

Sahar pulled back. She refused to be touched intimately.

That was enough for everything to fall apart.

Within minutes, she was surrounded. Her wig was pulled away and the fake beard identified.

She was arrested and carted away in a van by the *morality police*, a religious vice squad charged with enforcing strict Islamic codes, especially for women.

For three nights, Sahar was held in Shahr-e Rey prison, a facility better known as Qarchak. Once a chicken farm, it remained an extremely grim place, overcrowded and unhygienic, with little in the way of medical care.

It was a holding pen for women convicted of violent crimes and for sex workers.

She was eventually bailed and ordered to return to court on 2 September 2019. She faced charges of 'openly committing a sinful act by (. . .) appearing in public without a hijab' and 'insulting officials'.

She returned to the court on 2 September and was told that her case had been delayed again. She was warned she eventually faced up to six months in prison. Her resolve crumbled.

Outside the courthouse, Sahar poured petrol over herself and lit a match. She suffered burns to ninety per cent of her body. She died six days later.

Her death sent shock waves through Iran. On social media, the hashtag #BlueGirl, a nod to Esteghlal's colours, became a rallying cry against the stadium ban for women. Protests erupted and vigils were held.

But then a narrative began to emerge.

Her father told the world his daughter had a bipolar disorder diagnosis, explaining that she'd stopped taking her medication over a year earlier. The implication was that she was unstable and that her actions were the result of a particular manic phase.

I couldn't stop thinking about Sahar. I'd seen pictures of her online before her horrific suicide. In one she's lying on the grass, a scarlet headscarf framing her beautiful face, her wide, doe-like eyes inviting you into the frame and beckoning you to find out more.

In another, taken a couple of days before her death from her hospital bed, she is unrecognisable, swaddled in yellow blankets, bandaged from head to toe.

Her story haunted me. The risks she took for football resonated with me. I couldn't accept her death being repackaged as the result of mental illness.

There must be more to this awful story. I tracked down someone in Iran who knew much more about Sahar.

She was a massive football fan too and has risked her life to secretly lead a campaign calling for a lift on the football stadium bans for women.

For obvious reasons she was hard to find and even when someone connected me to her, I didn't have much confidence she would reply to my request for a chat.

But one day in spring 2024, I received an email from her agreeing to meet me. She went by the name of Sara.

* * *

The Zoom screen flickers to life. Sara asks to keep her camera off, afraid of reprisals if the footage is somehow leaked.

She laughs when I tell her I'm a Wolves fan. She knows we're having a shit season. I can hear her giggling at the thought of my habitual emotional meltdowns.

She reassures me that her own emotions are just as volatile. She gets terrible headaches when her team loses and sometimes can't even go to work.

Sara was born after the revolution. Although she and her friends loved football, it was taboo to play, even at school.

Football was the domain of men. Bizarrely, girls were allowed to play basketball, though. And when the teachers weren't looking, they'd kick the heavy, oversized ball around between makeshift posts.

When Sara played football with her friends, they felt like they belonged to the society that excluded them. Although girls were banned from stadiums from 1981, Sara and her friends devoured football anyway – watching televised replays, often Premier

League games, then turning up at school the next day to dissect every moment.

She responded to the stadium ban by learning everything. She knew more than most of the boys. Her knowledge became her currency – a way to belong, to earn respect, to carve out an identity where she felt it had been flattened by patriarchy.

'Football became something you could share with the other half of the country,' she says. 'With men.'

She slips into the voices she heard growing up. '*Football is a man's sport. You don't know anything. Do you even know what offside is?*'

There's a short silence.

'I became equal to them.'

She pauses, weighing what to say next. 'I know things,' she says, starting to giggle, 'maybe even better than you.'

She creases up in the dark.

'I bet you do,' I concede to Sara. We laugh; two strangers in the dark, two minutes into a conversation, different countries, and football's already given us an easy conversational intimacy, licence to tease.

Sara dreamed of going to a game, especially the famous Tehran derby between her team Esteghlal and Persepolis.

The derby is one of the most hotly contested in the world. In 1983, 128,000 crammed in to watch. Only men.

In the years after the revolution, high-profile football players who actively opposed the regime were tortured and executed. Among them was Habib Khabiri, captain of the national team.

Khabiri had scored a dramatic 25-yard goal against Kuwait in December 1977, leading to Iran's first appearance at a World Cup, Argentina 1978.

I found some grainy footage of that game: Khabiri, in a number 7 all-white strip, wheeling away to celebrate with teammates after his second-half equaliser.

Iran came last in their group at that Argentina World Cup, but they did draw 1-1 with a Scotland side featuring Joe Jordan, Archie Gemmill, Asa Hartford, Lou Macari and Kenny Dalglish. Khabiri was a centre-half.

Seven years after leaping into the arms of a teammate to celebrate his World Cup-qualifying wonder goal against Kuwait, Khabiri was shot dead by a firing squad, aged twenty-nine.

He was accused of being a member of the People's Mojahedin Organization of Iran, an armed opposition group to the regime. Sara had to wait until she was thirty-five to go to a game in an actual stadium. She watched Iran beat Morocco 1-0 in St Petersburg at the 2018 World Cup in Russia.

Sara tells me young women were furious at being locked out of stadiums. But any female protesters were dealt with brutally. The regime rolled tanks into the streets to intimidate them. Others were interrogated, tortured and jailed.

'These girls were not jailed with the political prisoners,' Sara says. 'They were thrown in with thieves and killers.'

Sara decided to step up her activism. She launched the Open Stadiums campaign, a secret mission to grant females access to the football family again. Young women embraced the cause. They disguised themselves as men to sneak into stadiums.

Sara and her fellow fans had gone through the same initiation as football supporters everywhere. Football was initially the ticket into belonging in a tribe. But for her it wasn't about bonding with her biological family, it was a way of belonging to society at large.

Her fight to watch the matches fused her to the team but also to the other women resisting oppression. Harvey Whitehouse and colleagues have seen this kind of deep fusion elsewhere too, like the fierce bonds forged between women after traumatic childbirth.

Sara spoke of an allegiance to Esteghlal that sounded as visceral as mine to Wolves, but it was also soldered to gender and resistance too. That double charge of identity fusion meant young women were willing to make extraordinary sacrifices for football.

She said many female fans – most in their teens – were arrested, detained and sexually assaulted by the *morality police,* who called them prostitutes.

'They forced them to take off all their clothes and searched their bodies, even their vaginas,' Sara says.

'They wanted to humiliate them. They were saying, "Why are you trying to look like boys?"'

Sara herself had been interrogated and detained many times.

After Sahar's death, Sara developed an eating disorder and became suicidal. She experienced panic attacks. It was the saddest time of her life.

I ask her about the Blue Girl's bipolar diagnosis and how it fed into what had happened to her.

Sara cuts me dead. Her tone changes, a little sharp, as if she wants to make something very clear.

'This is *not true,*' she says sternly.

'Do you want to know what *really* happened to Sahar?'

She takes a breath and starts to tell me the story.

* * *

Sahar was born in the village of Salm in Chaharmahal and Bakhtiari province, later moving with her family to Qom, a deeply conservative city, two hours south of Tehran. It is home to many of the ruling mullahs, the country's leading religious leaders and scholars.

She was one of eight children in a traditional, religious family and wanted to be a police officer. But her father told her that she could not do this because she was 'a girl and weak'.

Her father agreed it was inappropriate – criminal, in fact – for her to go to the stadium, but he allowed her to watch the game on the television with her brothers and sisters.

From a young age, Sahar was passionate about football. Watching the games on television enabled her to express herself emotionally and bonded her to her siblings. She kicked a ball in the streets with friends while the stadium ban played out.

Like Sara, she devoured news about Esteghlal. Sahar was bright and ambitious, earning degrees in computer science and English translation. Friends recalled her as independent-minded, railing against the regime's restrictions.

When Sahar was thrown in jail with sex workers after being arrested in disguise, the stigma was unbearable for her family. 'The reason she stayed there so long,' Sara says, 'was that her father didn't want to bail her out.'

Inside prison, she became depressed and anxious, and Sara suspects she was sexually assaulted like other girls. She heard she experienced white torture, a form of psychological persecution relying on isolation and sensory deprivation. Prisoners are placed in solitary white cells, with constant light, wearing white clothes, in total silence. The idea is to break an individual without leaving physical marks.

Someone in the family eventually paid Sahar's bail but, on her release, the police took all her possessions, including her phone. This was her lifeline and too expensive to replace.

Sara's voice quietens to a whisper.

She was bailed several times and each time she returned to the court and asked for her phone back. Each time she was denied. She asked for her bail money but that was denied too.

Her failure to retrieve the bail money angered her family. She was a selfish woman who had dishonoured her family and put them into debt because of a stupid football match.

But it was what Sara told me next – about the Blue Girl's bipolar diagnosis – that she was most desperate for me to understand.

After Sahar burned herself on the courthouse steps, the regime panicked. Headlines appeared around the world. Sahar was becoming famous, a martyr, and the regime hated it.

So, according to Sara, state television went into propaganda overdrive. They went to talk to her father and encouraged him to collude with a lie; his daughter was mentally ill with bipolar disorder and this was the reason she had killed herself. Sara had spoken to Sahar's fellow inmates and they had said how scared she was of her father, and there was no mention of mental illness.

According to Sara, bipolar diagnoses are often weaponised in Iran – rolled out when the regime needed to discredit a young woman whose defiance had become inconvenient or embarrassing. Some psychiatrists and psychologists, she says, are directly complicit, working with the state. Girls would be declared 'crazy' with bipolar diagnoses and locked up in psychiatric wards instead of jails, under regime supervision.

I was horrified. According to Sara, the Blue Girl had been arrested for trying to watch football, and then pathologised as insane for her defiance. It sounded too grotesque to be real.

* * *

Dr Fahimeh Mianji is sitting in her car, waiting for her daughter to finish a drama class in Vancouver on a Tuesday morning. It's morning time there, but here in the UK there's just minutes to go until Wolves kick off against West Ham in the EFL Cup. An ungrateful, resentful part of me hopes the interview will dry up quickly, so I can sneak away for kick-off.

Fahimeh is wearing a tracksuit top under a big beige anorak, looking like a mum in a rush. She props her iPhone up on the dashboard, apologises for being slightly late and for the unconventional setting. She has glasses, a warm smile and a soft voice that settles my nervous system ahead of the game.

I reassure her that talking to people on video calls in their cars feels like normal clinical practice to me now. Post-Covid, patients log in from dashboards with phones sliding around, motorbikes roaring past and traffic wardens hammering on the glass. Therapy has changed a lot since Freud.

Wolves are 1-0 up at half-time and my phone starts pinging relentlessly.

Fahimeh is an Iranian clinical psychologist. She started to realise all was not what it seemed in the world of Iranian psychiatry during her undergraduate degree in Tehran. She noticed more and more girls being labelled bipolar.

They were being prescribed powerful second-generation antipsychotics that numbed and sedated them, so they stopped doing things, like trying to watch football. She was suspicious that while there was no supposed gender difference in bipolar prevalence, she was only hearing of girls being diagnosed – and it was the ones who didn't meet the modest, obedient, patriarchal norms.

After completing her first doctorate in Iran, she left for Canada in 2011 to begin her PhD in cultural psychiatry under Professor

Laurence J Kirmayer at McGill University. She told Kirmayer what she had noticed about the bipolar diagnoses in Iran, and he encouraged her to investigate further.

Fahimeh threw herself into the project. She returned to Iran, visiting psychiatry conferences, hospitals and universities to interview prominent mental health doctors. Most were unaware of her hypothesis.

What she found was that many psychiatrists *were* medicating young women – including football fans – who weren't conforming. When she spoke to trainee psychiatrists as part of her research, they told her bipolar diagnoses were handed out like sweets in a playground. It was so common that residents developed a tongue-in-cheek *Time until Bipolar Diagnosis Scale* to measure how long it took in clinical rounds before someone suggested it for a young female patient. One psychiatrist told Fahimeh it usually took one or two minutes. They were diagnosed for wearing 'harsh make-up', for 'being happy', using social media – and for being emotional about football matches.

'In order to stop them from,' she does the bunny ears, '"causing trouble", they get diagnosed.'

We turn to the case of the Blue Girl, Sahar, the girl who burned herself to death. 'So this is who gets labelled bipolar,' I say. 'Young women sneaking into stadiums in disguise?'

'Yes,' Fahimeh says, without hesitation. 'If you are emancipating, this is not going to be tolerated at any level.'

After collating her data, she wrote it up in Canada, then returned to Tehran to present it at psychiatry conferences full of male colleagues.

Things got even weirder. Many male psychiatrists were furious with Fahimeh's findings and told her so. On the way back from one conference she sat with a prominent male psychiatrist.

As she drove, she sensed she was being observed like a lab specimen. Eventually he told her he suspected she had bipolar too. She needed to be assessed.

'Oh my God,' I say.

She creases up laughing.

'Because of my energy. Because of my energy . . .' she can't stop laughing.

I ask whether she was surprised when the media claimed Sahar had bipolar disorder, using it to explain both her love of football and her suicide.

'No,' Fahimeh says, shaking her head. 'I wasn't surprised at all.'

She exhales.

'I could see it coming. It just made me very sad.'

She falls quiet, gazing out of the window. Her daughter returns to the car. I head back to the lounge to catch the end of the match. Two late goals by Strand Larsen and we win 3-2.

12

Cup Upset at Blundell Park

The next day, news breaks of a potential cup upset. I tune in to the game at Blundell Park – League Two Grimsby against Premier League giants, Manchester United.

If you ever wanted to see identity fusion in action, this is it. Grimsby, with a squad worth £3.1 million are 2-0 up against United, whose squad is worth £766 million.

Rain is pelting down.

Charles Vernam and Tyrell Warren have given Grimsby the lead, but now they're under siege.

United enjoy seventy-seven per cent possession. They've had eighteen shots in the second half compared with Grimsby's four. The footage is so dark and rainy I can barely make out the players.

Still, Grimsby hang on. The crowd sways and gasps together, thousands of bodies locked into one nervous rhythm.

United wheel out the heavy artillery. On come Bruno Fernandes, Bryan Mbeumo, Mason Mount and Matthijs de Ligt.

On seventy-four minutes, Mbeumo scores. He sprints into the net to grab the ball for a quick restart. Grimsby players hold their heads. In the stands, thousands mirror the same grimace. Then, at eighty-nine minutes, Harry Maguire ghosts in at the back post to equalise from a corner. There's five minutes of added time. The siege is unremitting. United somehow manage to sky one over the bar from close range. The whistle goes. It's time for penalties.

Grimsby blink first, missing one of their first five. All United's Matheus Cunha must do is score to kill them off. He takes a well-rehearsed run-up and strokes it to the right. Christy Pym guesses correctly and saves. The crowd explodes, rising as one body. Fans clutch one another like lifelong brothers and sisters.

Now it's sudden death. But everyone keeps scoring.

It's eleven penalties each.

Darragh Burns steps up for Grimsby. The camera cuts to two teenage girls in the stands, side by side, identical, both hiding behind match programmes. They look like Geishas holding fans. Burns sneaks it in. The place erupts, and United's Mbeumo has to score to keep United alive.

In the corner, a steward is half-heartedly trying to restrain the Grimsby mascot, who's desperate to edge closer to the goal. Mbeumo hits the bar. Grimsby win.

Children spill on to the turf, bouncing up and down. Players are hoisted on to shoulders. Eight- and nine-year-old boys dart forward to high-five their heroes. Inflatable Harry the Haddocks ricochet through the delirious mass, drenched by rain. It looks like someone has spiked the jelly at a children's party with MDMA. Stewards abandon all pretence of control. Fans hug strangers, hug players, hug themselves. The unmitigated affection and love for strangers reminds me of the rave scene in the '90s.

I ring Bill Brewster, a Grimsby fan and one of the country's most respected dance DJs. He was a founding resident at Fabric, co-wrote the seminal 'Last Night a DJ Saved My Life', and once edited *Mixmag*.

I'd already spoken to him once, after reading about how football hooliganism declined alongside the rise of the rave scene in the 1990s. Commentators suggested that hooligans had swapped the thrill of belonging to a violent mob for the gentler, but no less intoxicating, communion of MDMA-fuelled rave culture. They had become 'love thugs'.

I catch Bill on his way back from the match. He tells me that taking ecstasy for the first time in 1989 was one of the most transformative experiences of his life.

The game against United, he says, was on a par.

The atmosphere was unbelievable.

It made me wonder what was happening inside the bodies of these fans to make them so tender, to bond them so tightly – without (as far as I knew) a trace of ecstasy.

I found a clue in research suggesting that MDMA works by triggering the release of oxytocin, often dubbed the cuddle hormone. It is released when a mother holds her baby and when we have sex. It typically rockets at the start of romantic relationships, marking the 'honeymoon' phase, which for many people seems to last about three months.

This is when you can't keep your hands off each other and your partner has no flaws whatsoever. It's like wearing a virtual-reality headset that airbrushes out their irritating habits. Nature expects you to reproduce during this intense, blissful window. After that, the headset slips and you notice they crack their knuckles every five minutes.

Oxytocin also operates in larger groups – especially when people sing and dance together. Chanting and moving in unison increases oxytocin and feelings of social closeness. Other studies show that when people are given oxytocin through a nasal spray, they become more trusting. It appears to act as a kind of social glue – and may provide the biological basis for identity fusion.

I say goodbye to Bill and flick back through the crowd footage on YouTube. One image stands out. A little girl, maybe seven, perched on the shoulders of her thick-bearded dad. She's wearing a Grimsby shirt, her legs clamped around his neck, right in the middle of the chaos. Thousands of fans surge and roar beneath her, and she just turns her head slowly, taking it all in.

I can't help wondering what she'll think about when she falls asleep that night. How her dreams will start to process all that noise and colour and emotion. In the days to come, she'll replay it, frame by frame, the night weaved into her autobiographical story, the sense of who she is.

It feels like a rite of passage. It reminds me of being six, on my dad's shoulders at Wolves versus Sunderland.

I have the sense I'm watching the exact moment this girl stops belonging just to her parents and starts belonging to a club. The moment an alloy between fan and club is formed.

On the downside, she may now be condemned to a lifetime of following Grimsby Town.

* * *

For a while, scientists dared to dream. Could oxytocin be the miracle cure for humanity's nastiness?

Here was a nasal spray which, with a few puffs up each nostril, might turn us from snarling tribalists into teddy bears. Billie Eilish even named a song after it. Was it possible that the antidote to war and hatred could be hiding on the shelves of pharmacies between hay fever spray and lip balm?

The commercial opportunists piled in. Oxytocin sprays were marketed as aphrodisiacs.

PherLuv Oxytocin Pheromone Spray, for instance, promises more dates, better sex and improved social confidence. Oddly, it also claims to be 'great for salesmen'.

Some reviews were glowing.

'The first time I felt it, I felt a sense of love and homeyness,' wrote one user. 'I wanted to call friends and family.'

Another crowed: 'My favourite time to use is right before sex. The rush comes in waves. I feel more verbal, more connected.'

Then, muddying the waters slightly: 'Works alone as well.'

Others were less certain.

'She held my arm and sniffed my neck several times,' reported one man. I couldn't tell if that was good, bad or grounds for professional help.

Some were disappointed.

'I felt a burst of euphoria followed by a migraine,' said one.

Another wrote: 'I got romantic, then angry. I had to sit down.'

Yet another: 'I think it makes me ejaculate faster than usual. Much faster.'

One man said it simply made him more aggressive in the pub.

At this point it was starting to sound like Russian roulette. You might get cuddles. You might get a headache. You might orgasm too quickly. You might get a fight.

The more I read, the more it was obvious that oxytocin was not chemical fairy dust. It has a darker side.

One reviewer warned: 'It makes me care more but also more dangerous, because you become overprotective.'

More dangerous?

Some unsettling evidence began to emerge in the research. In one study, people who put oxytocin up their noses were nastier to Arabs and Germans. In another, oxytocin led participants to give more money to their own group and actually *waste* resources rather than give them to outsiders.

The dream that oxytocin might be a panacea of universal love began to evaporate. Sniffing oxytocin made us kinder to our own group and harsher to everyone else.

Psychologists call this ethnocentrism.

If you met oxytocin in a bar, it would be leaning against the jukebox with LOVE and HATE tattooed across its knuckles.

Which takes us headlong into Part III, and some unsavoury behaviour at a Boxing Day football match.

PART III

Them

13

The Delicious Downfall of Bruno Fernandes

It's still 0-0 in the Boxing Day clash between Wolves and Manchester United at Molineux in 2024. I'm wedged into our living room in Hastings with eight of my Wolves-supporting family members. We span three generations. The mood is taut.

Then, early in the second half, Bruno Fernandes, United's captain, lunges into a challenge on Nelson Semedo. It's high and reckless. Even if he hadn't already been on a yellow card, there's a strong argument for a straight red. With the yellow, though, his fate is sealed. Fernandes is off.

And our living room? Pandemonium. We erupt as if Wolves have just won the Champions League. Fernandes, dragging his captain's armband down his arm in slow motion, looks distraught, possibly on the verge of tears.

I find myself screaming, 'Petulant cunt!' at the TV, which earns an approving cackle from my elderly mother, who is brandishing an imaginary red card from her armchair. 'See you later, you sulky twat!' she shrieks.

My sister – a nurse – rushes the TV, flashes a wanker sign, and performs a small, triumphant jig. We all join in – even my devout father, gently flapping his hand like he's blessing a sinner on their way to Purgatory.

When my nephew gleefully announces it's Bruno's third sending-off this year, we high-five as though we've personally brokered peace in the Middle East.

Ahhhhhhhhhhh, the warm embrace of festive cheer.

But as the euphoria dies down, I catch myself wondering: what has happened to us?

Less than twenty-four hours ago, we were sitting in church, solemnly absorbing a Christmas sermon on compassion, forgiveness and the virtue of sitting alongside someone in their suffering.

Yet here we are, practically foaming at the mouth, celebrating another human's humiliation with a fervour usually reserved for finding a tenner in an old coat.

I recalled the images of smiling Blues fans clapping with delight after Paul Mitchell landed his punch.

I began to wonder whether I was gripped by something similar. I understood more clearly now how my identity had fused with my team's, why everything felt so personal. But the depth of my vitriol towards the other side still demanded explanation – particularly when, as my wife so helpfully likes to point out, it's 'just a game'.

14

Tall Poppies

The German word *Schadenfreude* comes from *Schaden,* meaning damage, and *Freude,* meaning joy. It is the pleasure we feel at another person's pain or humiliation. It offers the clearest window yet into our tribal human brain. I sit in my office Zooming with the historian of emotions Dr Tiffany Watt Smith. I'm showing her some images of the day Paul Mitchell punched Grealish.

'Can you see any images?' I ask.

'Not yet,' Tiffany says politely.

I start clicking around. Nothing happens. I hit 'Share Screen' again and accidentally broadcast my entire browser: beard oils, kettlebell workouts for middle-aged men, and a tab labelled *Why Am I Always Tired?*

'What about now?'

'Oh yes, now I can.'

'Is it the one of Paul Mitchell wearing a cap punching Jack Grealish?'

'No, it's another one. It's a crowd . . . some of whom look quite pleased.'

I point out a young woman in the crowd – a Blues fan – beaming with joy. Tiffany notices too, and she spots another man clapping, his face lit with delight.

Tiffany believes we are living in an *age of schadenfreude* and has written a book about it. With all the digital platforms and social media, we get to see rivals and rule breakers being shamed like never before.

She began writing about the topic after catching herself in the act: watching a reckless cyclist in South London go skidding off the pavement after nearly clipping her baby buggy; reading reports of celebrities in their mansions, abandoned and lonely.

Their distress felt like a hot bloom in her chest, a rush of warmth as people suffered.

Then, inevitably, she felt a flush of shame for feeling it. What did that make her? A psychopath? A sadist – someone who took pleasure in other people's suffering?

Turning to the world's great thinkers didn't reassure her. She discovered that schadenfreude has long been treated as a bleak indictment of human nature.

The philosopher Arthur Schopenhauer was particularly unforgiving. He said it was so corrosive that anyone caught indulging it should be shunned from society.

Then again, he was a cantankerous misogynist who once pushed a woman down the stairs for making too much noise and was famously cruel to his servants. It's not obvious he was in a position to lecture the rest of us about virtue. Tiffany carefully looks at the pictures on the screen. She wants to know more about Grealish as a player, admitting she doesn't really know anything about him. I explain that those who know him talk about his kindness and sensitivity – while, to many watching from the stands, he's a diving cheat with floppy hair held back by an Alice band.

She adjusts her wide-rimmed round glasses and peers in closer at the picture of the crowd. She says one of the reasons people experience the pleasure of schadenfreude is a sense of justice being served.

Children, she explains, love watching wrongdoers get their just deserts. In Leipzig, researchers set up a puppet theatre for an audience of six-year-olds. Some puppets were kind and generous, others were sly, selfish cheats. The selfish ones offered toys – only to snatch them back at the last second. The children then watched as the puppets were individually beaten. Seeing the good puppets punished upset them, but watching the bad puppets thrashed brought huge smiles to their gloating little faces.

It didn't end there. After a short glimpse of punishment, the theatre's curtains were drawn shut. The children were given a choice: they could wander off and do something else or they could hand over tokens to see an encore of the bad puppets being mercilessly beaten. They paid up gladly, eager to watch more suffering.

The puppets reminded me of Grealish toying with the ball in front of defenders.

'I'm sorry to drag you into the football with Jack Grealish,' I say, 'but that's exactly what Grealish does. He's a bad puppet.'

Tiffany raises an eyebrow.

Grealish is the puppet with the toy everyone wants – the football – dangling it just close enough to tempt, taunt and enrage.

Opponents lunge, flail and swipe, but each time Grealish whisks it away with balletic cruelty, as if the ball is tethered to his boots by invisible string. He makes defenders look ridiculous, humiliating them like the six-year-olds deprived of their toys at the puppet show. And then, to make matters worse, he falls over anyway, drawing a free kick.

To rival fans watching, it feels personal and unfair. It's like he's trying to humiliate *us* as well.

So, when Grealish is really scythed down, or someone in the crowd runs on to the pitch and punches him in the head, we savour it with the same gleeful appetite as the children at the puppet theatre. A selfish cheat getting his just deserts. It feels like justice. We are the children now.

* * *

The joy we get from watching cheats being punished is not surprising, given that cooperation is perhaps the main reason humans have prospered over other species. Our ability to collaborate and trust others has led to huge advances in civilisation. It is probably the reason that gossip evolved – to root out cheats and moral rule breakers.

It should be said that while Grealish is treated like a cheat, I could not find any real evidence that he *cheats* more than anyone else. Yes, he gets fouled a lot, but that's because he draws fouls with his incredible skill. It's difficult to nail down the stats, but it appears that in 2019/20, when Grealish was playing for Villa, he set a Barclays Premier League record for being fouled more than any other player, with 167 fouls blown against him in thirty-six appearances.

Most sports journalists have acknowledged he's not a diver but invites contact.

In 2020, Grealish was interviewed by *Soccer AM*. He was asked about the 167 fouls he drew in 2019/20.

'I get so much stick on social media from opposition fans saying you go down too easy which . . . at times I probably do, but that's just the player I am. Sometimes you have to slow the game down. It's part of my game, part of what I do . . . that's not saying that I dive at all. There's a difference between winning fouls and diving.'

He's asked whether it bothers him.

He grins widely. 'Not at all . . . it's all just banter at the end of the day.'

* * *

During a recent Wolves game against Everton, my wife observes me as I'm muttering abuse at Grealish. She asks me why I hate him so much. It was one of those offhand questions, the kind where you know the asker already has an answer lined up.

Still, I dutifully launch into my well-rehearsed spiel. Echoing Paul Mitchell, I say, 'He's a cheat.' 'Look at him. Always diving, always rolling around like he's been shot. It's pathetic.'

'Bollocks,' she says, barely looking up from her phone. 'It's because he's good-looking. You're just jealous, like the rest of them.'

I open my mouth, ready to retaliate, but I keep quiet.

As well as justice, Tiffany has a whole chapter on envy as a precursor to schadenfreude. In fact, she says, 'Few things elicit such guilty spasms of delicious schadenfreude as the disappointments of our most successful friends.'

The seventeenth-century philosopher Thomas Hobbes saw a link between other people's failures and our own sudden rise in *status*. Laughter, says Hobbes, comes from realising our own superior status in comparison with others.

Envy-fuelled schadenfreude does strange things to us.

I had an awkward experience on the phone with a friend, exploring the topic.

'You were hoping we'd gone bankrupt?' she said.

I'd been trying to explain that I wanted to include my experience of schadenfreude towards their absurdly successful family in the book.

'Really?' she said.

'Well, erm . . .'

'I don't know, Dame,' she cut in. 'It sounds a bit sick.'

Silence.

These are some of my closest friends, but I've always envied their lives. They retired at fifty, built a glass extension that doubled the size of their kitchen, complete with a floating log burner. So, when I got a text saying something was wrong in the family, my eyes widened with excitement.

Maybe their investment portfolio had imploded. Maybe a pheasant had flown into their bifold doors, shattering them. Maybe one of the golden, Oxbridge-educated daughters had been kicked out of college for smoking weed.

The call ended on an uneasy note. I stared at the phone for a while, replaying the word *sick*.

An hour later, she called back.

'I've been thinking,' she said. 'And . . . I've had similar thoughts. Every time you call, I have a faint hope you'll tell me your book deal has collapsed.'

She said she'd imagined my editor finally realising that beneath the overinflated proposal, the subsequent drafts had exposed me for what I was – an impostor, my limited talent laid bare.

'And do you remember when you got married in that swanky French chateau . . .'

She was on a roll, but I stopped her. I got the picture. The book deal example already hurt, but to hear she had hoped I'd been dredged from the swan-speckled lake on the morning of my big day after cracking under the pressure of the seating plan would have been too much.

Still, it was a relief to learn she didn't think I was a psychopath. And like Tiffany, she seemed to be coming to terms with the grim neural hydraulics of being human.

But the question remained – was I envious of Grealish?

It's true that I'm annoyed by how girls bang on about his looks all the time. The thing that really bugged me was the way women would go on about his calves. I'd see a shot of him strolling off the pitch, his shorts riding up ever so slightly, and there they were bulging out like two bronzed bowling balls. *Oh, those calves! Have you seen his calves? Look at those calves!* They would say through blushes. I hated it.

During my childhood, 'friends' called me chicken legs. I wore leg warmers under my trousers to bulk them out. My hair was a frizzy, mutinous mess of blond curls, sticking out in all directions. I looked like a little Art Garfunkel on stilts. The popular boys had straight hair, like Grealish, the kind that flopped nonchalantly.

I remember sweet, well-meaning hairdressers cupping my face in the mirror and saying, 'Haven't you got lovely curls?' *No. No, I haven't. I hate them. Burn them with your crimpers. I don't care if my hair turns to dust – just make it straight.*

So maybe my wife had a point. Maybe, when I watched Grealish strut around a football pitch, something deep stirred up. Maybe I envied him and that's why I felt unfettered joy when I saw him taken down.

But honestly, I'm not convinced that's it. There are plenty of good-looking players I admire, and I don't feel the same schadenfreude when they suffer.

I don't think it's envy exactly, it's something adjacent, something that Tiffany devotes another entire chapter to in her book.

Smugness. That unmistakable sense that someone thinks they're better than the rest of us.

Hubris is the flaw we most love to see punished, Tiffany says, and it is related to a phenomenon called *tall poppy syndrome*.

The phrase harks back to a story told by the Roman historian Livy. Livy told how King Tarquin the Proud demonstrated how to deal with threats to power. He went into his garden with a stick and swept off the heads of the tallest poppies. Those who dared to stand above the rest should be cut down to size.

The myth of Icarus carries the same warning. Given wings glued together with wax by his father Daedalus, Icarus soars too close to the sun, intoxicated by his own brilliance, until the wax melts and he falls into the sea.

Grealish is a prime example of someone who is considered a tall poppy. The socks rolled down to his ankles, shin pads the size of beer mats; everything about him suggests a player who thinks he is too good to bother with normal rules. He plays with an unbothered swagger, like a street footballer who's wandered on to a Premier League pitch by accident.

And then, obviously, there's his hair. When I see all this, it tells me he thinks he's too good to conform to the normal rules of men's football. *Male footballers don't wear hairbands.* I think to myself that I wouldn't like him even if he were on my side. He's not the warrior I want. I don't want some pretty boy applying self-tan before he goes out to battle. What if the fortress falls while he's exfoliating?

'So that's it,' I declare to Tiffany, pleased with myself. 'He's smug – he's a tall poppy, so he deserves everything that comes to him.'

Case closed, surely?

Tiffany sighs. It's not that simple. She urges me to speak to someone who knows more about football: the Dutch professor Wilco van Dijk. Wilco is professor of psychology at the University of Leiden, is a massive Ajax fan and is an expert on football and schadenfreude.

15

Frankenstein's Monster

'How are Ajax doing this year?' I ask genuinely.

'Is that a joke?' Wilco says, face completely serious.

I laugh nervously. I realise I haven't done my homework on the Dutch season.

'Okay,' he says, raising a hand to stop my grovelling. 'Let me give you a short summary of the season we had.'

Wilco explains that Ajax were nine points clear of Eindhoven with five games to go and still came second. Asking him about Ajax's season was the blundering equivalent of asking Kevin Keegan if he fancied curling up on the sofa with Sir Alex Ferguson at the end of the 1995/96 campaign.* He tells me that he was the victim of lots of schadenfreude, because Ajax were considered so arrogant – they called themselves the Sons of God.

He tells me he has a shameful little football fan habit he can't shake. When the Germans are playing – and losing – he switches the broadcast from Dutch TV to a German channel, just to hear the suffering in the pundits' voices.

* Keegan's Newcastle famously blew a twelve-point lead at the end of the 1995/96 campaign, allowing Manchester United to win the title on the final day. Sir Alex played relentless mind games with Keegan throughout the season leading to an iconic TV rant from Keegan ahead of the final match – 'I would love it if we beat them, love it!'

He once wondered if he was alone in this, so he decided to check. He obtained viewing figures for various Dutch and German channels after Spain played Germany in the 2010 World Cup semi-final. Spain won 1-0 after Carles Puyol's 73rd-minute header. Wilco found two huge spikes in Dutch audiences switching from local to German channels. The first came immediately after the goal – around 300,000 viewers couldn't resist tuning in to hear the German commentators choke back tears.

'The second peak,' Wilco says, rocking back and forth with delight, 'was at the end of the game, when Germany was eeeeeeeee-liminated from the tournament.'

The peak at the end of the game was even bigger and even more enjoyable.

'You could actually see all the German players crying on the pitch, and the German commentators having to comment on it,' he says, eyes gleaming.

'They emphasise how INCREDIBLY. SAD. THIS. IS.' He delivers it in a perfect robotic monotone, drained of all feeling.

* * *

As I listen to Wilco talking about switching channels, a memory surfaces. It's a Sunday and Wolves have lost again the previous day. I tell myself that on no account am I wasting my time by watching Sky's *Soccer Sunday*. I'm above it. I'll watch Guillermo del Toro's *Frankenstein* with my wife instead.

Then an advert for Man City–Liverpool flashes up on my phone. I start doing the emotional maths in my head – calculating the odds of another blow for Liverpool, a little joy borrowed from my brother's misery. I imagine him and his smug mates, all sad and silent in front of the TV, muttering, 'We'll be okay, we're Liverpool, it's just a blip.'

But even togetherness has a breaking point. Every defeat chips away at their specialness until it starts to look like everyone else's. And the thought of that, their own myth crumbling, the aura dissolving – oh, that would be better than *Frankenstein*. Wouldn't it?

'I thought we were watching a movie?' my wife says, forlornly.

'Why don't you watch it without me – you can have the lounge, in front of the fire?'

Her face drops.

'You can even watch the final of *Celebrity MasterChef* if you like?' I'm manipulative, desperate. After another depressing weekend watching Wolves, I'll suffer the cold kitchen and smaller TV for the potentially warm glow of schadenfreude.

I'm making a fish stir-fry when Doku slams in City's third. The Liverpool players trudge back to the halfway line, shoulders sagging. I mutter, 'Ha. Bet my brother's not laughing now.'

My wife, who has decided to stay and do some 'admin' on her phone, hears me and looks up. 'That's so bad. He's your brother.'

I continue stirring the food with an evil grin. The fish crackles and spits. Steam rises from the pan.

The Scouse Republic of Liverpool – the moral conscience of football. The people's club.

Too pure to sing the anthem, eh; too special to lose. Not tonight, though.

I know how pathetic it is – how utterly inverted that football has turned family into proxy enemies, that my brother's unhappiness is, for a moment, my own reward. It doesn't help that Ben was always better than me at football, a gifted youth player, while I was mediocre. Now he supports a great team, and mine is shit. I envy him. He's a tall poppy and this evening Manchester City wield Tarquin's stick.

Liverpool lose 3-0, and later we do watch *Frankenstein* – a creature assembled from fragments, cursed to lurch through life under urges it barely understands.

16

The Darker Side of Schadenfreude

It would be easy for me to feel deeply ashamed of my attitude towards my brother – and even towards Grealish – but Wilco's confession about switching channels just to enjoy the other side's misery makes me feel marginally less unhinged. And it turns out neuroscience is on my side too. The evidence suggests that this little surge of pleasure arrives without any conscious choice at all.

Tiny electrodes were strapped to the faces of thirty-two German football fans during the 2012 European Championship. The electrodes recorded every flicker of muscle movement while they watched short TV clips of football penalties taken by the German team and their arch-rivals, the Dutch.

The electrodes tracked the activity of two facial muscles involved in smiling; one raises the cheeks, the other tightens the skin around the eyes. Crucially, the penalty clips were selected from games where the teams were not playing against each other. In other words, there was no competitive advantage to the Germans when the Dutch missed a penalty.

The German fans confidently reported that they were happier when their national team scored than when the Dutch missed. In other words, their subjective self-reports suggested patriotic pride, not malice.

But the electrode data told another story.

The facial readings showed that when a Dutch player failed to score, the German smiles appeared faster and spread wider than when their own team scored. These were genuine grins, not simply looks of surprise.

The researchers described it as an emotional dissociation – what we say we feel isn't always what we show. When the emotion is socially undesirable – like taking pleasure in someone else's pain – it slips below the level of awareness, surfacing only in the twitch of a cheek or the brief, involuntary lift of a smile.

* * *

There's a difference between feeling schadenfreude and really participating in harming someone. But a professor at Harvard University fears there's a sinister overlap. Mina Cikara, usually a mild-mannered academic researcher and mother, decided to study schadenfreude after discovering how tribal her own brain was in sports contexts. On one occasion her husband had to prevent her fighting a New York Yankees fan who antagonised her while she was wearing a Boston Red Sox hat.

Cikara was confused by her behaviour. She saw that humans were, by default, surprisingly reluctant to hurt others. Studies show consistent patterns of harm aversion. In lab experiments, people are willing to pay money to stop pain being delivered to someone else, and they actually avoid harming others more strongly than they avoid harming themselves.

When participants are asked to perform 'violent' actions that are actually harmless – like firing a fake gun at someone – they show real physiological stress responses. Evidence from outside the lab suggests the same thing. Analyses of activity in the American Civil War and the First World War suggest that many soldiers deliberately fired over the heads of enemy fighters rather than kill them.

Other primates appear to demonstrate the same instinct. In one laboratory experiment, rhesus monkeys showed they would rather go hungry than inflict pain on others. They were offered a chance to pull a lever for food but when they realised this would also deliver an electric shock to a fellow animal, they refused to pull it. One monkey even went twelve days without food to avoid hurting a neighbour. The primatologist Frans de Waal argued that such findings suggest that hurting fellow animals violates a deep biological instinct.

The problem, however, is that throughout history, groups have *required* their members to hurt or even kill outsiders under situations of threat or when resources are scarce.

So how do we switch off our empathy circuits when the group demands it?

In humans, there are various moral disengagement strategies that make it easier to justify harm. Dehumanisation is an obvious example. This is where we label members of another group as 'inhuman', so our brains fail to register their pain as relevant. There are many terrible examples of this. Tutsis in the Rwandan genocide were called 'cockroaches'. Armenians were described as 'weeds' or 'tumours', and Jews were labelled 'vermin' in Nazi Germany. Entire villages in Vietnam were attacked and justified under the metaphor of 'weed control'. Football culture contains similar patterns, where rival fans are 'scum', 'rats', 'vermin' and so on.

Infrahumanisation, a term coined by the Belgian psychologist Jacques-Philippe Leyens, is a subtler but equally dangerous cousin of dehumanisation. The rival is still human – but only in outline. Our minds deny them the richer inner states that make someone fully real. Outgroup members may feel basic emotions such as anger, fear or pleasure, but not the more complex, self-conscious ones like grief, guilt, hope or love. By emptying them of these emotions, we make it easier to bypass the usual brakes of empathy.

Another well-researched way we override our natural tendency to be kind is through obedience to authority. Stanley Milgram's work in the 1960s showed how easily ordinary people will deliver what they think are dangerous electric shocks when a figure of authority tells them it is required. Displacing the responsibility on to an authority figure helps override a natural aversion to causing harm.

But Cikara thinks schadenfreude may hold the real neurobiological key, a way of hacking our good-naturedness from the inside. She argues that the neurobiology of schadenfreude teaches our otherwise cooperative brains to associate a rival's suffering with pleasure. Repeated learning that other people's pain is pleasurable creates a neural bridge which makes actually harming others easier.

She cites a study where sixteen fans of rival Swiss clubs were recruited. Each was given a wristband in their team's colours and emblem.

To stoke team rivalry, the rival clubs first took part in a competitive football quiz against each other. Then each fan was placed inside a brain scanner and shown electric shocks – from *mild discomfort* to *extreme pain* – being delivered to the hands of fellow fans and rival fans.

When the shocks hit their own fans, the brain's empathy hub – the *anterior insular cortex* – lit up brightly. These were their people, after all. But when the same shocks were delivered to members of the rival team, the insula was less engaged. Empathy, it seemed, was selective.

More striking still was that when rival fans were in pain, a different part of the brain – the *nucleus accumbens*, associated with pleasure and reward and dopamine – lit up like a floodlight. This all happened in fractions of seconds, below the level of awareness.

In other words, brains were rewarding fans for experiencing their rivals' suffering. Schadenfreude was hard-wired in.

Cikara was most intrigued, however, by what happened next in the experiment, when the moral heat was turned up further. The fans in the scanner were given a choice: they could reduce the intensity of another fan's pain by absorbing half of it themselves. Or they could refuse to help and either choose to watch a football clip or sit back and actually watch the other person suffer.

The results were grim. Fans were far more likely to share the pain if the person was one of their own. And when the victim was a rival, they tended not to reach for the football clip – they chose to sit back and watch.

Cikara found similar results in her own research with baseball fans (Red Sox and Yankees). She demonstrated that fans whose brains lit up most when watching the rival team suffer were most likely to advocate throwing food or beverage at rival fans when asked in a follow-up survey two weeks later. This was after controlling for general levels of aggression in each participant. She began to wonder whether schadenfreude might be a training camp for actual harm.

Each time the reward circuits light up during schadenfreude and dopamine is released, it acts like a reinforcement-learning trial; the brain encodes *out-group harm = good feeling*. Repeated doses of seemingly harmless schadenfreude dull the guilt we would normally feel about someone else's pain. The neural pathway for *enjoying* out-group suffering becomes more accessible, making the leap to *endorsing* or even *inflicting* harm less unthinkable.

William James, a founder of modern psychology, summed it up, back in 1890: 'If evolution and the survival of the fittest be true at all, the destruction of prey and human rivals must have been among the most important of man's primitive functions.

'The fighting and the chasing instincts must have become ingrained. And so inflicting violence or seeing an enemy mangled or destroyed would have become intensely pleasurable.'

* * *

'Are you OK for time?' I ask Wilco.

'Yes,' Wilco, says, hopefully enjoying a relatively low-brow conversation.

I share a screenshot of a Twitter message sent by a Birmingham City fan on the day of that fateful derby between Blues and Villa when Paul Mitchell invaded the pitch.

Wilco leans in, his glasses slipping down the bridge of his nose, and the moment the words come into focus he jerks back in his chair as if he's been bitten by the screen.

'That's terrible,' he says.

He seems a bit rattled.

'That's not schadenfreude.'

He shakes his head.

'That's sadistic.'

17

Robbers Cave

In July 1954, Muzafer Sherif, a Turkish-American psychologist, was sending letters to parents inviting their children to what he promised would be a 'wholesome cooperative living experience'. He was lying through his teeth.

Sherif was born in 1906 in Ödemiş, in what is now western Turkey, and he spent his childhood surrounded by war; the Italo-Turkish War, the Balkan Wars, the First World War and finally the Greco-Turkish War.

As a teenager he watched neighbours – Turks, Greeks, Armenians, who once lived side by side together – fracture into hostile camps. He lived through the city's alternating occupations by Greek and then Turkish soldiers. Sherif saw how quickly ordinary people could turn on each other.

Decades later, he staged one of the most audacious psychological experiments to test his idea that human behaviour could be understood by looking at group dynamics.

The stage was Robbers Cave State Park in Oklahoma, where two groups of eleven- and twelve-year-old boys arrived by separate buses. They'd been chosen because they came from two-parent middle-class families. They thought they were off to hike, swim and toast marshmallows in the 8,000 acres of woodland and caves. Sherif had other plans.

For the first week the groups never met. They bonded internally by setting up their camps and playing together. One group named themselves the Eagles, the other, the Rattlers. All the while, hidden microphones and cameras recorded their every move. The researchers posed as counsellors, watching.

When the groups were finally introduced, the competitions began. There were tug of wars, treasure hunts and baseball matches. Points became trophies and medals. Pocket knives were among the prizes. Hostility escalated. The Eagles arrived late to a picnic once and found the Rattlers had eaten all their food. What started as name-calling quickly degenerated into violence. Flags were set alight, cabins were ransacked and physical fights broke out.

Apples were stockpiled as missiles and socks were filled with stones and carried 'just in case'. Leaders unable to handle the heat were toppled and replaced by bullies.

Sherif wanted to show how quickly hostile tribes could form when competing for scarce resources. But he also wanted to test whether enmity could be undone. He staged joint meals, but the boys fought in the queues and hurled insults across the room. The meals ended in food fights.

He screened a film together but it was ruined by insults and scuffles.

Sherif's findings were sobering. Well-brought-up boys, divided randomly into two groups, spiralled almost instantly into violence and cruelty when competing for the same resources.

The Robbers Cave study demonstrated that if you put two tribes on the same small patch of land, things are likely to unravel fast.

It mirrored football rivalry in general. But more than that, it mirrored the particular savagery of local derbies, where shared geography tightens the screws. Freud, of course, had a name for the hatred that flares up between closely related groups. He called it the *narcissism of small differences*. In football terms, it translates as this: the closer two clubs are in geography, history and culture, the more ferociously they need to hate each other in order to maintain status and identity. Which brings us back to Wilco's look of horror when I showed him what happened next – *after* Paul Mitchell punched Grealish on a shared patch of land in Birmingham in 2019.

18

Condolence Page Vigilantes

I stumbled across the next part of the Paul Mitchell story during a break from my interview with his mum and sister in Glastonbury.

For lunch, I headed into town, hoping for a quiet corner where I could digest what I'd learned so far about Paul's attack on Grealish.

I end up parked outside Papa John's Pizza. I order myself a pizza and sit on a bench outside. I start to do some research on Paul's story on my mobile, but suddenly I am surrounded.

People in tie-dye shirts, flowing linen trousers, flapping like sails, draped in beads and jewellery that jangled with every step. There are multiple Afghan hats and a man walks past clutching a pineapple under his arm like a briefcase. No one bats an eyelid. It's as if I've stumbled out of Somerset into some Goan traveller enclave.

I feel anger bubbling up inside me. I stare at the man with the pineapple and I feel complete hostility. *Who the hell are you?* I think. *Why are you carrying a pineapple? Why do you look like that? When are you going to grow up?* In my head, I see myself marching over to him, grabbing the Afghan hat from his head, tossing the pineapple into the gutter and shouting, 'Grow up, for God's sake!'

Of course, I don't do it. I'm sitting on a bench eating a Papa John's pizza – alone – and I know how it would look. A middle-aged man, holding a half-eaten pizza, shouting at a stranger about fruit. I'd be the mad one, not him. Instead, I text my friend Dan, sharing a picture that I've taken, covertly, of the man with the pineapple. 'What a tosser,' I say. Just one tick. I wait. Still one tick. Dan's clearly doing other things. The hatred lingers.

I finish my pizza and head to somewhere less distracting, a field that sits beneath Glastonbury Tor. The fifteenth-century monument is considered one of the UK's most spiritual sites. From the summit, you can see the Somerset Levels sprawling out beneath you, Dorset and Wiltshire melting into the horizon, and, if you squint hard enough, Wales. And, of course, there's a farm, where, every June, a handful of bands gather to play music to a few friends.

The paths that climb up to the tower are grassy and full of people moving slowly, almost like pilgrims from all sides. I sit there scrolling through Paul Mitchell stories on my phone, as the devotees file past me to the optimistic sound of Spanish guitars and the beat of tiny drums, those deep, reedy, handmade ones. Incense – sweet and cloying – drifts lazily in the warm air. It reminded me a little of match days at Molineux: bodies converging from all directions, united by a shared ritual. Their tribal uniform is beads and flowing fabric, carried along in a haze of Nag Champa; ours is scarves and hats and the buttery smell of hot dogs. Maybe it's because I was in my smart clothes, clearly not one of them. Maybe that's why the anger bubbled up. Maybe it was envy, watching them drift about weightless and unbothered while I was all knotted up and stressed. It didn't take much for my mind to create an outgroup, worthy of my ire.

I clicked on a story which followed Paul's death. It was an online condolence page on the local *Evening Mail* website. The headline: 'Birmingham City Fan Jailed For Punching Jack Grealish on Pitch Dies, Aged 32'. The story had very few details about Paul's death, other than to say that he had been found dead at his father's home.

The first few reader comments under the story were sensitive enough. Some observed that Paul must have been unwell at the time and must have needed support.

'RIP mitch – only met you a few times,' one wrote, 'but you was a funny person whose troubles got the better of you and you will be sorely missed.'

A colleague, who worked at a pub with Paul in the weeks before his death, posted: 'Paul it was a pleasure working with you the last few weeks rip'.

Some were more critical of him but measured, as if giving him a stern but loving telling off. 'RIP Paul – what you did was wrong but how many of us are squeaky clean?'

Villa fans were reflective too. 'What he did was foolish and he deserved to be sent to prison but no one with an ounce of compassion would want him to die. He's only 32 and has clearly left a loving family behind. I'm sure Grealish would feel sad for them. My heart goes out to them and I'm a Villa fan. I hope he's at peace.'

There was one comment I didn't understand straight away. A man named Michael had written: 'He didn't have the *"kindest heart"* when he ran on to the pitch and punched Grealish.'

Why the quotation marks around kindest heart? I tracked back and discovered that the original headline on the condolence page had described Paul as having 'the kindest heart'. It struck me as a modest offering. Paul was dead. This was how his family remembered him. But the phrase was removed – perhaps in response to Michael's comment, or the flurry of vitriol that followed.

Because things got much crueller.

One female commenter called Andrea stood out.

Andrea called Paul an 'oxygen-stealing thug', among other things.

Her words had momentum. Others piled on. 'Rest in peace, thug,' someone called Tracey said.

A swarm of laughing emojis, loves and likes acknowledged the sentiment. Rachel added, 'karma got the better,' Jennifer sneered, 'bet his parents are so proud.' I was struck by the fact that all of these were coming from women.

I wanted to know more about Andrea.

I clicked on her profile and found all the normal stuff; pints of beer with friends, dinner parties, cappuccinos and cats. Her grammar was meticulous, and her posts revealed someone who was normally thoughtful and measured. She used words like *segue* and *poignant*.

She looked like someone you might trust to water your plants while you were on holiday or find on a 'Meet the Team' page of a charity's website. On the face of it there was nothing to suggest she fitted the profile of a digital vigilante hammering hatred into her keyboard. And yet, here she was, orchestrating a virtual hate campaign against a dead man.

I noticed she was obsessed with Aston Villa. There were photos of her queuing overnight at Villa Park, tucked into her sleeping bag, thumbs up for the camera.

* * *

Back in Hastings, I message Andrea on Facebook to ask if she'll talk to me about why she felt the need to desecrate Paul's condolence page. The message is sent early in the morning. It's polite and careful. I've already decided I won't use her full name in the book.

By mid-afternoon I hear nothing. I send another message. I even contact a friend of hers. Days pass.

A week later I'm walking the dog on West Hill, where the old town meets the new, and where Hastings Castle – one of the least impressive relics I've ever seen – squats in crumbled glory. My messages remain unanswered.

This is the point at which my mind starts to get agitated and sensitive to rejection. I'm not even worth a basic 'Thanks, but no thanks.' Stephen Fry managed it. Stephen Fry – national treasure, famously busy – still found time to send back a courteous refusal to my book interview request (he's a massive Norwich fan and obviously speaks a lot about mental health). But mortal Andrea? A civilian with no public obligations? Again, it staggers me how quickly my mind makes an enemy out of a stranger, this time because I feel rejected.

I'm just about ready to give up on the whole Andrea thing when I glance back over the thread one last time, wondering if I've missed something. And that's when I realise she's got something wrong.

Andrea is speaking to someone called Louise about Paul running on to the pitch, but then adds: 'That was bad enough . . . but especially galling was his desire to "put Jack in the ground with his little brother". Sick beyond belief . . . I won't be shedding any tears over losing that sort of pure evil.'

What did Andrea mean about Paul's desire to 'put Jack in the ground with his little brother'?

Andrea is confronted by another person on the thread who says, 'get ya facts rite div'.

Andrea clearly checks her facts and backtracks.

'It has come to my attention that I am WRONG about the vile tweets that were made by another Birmingham fan re Jack's brother.

'Hands up HUGE apologies to all who read that and knew I was wrong. The tweets WERE evil. And I have attributed them to the wrong person. I am so sorry.'

I do a bit of digging. What is this stuff about 'putting Jack in the ground with his little brother'? And it soon becomes clear that Paul Mitchell wasn't the only young man arrested at the derby on 10 March 2019. Someone else screwed up catastrophically that day. And somewhere along the way, Andrea had confused the two.

19

When Hate Finds a Target

Not far from where Paul Mitchell had his first pre-match pint before the Birmingham derby, a fresh-faced university student called Alfie Perkins cracks open his first can. It's 7 a.m., the kind of morning already heading off a cliff. By kick-off he's nine beers in. He's at the game with his mates.

Like everyone else, he sees Paul Mitchell steam on to the pitch and punch Grealish. He's among the fans cheering as Paul is frog-marched away, blowing kisses.

But, as we know, Grealish isn't done. Two-thirds through the game he's still darting and jinking, needling the Blues fans like a mosquito that refuses to be swatted. And then he scores the winner.

Alfie pulls out his phone and tweets a photograph of a gravestone:

'HE MAY HAVE SCORED, BUT HE'LL NEVER BRING HIS DEAD BROTHER BACK, AND THAT BRINGS ME MORE SATISFACTION THAN ANYTHING ELSE EVER COULD. HAHAHAHAHAHHAHAHAHAHAHAHA'

Then he tweets again: 'GREALISH WENT DOWN QUICKER THAN HIS BROTHER GOT LOWERED INTO THE GRAVE'.

Then another blow:

'WHERE'S YOUR BROTHER GONE? COME ON!'

The tweets refer to Grealish's younger brother, Keelan, who died in 2000 from sudden infant death syndrome. Grealish was four. He has spoken movingly about the loss and dedicated goals to him.

These are the tweets that made Wilco recoil.

Alfie's friends beg him to delete the tweets but he refuses. Police are tipped off and the media descends on his family home in Chelmsley Wood, east of Birmingham. A relative reportedly tells journalists, 'He has no regrets,' which only fuels the fire. Alfie has already fled back to Manchester, where he is at college.

Three days later he turns himself in. He's taken back to the West Midlands where he admits sending the tweets. His solicitor calls the posts 'reactive, not premeditated', saying they were only meant for mates. He is fined £120, ordered to pay costs and banned from Birmingham City for life.

Seven months later, Alfie fractures his skull when he is hit by a car while crossing a road in Manchester. From his hospital bed he tweets photos: tubes everywhere, face swollen and bloodied, a red slash across his cheek. The papers get hold of the story and the headline writes itself: 'CRUEL TEENAGER WHO MOCKED COT DEATH SUFFERS FRACTURED SKULL'.

You could taste the glee. A reader at the bottom of the story calls it karma.

The comments light up and, from his hospital bed, he gets a digital stoning.

'I wish him nothing but dead in the near future.'

'He should have been hit by a train.'

And then Alfie disappears.

* * *

I only stumbled on Alfie's story because of Andrea and her fellow keyboard executioners. They'd made a mistake. Andrea believed Paul Mitchell had written the tweets about Grealish's dead brother as well as punching him. But the real culprit was Alfie.

I thought back to the Liverpool game. The way I'd piled on to Gary O'Neil. How good it had felt to see other fans comparing him to Phillip Schofield. I wasn't just a spectator: I was taking an active role, deliberately liking malicious posts, adding crying-with-laughter emojis, yelping along as Gary's carcass was picked clean. It went beyond schadenfreude.

Of course, I hadn't gone anywhere near the territory Alfie entered. There's a gulf between mocking a manager and taunting someone about a dead child. But the emotional mechanics – the thrill of outrage, the group-fuelled cruelty, the way a crowd can make you feel licensed to lash out – felt familiar.

I've sat in forensic units with people branded monsters. I've seen their names scrawled in red pen on incident boards and risk matrices. I've been in rooms where senior police officers referred to young children as 'nonces' and 'sociopaths'. But when you sit across from them and start to ask the questions and build the timelines they stop being monsters. They start to make a broken, human sense. So I decide to try and track Alfie down.

* * *

Alfie's camera is off. He says he is on his phone and can't turn the camera on. All I see is big white writing 'Zoom user' on a black background.

I carry on, but part of me can't shake the feeling I am walking into something. Any second now, the screen will flip and there they'll be – his mates, swilling pints, in hysterics at the do-gooder psychologist who thought he could understand the internet and youth culture.

But I press on, earnestly explaining the book to the monochrome screen.

Then I start oversharing again. It's something I do too often. With friends and family, and occasionally, embarrassingly, with patients.

'You know, I shout at my wife,' I tell Alfie. 'I even stole a JCB digger once from Wolverhampton when I was pissed. That's what ended my legal career.'

Maybe it is anxiety but sometimes, I wonder if I'm not strategically deploying my vulnerability.

Look, I'm not here to expose you. I've nicked heavy machinery while drunk; I'm safe.

'I'm happy to help you,' Alfie says. 'If I was doing something similar, I'd appreciate the help too.'

While I wasn't expecting Alfie to be the same raging character who'd tweeted hate from the terraces, his conscientiousness was jarring.

At first glance, he was the picture of potential; a fresh-faced university student at the University of Salford, studying business management. From pictures I'd seen, he was stylish and good-looking, of British-Jamaican heritage, with warm brown eyes. There was the faintest dusting of stubble across his chin and lip, an attempt at adulthood that couldn't quite mask the boy underneath. On Facebook he poses with other young men, in tailored-fit shirts and pink Lacoste polo tops, with their tiny green crocodile motifs. And yet, beneath the composure, Alfie tells me there has always been something darker moving inside him. All it needed was a space.

Alfie grew up in Chelmsley Wood, a densely populated town, built on ancient woodland in the late 1960s for families on the council house waiting list. It has just over 13,000 people living there. Among its famous residents is the footballer turned talk-SPORT pundit Troy Deeney.

Like Paul Mitchell, Alfie was from a working-class family and his parents had separated when he was an infant. Alfie's Jamaican-born father worked at the Jaguar car plant in Castle Bromwich, and his white mum took on cleaning jobs to make ends meet. He'd spent his formative years with his mum, stepdad and siblings – an older sister and a younger brother.

Alfie says his childhood was 'fine', but when he was six, the divisions and disillusionment within the community led to the election of a British National Party councillor George Morgan who pipped Labour to the post by nineteen votes. At the time, the BNP was led by Nick Griffin. Reports of race-related hate crime in Chelmsley Wood doubled after Morgan was elected. It's easy to imagine a kid like Alfie feeling unanchored there.

Alfie did well in school, getting GCSEs and A levels. He has recently been diagnosed with ADHD, but back then he didn't know it.

He tells me he started gambling on football matches at fifteen. It gave him a sense of perceived control. He would stay up through the night betting on sports from across the world. By the time Alfie went to university he was in serious debt.

His grandmother acted as guarantor for his university accommodation. But as soon as he got his student loan, he gambled it away instead of paying his rent. His gran took the hit. Three weeks before the game he was at his lowest ebb. He found himself wandering down the rail tracks late at night in Manchester, hoping he might get hit by a freight train.

I told Alfie I could identify with the destructive power of addiction. In my twenties and thirties, drink and drugs tore through my world like a tornado. My life splits cleanly in two:

Act One – the journalist riding deadlines and hangovers, chasing bylines through a haze of adrenaline and alcohol. Reporting on England football hooligans at the World Cup in 1998 and Euro 2000, as the Press Association's crime correspondent. In amongst them drunk and loving it, filing copy through the static of beer breath and gum.

Act Two – the slow, painful climb from the wreckage and into a new career. My journalistic colleagues used to call me The Cat, always landing on my feet, somehow. But by the end, I was flat on my face, and everyone knew it.

So, when Alfie told me about walking down the train tracks, crippled by shame, having trampled over his grandmother's kindness, he didn't need to convince me it was true.

We talk about the tweets.

'What possessed you?'

Alfie thinks that people react in different ways to depression. Some reach out for support, some self-harm, some lash out with violence.

'I've always used hateful words,' he says.

'I'm not making any excuses now. What I did was terrible, but everything just came to a head.'

After Grealish scored that day it tripped a wire in Alfie's brain.

'It was like this outpouring of anger. It wasn't about Grealish, not really. It wasn't personal. Football means a lot to me but this was just an excuse to be as hateful as I could be in that moment.'

He hadn't tagged Grealish, but he knew the tweets could travel beyond his followers. It was as if he didn't care. He wanted his hatred to be seen – absorbed – and Grealish and his family were caught in the crossfire.

If Grealish doesn't really feel grief anyway, then what's the harm in mocking his brother? He wasn't a person, or a young man still grieving his baby brother. He was simply the 'other' and not *fully* human.

What struck me most about Alfie was how he wasn't hiding behind the usual shield of impulse, even with his ADHD diagnosis. Nor was he hiding behind the nine pints either. Decades of research show that alcohol reliably increases aggression. In laboratory after laboratory, intoxicated participants deliver stronger electric shocks to people who provoke them.

For Alfie, football bestowed belonging, a place where he could let his hatred out. Hatred does something, after all. It offers power when you feel helpless. Like the crocodile on his polo shirt, hatred gave him teeth.

* * *

After the court case, Alfie says he sent a letter of apology to Grealish, though he doesn't know whether it was received. He received a flood of abuse and death threats. But among all the bile, one tweet caught his attention. It confused him at first.

It came from someone with the handle @Iamzulubaz. Alfie recognised the 'Zulu' part straight away, a nod to Birmingham's hooligan firm. But who was this guy?

The tweet started out as menacingly as the others.

'Tell u what, in a few days I'm going to come round your house, pick u up and we are going to have a chat about some old skool ways.'

Alfie almost deleted it. It sounded like someone was planning to give him a proper hiding. But then it continued:

'Then u are coming out to do some homeless outreach graft and hopefully u will learn.'

'So inbox me your phone number or someone else do it. Let's get this sorted – ball's in your court, kid.'

Alfie stared at the profile picture. It became clear this wasn't a vigilante. The man behind the tweet was an eighteen-stone hulk who had once fought in the ring with Wladimir Klitschko, one of the greatest heavyweight boxers of all time.

Barrington Patterson was known as 'One-Eyed Baz' because, when he was seven, he was blinded in his left eye when his young sister threw a can of Coke at him. He was brought up in Handsworth, Birmingham and was breaking into shops at eight years old and robbing people at twelve. He appeared in an episode of *Danny Dyer's Deadliest Men* series. Dyer described Barrington as 'one of the most intimidating individuals' he had ever encountered.

But Barrington turned his life around – from criminal and hooligan to one of the world's top kickboxers. He also worked for charities reaching out to the homeless. He didn't want to pass on the legacy of crime and violence to his children.

Alfie replied to Barrington's invitation and they agreed to meet. In another tweet, I found a picture of Barrington and Alfie in orange high-vis jackets, VOLUNTEER on the back, the Birmingham Homeless Support Team logo clearly visible. The charity collects and donates clothing and other practical supplies to the city's rough sleepers.

Barrington, in a black hoodie, has his arm around Alfie's shoulder. And while the picture is taken from behind you can see enough from the angle of Alfie's face that he is smiling.

One-Eyed Baz tweeted a message to those who demanded a 'public flogging'.

'Youngsters deserve a chance to redeem themselves.'

'Trust me, he's not getting an easy ride.'

Barrington died of a heart attack on 22 March 2022, aged fifty-six. So many people wanted to attend his funeral that organisers had to issue wristbands and stream the service online.

He remains a symbol of the possibility of redemption. Debbie, Paul's mum, said Paul admired him greatly.

* * *

I ask Alfie what he is up to now. He tells me he's no longer gambling and since the ban, he doesn't even watch the Blues on TV any more. What he loved wasn't so much the football as the day out with his mates and the atmosphere in the stadium.

He tells me he got a First in his degree.

'Are you working?' I ask.

'I'm a civil servant,' he says.

'A civil servant?'

'Yeah,' he says, after a pause. 'It's a good, steady job.'

'Congratulations,' I say, catching the note of surprise in my own voice.

We say our goodbyes. 'All the best, Damien. Good to speak,' Alfie says.

And then Alfie – monochrome Zoom user – vanishes into the ether and, I assume, back into the comfort of nine-to-five normality.

20

Deluded by Design

A few months after Alfie's cruel tweets, Villa were promoted to the Premier League via the play-offs.

Early in the new season they beat Newcastle 2-0, and Grealish was met with the familiar chorus of boos and accusations of diving.

The jeering came after the opener when DeAndre Yedlin shoved him over on the edge of the box, and Conor Hourihane curled the free kick into the net.

Villa fans leapt to Grealish's defence with the fervour of believers shielding a saint.

News sites even ran pieces collating the competing realities. Villa fans fired off tweets like 'Blatant push', 'Anyone would've gone down from that', and 'Can't believe there wasn't a card for that'. The Geordies accused him of being a cheat.

On one side of the tribal divide, it was simulation. On the other, it was sacrilege even to suggest it. It was the same shove and the same fall but two completely different universes.

Group membership not only sets us up to hate the 'other', it also skews our perceptions of reality. Children, as young as three, divided into groups based only on the colour of their T-shirts, said their own group was 'nicer', 'smarter' and 'more fun'. When shown pictures of kids doing something good or bad – like sharing toys or knocking over blocks – they misremembered what they'd seen. Good deeds were credited to their own group; bad behaviour was blamed on the other.

It reminded me of one of the first studies we were shown in social psychology: *They Saw a Game*. It was published in 1954, the same year Muzafer Sherif was posting invitation letters to parents for the Robbers Cave experiment.

It demonstrated that our tribal brains can actually bend what we think we see on the pitch.

Two psychologists, Albert Hastorf and Hadley Cantril, analysed the perceptions of rival fans in a notoriously rough American football game between Princeton and Dartmouth.

They showed footage of the match to students at both universities, asking them to record any fouls they observed.

Princeton students saw more than twice as many Dartmouth fouls as Dartmouth students did. Dartmouth students judged Princeton's play as rougher than Princeton fans did.

Each side was convinced they were seeing the 'truth'.

The researchers concluded that 'there is no such "thing" as a game existing "out there" in its own right . . . the "game" exists for a person and is experienced by him only insofar as certain occurrences have significance in terms of his purpose.'

In other words: your eyes don't see football; your bias does.

The landmark study inspired a neuroscientist at the University of York to investigate British football fans to see if their brains were bending reality too.

Professor Tim Andrews put nine Chelsea fans and nine Manchester United fans into a brain scanner. They were then shown the same clips of matches involving the two rival teams, including goals, missed penalties and fouls.

What Tim found was that activity in the basic sensory areas – vision and hearing – was practically identical across fans. They literally saw and heard the same game.

But fractions of a second later, everything splits and realities change.

Brain activity in the regions that interpret what's happening diverged sharply between the rival fans. Different areas of the brain light up depending on allegiance, suggesting that an interpretive layer switches on automatically after the raw data hits the eyes and ears.

'So, they're seeing the same offside, but their brains are interpreting it differently?' I ask.

'Exactly.' Tim nods. 'Their brains are telling different stories about the same event.'

I was starting to understand why Tiffany had sighed so deeply when I was congratulating myself for my condemnation of Grealish as an arrogant tosspot. My brain wasn't seeing him straight. Perhaps if Grealish was on my side, I'd interpret his hairband as endearing.

Tim tells me he is now applying the same approach to politics, scanning the brains of left- and right-wing voters while they watch the same debates. Although he hadn't completed his study when we talked, the data was pointing in the same direction.

My brain is apparently also skewing my perception of Donald Trump, long before I'm aware of it.

Which feels unfair given that I truly want to believe my opinion of him as a lunatic comes from a place of calm, rational judgement.

* * *

I think it's fair to say that referees get the brunt of our perceptual bias. They are physically attacked and abused by fans every year, from grassroots matches to professional games.

Even teenage referees are being targeted by furious parents convinced their children are suffering some historic injustice.

They are reduced to tears or ambushed in car parks by unhinged parents, the kind of people normally supervising a school raffle, not hunting down a fourteen-year-old with a whistle.

One of the young refs, Luca Sinclair, was forced to quit aged eighteen after four years as an official.

'I felt quite scared,' Luca told the BBC, after a player's mother invaded the pitch and started yelling at him. 'She kept shouting at me, saying I was blind.'

In the 2023/24 season, there were 1,716 serious cases of abuse or physical assault against match officials in grassroots football – a rise of seventeen per cent on the previous year, according to the FA's Grassroots Disciplinary Review.

One fourteen-year-old ref was chased by the mother of an eight-year-old at a youth tournament. Meanwhile, an under-eleven girls' match had to be abandoned after parents turned on a young referee, leaving him unable to continue.

Amateur referees are now even offered training courses to help them cope with the abuse.

Beyond grassroots football, there's a long history of terrifying attacks and death threats against referees by fans, convinced they are being cheated.

Several professional referees – including Mike Dean, Michael Oliver, David Coote and Anthony Taylor – have received death threats.

And away from the UK, referees have been punched, kicked, stabbed, even shot dead. The most brutal attack on a referee happened during a 2013 amateur game in Brazil.

Otávio Jordão da Silva, twenty, was officiating a match in Pio XII, Maranhão, when he sent off a 31-year-old player named

Josemir dos Santos Abreu. Abreu threw a punch, and da Silva, the ref, responded by stabbing him.

Abreu's friends and family invaded the pitch, stoning da Silva to death before decapitating, quartering him and putting his head on a stake on the pitch.

It reminded me of John – one of the Wolves fans I mentioned earlier.

He was aware of how his brain might be biased, and he prepared for it by moving to the upper tier of the stand. Unlike the furious mums, he built in a physical barrier between himself and the referee.

Unfortunately for referees, there's an uncomfortable truth that spoils the moral clarity here. We'll come to that later.

PART IV

Revenge Junkies

21

Hunted

On Dale Houghton's Facebook page, there is a photo of him when he was much younger – maybe in his early teens – with another boy tagged as Nick. They're in a classroom in their school uniforms. Dale has spiky blond hair, Nick cropped dark hair, both smiling at the camera. Nick's wide, green-striped tie is pulled low over a green V-neck jumper. On 11 March 2020, Dale had written: 'Can't believe it's been 12 years pal, still love and miss you every day. ❤'

As I read, it becomes clear that Nick and Dale had been friends at school and that Nick had died. The original post was a tribute to Nick, on the anniversary of his death. There are hundreds of comments beneath it, from men and women alike. The page has been hijacked by people keen to attack Dale for what he did – and to mock Nick's death.

'Sick bastard.'

'Sick cunts.'

'This is what the two pretty boys looked like before the country got hold of the sick bastards.'

'Probably died to get away from you, you vile cunt.'

'Your mum's a slag, mate.'

'You might get to see him soon.'

'Rest in piss 🤣🤣🤣🤣🤣.'

The commenters are referring to something Dale had done at a match between Sheffield Wednesday and Sunderland on 29

September 2023. He was photographed – face beaming with joy – in the crowd, next to his brother Drew, holding his phone high above his head, taunting Sunderland fans with an image on the screen.

The image was of Bradley Lowery, a young Sunderland mascot who had died six years earlier. Bradley had been taken to the nation's heart as he battled, and eventually succumbed to, a rare childhood cancer. He became a mini-celebrity after leading Sunderland – and England – out of the tunnel before matches, often grinning into the camera, thumbs up in his red-and-white mittens.

A camera picked out Dale, high on cocaine and alcohol, holding the phone aloft, and the image spread rapidly on Twitter. I already knew that Dale had been arrested and banned from attending matches. What I hadn't grasped was the scale of the carnage that followed.

I wanted to include Dale's story not only because it shows how easily we dehumanise people outside of our tribe, but because it exposes a theme lurking beneath many of the stories in this book.

Revenge.

I also wanted to include it because it isn't only about the calamitous consequences of crossing a line at a football match and the mob justice that followed; it's also about loyalty, forgiveness and redemption – and some hope about what can be done with our tribal human brains.

I tried to reach Dale through his Facebook page, but it had long been abandoned. He wasn't anywhere else either.

But there was one other comment beneath his, on the tribute to his friend Nick, posted before the Facebook pile-on began. It was from someone called Kallum Nix. He had written: 'Love you, brother ❤.'

* * *

Kallum, thirty-three, sits on a sofa in a grey hoodie while a dog pads back and forth along the cushions behind him. He rubs a hand through his cropped brown hair and over his stubble and speaks in a strong Lancashire accent.

I'd sent Kallum a message not expecting to hear anything back, but a few hours later he replied that he'd be happy to talk.

Kallum is a Manchester United fan, and his whole life has revolved around football. His brother, Kyle, was a professional player who played for clubs including Bradford, and his father, Peter Nix, played for Rotherham.

Kallum himself came through several academies, including United.

He now runs a professional coaching business with the mantra 'More Than Just a Game', and when we spoke, his wife was expecting a baby boy. He was finishing his final year of a coaching and development degree at university. His dissertation was on mental health support for young players in academies. Kallum sees how many talented schoolboys are left vulnerable to mental health crises when their dreams of becoming professionals collapse in a ruthless culling process.

He tells me about Nick Walker, the boy in the photo with Dale. It was the morning of 11 March 2008. Kallum was sitting with his head of year, on report for being a 'naughty boy'. The phone rang. Kallum watched as his teacher turned white, dropped the phone and bolted out of the room. Kallum chased after him but eventually hit a crowd of pupils, all crying. He found a window and jumped up to see what was going on. He saw Nick's body crumpled on the road. He had been hit by a coach while trying to cross the dual carriageway.

After Nick's death, Kallum said he and his friends went 'a bit mad'. He left the Manchester United and Leeds academies, fell out of love with football, started drinking too much and taking drugs. He was kicked out of his parents' homes. Eventually, he moved to Australia to start again. He kept playing football and wore a tribute to Nick on his shirt and had a tattoo on his back. He returned to England at twenty-seven and began developing his football coaching business, K3. He became player-manager of Joker Wickersley football team. Joker are an amateur team who play in Sheffield's Blades Super Draw Premier Division, and Dale's brother Drew played for them.

On Saturday, 30 September 2023, Kallum was playing football for Joker and just before the game, someone messaged him to say there was something about Dale on Twitter. He didn't take much notice. When he finished the game, he noticed something strange: his phone was dead, even though it had been fully charged. He turned it on – and it went berserk, one notification after the next.

Although Kallum had nothing to do with what Dale had done, the threats started pouring in, thick and fast. The vigilantes had spotted Kallum's Facebook post on Dale's page and turned their venom on him as well.

A mob seeking retribution had already gone to Dale's parents' home, where Dale lived, smashing the windows and threatening to burn the house down. But Dale and his brother were in hiding, having fled to a hotel.

Fans of both teams – Wednesday and Sunderland – started calling Kallum using withheld numbers, threatening him. A coachload of vigilantes was on its way to Joker FC to seek revenge on its players. Others wanted information on where Dale was hiding, offering him thousands of pounds for information.

Even his brother and relatives in Australia were hounded. Meanwhile, wrong addresses were being shared online. Mobs gathered at the homes of innocent families, causing chaos and dishing out abuse.

Kallum was forced to untag himself from all pictures containing Dale on Facebook and other social media platforms. Fearing the Joker Wickersley club would be ambushed, he issued an emergency statement:

> I have been playing football and have only just finished our game to be made aware of everything that is circling online.
>
> Joker Wickersley Youth CC, Wickersley OVCC, our committee, players and all involved with the club do not condone the behaviour of the people in question in any way, shape or form.
>
> All we can do is apologise for the distress this has caused to so many people. ⚽🙏🤍

Drew was kicked out of the squad and the brothers were banned from the team's pub. But the threats continued, more windows were smashed and Kallum was even hunted down by the head of one of the country's main hooligan firms asking for details.

Kallum was furious with Dale and thought what he'd done was despicable and cruel. He took him for walks and spoke with him daily on the phone. 'I said, "Mate, you're an absolute fucking idiot. This is your comeuppance for everything you've ever got away with."'

Through everything, he stood by him as a friend and even kept him on as a groomsman at his wedding.

Kallum says Dale had never really grown up and confronted his demons. Dale had been especially close to Nick. They were born on the same day in adjacent hospital beds and they had walked to school every day together, apart from the day Nick died, when he had been staying at his grandparents. Dale had never done the necessary work on himself. Kallum believes *playing* sport gives people a way to vent frustration and regulate emotion. Without that outlet, people – especially men – need somewhere to dump their pain and 'pent-up masculine energy'. It can often be dumped at football stadiums. Effing and blinding in the street would get you arrested – in football stadiums it's socially acceptable.

'On the terraces, people say some pretty despicable things,' Kallum says. 'If everything said in a stadium was recorded, a frightening number of fans would lose their jobs.'

'Same with WhatsApp groups.'

Kallum believes Dale should have apologised publicly. There were times, he says, when Dale tried to evade responsibility when he should have just owned up.

'That's the first thing you do as a man,' Kallum says. 'You say, "I've absolutely, royally fucked up. I am so sorry."'

But the hypocrisy and scapegoating among those calling for him to be lynched was also staggering. Kallum would scroll through their social media profiles – and a few posts below their fury were jokes about Madeleine McCann.

I wondered what had happened to Dale since as there was no trace of him anywhere. Kallum said he'd speak to him and maybe he could update me himself.

* * *

Bradley's mum Gemma Lowery, forty-two, speaks to me on the eve of Sunderland's play-off semi-final second leg against Coventry at the Stadium of Light. They'd won the first leg 2-1, so Gemma was hopeful.

She's just rushed home from work because the internet's down at her office. Alongside running the Bradley Lowery Foundation, she also runs a hair and beauty academy. The charity supports families who are fundraising for treatment or equipment that isn't available on the NHS. Bradley would have been fourteen next week.

Her husband, Carl, hovers in the background, occasionally crossing the frame.

Gemma looks a little unsure of my motivations, as I expected. She has her arms folded, wearing a navy sleeveless top with a name badge pinned to her chest. Her dark brown hair is tied back. By the time I've finished introducing myself and the book – three minutes and thirteen seconds – she's unfolded her arms.

Gemma was born in Blackhall, between Sunderland and Middlesbrough. Her brothers are Newcastle fans, but she is a Sunderland fan, like her husband Carl.

'Can you remember when we took him to his first match?' she asks Carl.

'Sorry, my husband's in the background. I think Bradley was three.'

A lot has been written about Bradley's short life and the extraordinary impact he had on everyone around him. I knew how Bradley had been diagnosed with neuroblastoma at eighteen months and about his popularity as a mascot for Sunderland and England. I knew that Gemma had worked very hard to raise money for treatment for Bradley that was not available on the NHS and that despite prolonging his life by some months it was unable to save him. But Gemma reveals many things I didn't know. I didn't know, for example, that it was an Everton fan who started the Christmas card campaign for Bradley when he was really sick. The Royal Mail was inundated: trucks and trucks of cards arrived. More than 300,000 were sent, along with gifts and donations. Gemma had to hire a warehouse to store them all. They've only recently finished auctioning off the gifts.

Yet it was Bradley's beautiful friendship with the Sunderland player Jermain Defoe that captured the nation's hearts more than anything. Gemma tells me about a tender moment between them that breaks mine. Bradley had only days to live, and knowing this, Jermain flew back from holiday to see him, privately, away from the cameras. He was used to visiting Bradley in hospital; they would sometimes fall asleep together. When Gemma told Bradley that Jermain had to leave, Brad would say, 'Just a bit longer, Mammy.' He was, Gemma laughs, 'pretty bossy'.

When Jermain arrived at their bungalow that night, it was 11 p.m. Brad was in bed and had not moved for days. Gemma was sitting with Bradley in his bedroom while Jermain spoke to her father in the living room. Bradley was too weak to see anyone, even his favourite footballer. But then Bradley heard something and stirred.

'Brad looked at us and said, "Mammy, is that Jermain?"

'I said, "Yes, darling," and he sat up. He hadn't sat up for days.'

Jermain went in to see him and the two lay on the bed together, cuddling. The contact seemed to energise Bradley and he moved into the living room with the others, sitting beside Jermain. They sat together on the couch for a while.

A couple of days later, on 7 July, Bradley died.

Since his death, Gemma has stood in the crowd at the Stadium of Light countless times, tears of pride streaming down her cheeks as chants of 'There's only one Bradley Lowery' echo around the ground.

We speak about Dale. I tell her about my conversation with Kallum and some of the fallout that followed.

'I get the revenge thing,' I start to say. 'I . . .'

Gemma cuts me off. 'I don't. I don't, because I don't feel like people should take that on themselves.'

Gemma has that rare gift of being firm but warm; she has a smile that tells you you're safe, even as you're being told off.

'I actually felt really sorry for Dale's family,' she continues.

She points me to an interview she did on a morning TV show where she pleaded with people to stop making threats against the Houghton family.

Revenge was not part of her plan.

22

Revenge at the Farmhouse

The 1980s. A farm in central Pennsylvania.

It's the middle of the night and James Kimmel, seventeen, is asleep in the farmhouse he shares with his parents and grandfather when a gunshot jolts him awake.

He'd moved there at twelve. His grandfather's farm was modest, a few Black Angus cattle, some pigs and a cute beagle dog called Paula. The smallholding was nothing like the big dairy operations nearby. James loved the rhythm of farm life, the smell of hay and oil and the rumble of old tractors. But he envied the big dairy farm boys with their gleaming machinery and massive herds. And by the time James rocked up, as a boy, their tribe was already closed. While their fathers rose at 4 a.m. in milk-stained overalls, his father, an insurance agent, left for work at nine in a tie and polished shoes. The difference marked him out and James was bullied by the other boys.

But, James still loved farming. He studied agriculture and joined the Future Farmers of America, visiting all the shows. The other boys watched and thought he needed taking down a peg.

That night, after the gunshot, he rushed to the window and caught the tail lights of a pickup speeding down the dirt road. He recognised it immediately as belonging to one of the boys who tormented him. The family went outside and found no damage, so they went back to bed.

One of James's jobs before school was to feed and water the cattle and pigs. After that, he always went to the pen to feed Paula, the dog.

Paula normally bounded over when she heard him. That morning, she didn't move.

Then James saw the blood.

Paula had been shot through the head.

The family called the police. A report was filed but nothing really happened.

Two weeks later, James was home alone when an explosion ripped through the night. He saw the same pickup speeding away. This time they'd blown up the family's mailbox.

The explosion destroyed what little self-control he had left. He snapped.

He'd been handling guns since childhood. So, he grabbed one, jumped into his mother's car and tore after the pickup, cornering them by a barn. Three or four of them got out of the car, clearly unarmed. They stood there, caught in James's high beams.

James got out his gun and prepared to shoot them dead. He wanted them to feel some of his pain. But as he stepped out of the car, he had a flash of insight – if he pulled the trigger, he'd never be the same again. He'd have to live with being a murderer. The price of revenge was higher than he was willing to pay.

He put the gun away and drove home, aware of how close he had come to destroying everything. But the sense of injustice didn't leave him. It lodged itself in his nervous system and he needed somewhere to channel it.

He decided to become a lawyer.

Lawyers, he says, are the only people with a licence to distribute revenge to the masses. They just call it justice.

He became a successful litigator, pouring his rage into the courtroom. Professionally, it worked. Personally, it nearly killed him. His fixation on revenge tipped into suicidal despair.

After twenty years as a lawyer he tried to quit but he kept getting sucked back in. He figured he was addicted. He craved revenge, got a brief hit of satisfaction, but the itch for avenging injustices returned and the cycle started over again.

Increasingly desperate, he had a thought. What if he turned his obsession into a question? Instead of being manipulated by it, what if he began to investigate what was going on in his brain?

And so, he began studying the neuroscience of revenge. He digested every empirical paper on revenge that he could find: he observed real-life examples playing out around him – school shootings, the War on Terror, gang violence – and he examined his own mind.

The research eventually led to a new career at Yale School of Medicine, where he's now Assistant Clinical Professor of Psychiatry. He's written a book on it called *The Science of Revenge*.

I'm talking to James because I am trying to understand the intensity of mob justice that keeps coming up in this research, both online and in the real world. I tell James what happened in the case of Dale Houghton and the innocent people it impacted. He shakes his head knowingly. He believes we've become a culture of 'justice junkies' – hooked on the neurochemical rewards of vengeance.

Revenge once served an evolutionary purpose, he says. In small Pleistocene bands, retaliation enforced social norms and deterred harm in the absence of police and courts. But now that adaptive instinct has mutated beyond recognition. Not only is there the unremitting cycle of violent retribution, there are also endless political witch-hunts, digital shaming and cancel culture.

He sits at his home in Connecticut, his book resting on a mantelpiece behind him. He's bald, bespectacled and wearing a red T-shirt.

He describes revenge as *neurochemically addictive*. Like schadenfreude, which rewards us with a burst of pleasure when we see wrongdoers being punished, actively participating in revenge can feel equally good. Recent research demonstrates that when we feel a grievance, brain areas implicated in physical pain light up. In response, dopamine activity increases, motivating us to repair the damage. In group contexts, oxytocin – the so-called 'cuddle hormone' – rises, binding us to the avenging mob. Subjectively, these changes in brain chemistry make us feel powerful and righteous, reducing feelings of humiliation. Even thinking about it can soothe the hurt of a grievance.

'It's the same pattern as drug or alcohol addiction,' James says. 'Your brain on revenge looks like your brain on drugs.'

'I knew this to my own cost – I became an avenger extraordinaire.'

The problem, however, is that, just as with drugs, the reprieve from hurt is fleeting. The underlying pain is not fully processed, while the appetite for a quick fix is reinforced. Worse still, a new 'victim' is created, and the revenge cycle gathers momentum.

James has founded a twelve-step addiction programme – 'Revenge Anonymous' – for those caught in the cycle. The first step reads: 'We admit that we are unable to control our revenge desires, and that this is ruining our lives.'

As James puts it, revenge is 'a drug sold under the brand name of justice'. Kids are sold the drug early.

'Take *The Lion King*,' he says.

'It's aimed at *children*.'

The film, he explains, sets up a terrible grievance – the death of a parent – and then delivers a sadistic revenge, that children are craving.

Scar, the movie's villainous murdering lion, is burned alive and torn apart.

We are, James says, a storytelling species – hard-wired to seek meaning through heroes, villains and justice.

Football, James argues, gives us a sanctioned theatre for revenge. Kick by kick, match by match, we are invited to feel wronged, to imagine payback, and to experience the release when it comes. Each loss or conceded goal sets up a grievance that requires payback.

Most of the time, it's harmless. But sometimes it isn't.

'Revenge is the secret sauce of sport,' James says.

'We crave victimisation just so we can feel the release of retaliation again.'

23

Finding a Way Back

Dale sits in his car, vaping like a man trying to breathe himself calm. The vapour drifts across his face in slow, uncertain veils, then up over his blond hair, tidy and flicked up at the fringe.

He speaks in the broad vowels of an old Yorkshireman. The mismatch is disorienting; Mick McCarthy's voice emerging from the soft, self-conscious face of a *Made in Chelsea* extra.

His orange railway work top glows and his pale blue eyes flick about, restless, as if expecting punishment to appear at the car window.

I thank him for agreeing to talk with me.

'It's my pleasure, pal. I mean, it's been two years now since it happened. So, if anything good comes out of it . . .'

There's something about the way Dale trusts me that feels like a burden. Here is someone who's had a wretched couple of years after doing something unthinkably cruel at a football match.

He's starting to get his life back on track. He became a pariah, lost friends, almost went to jail, was hunted down, with his family, and threatened for months. He was banned from attending Sheffield Wednesday for five years.

He lost his job but retrained on a railway scheme and went to drug counselling.

It feels like a fragile thing, this trust. He doesn't know me and his experience of journalists hasn't exactly been positive. So why talk? Why not just let it fade away? I can only assume something inside him still needs reckoning with.

I tell him I'm a Wolves fan and he sympathises, adding he worked there for a period and found it a welcoming city.

Football is doing its normal job of breaking the ice.

I give Dale my usual spiel about how I'm investigating the emotional and psychological power of football – how it affects our behaviour – and tell him about my own struggles with regulation.

'We've all been there, mate,' Dale says.

He was a season ticket holder at Hillsborough from the age of six, going with his grandad. The phases were obvious again; attraction to football generally and a bridge to his grandfather, then fusion with the club. In his early teens he got involved with the violent youth side of football, fighting with Wednesday's youth firm. He first got locked up at a Bristol City away game and it frightened him. He took a few years away from football before starting to go again with his grandad.

On the night everything went wrong, Dale had gone to Hillsborough with his brother Drew, their first game together in ten years. It was a 7.45 Friday night kick-off. They'd been drinking and taking cocaine since 1 p.m. He insists he knew very little about Bradley, but his picture had been circling on WhatsApp groups.

'Did it cross your mind that it was really cruel?'

'I'll be honest, mate – not at the time.'

He pauses.

'I know it sounds sick, but I'm here to be honest and it didn't cross my mind one bit.'

Dale says he's always been an impulsive person and the cocaine and alcohol removed any remaining moral brakes he had.

'I'm not here to make excuses,' Dale says firmly. 'That's not why I'm here. I was off my nut, I was pissed, I didn't think of any consequences.'

While Dale is trying not to make excuses, it's fair to say that cocaine use and football tribalism are a potentially explosive mix. Dale shakes his head behind the vapour. He looks sad.

'I sound a bit stuffy, mate,' he says, wiping his eyes. 'I've got terrible hay fever. I had a sneezing fit before I came on. Sorry.'

He left the game and went to sleep at his brother's home, blissfully unaware of the storm that was brewing. The next day he went for a KFC and at 1 p.m. his boss phoned him to tell him he was headline news. His friends warned him vigilantes were already looking for him, so he and his brother fled to the hotel.

He scratches his face, looking strained. Police tracked them down and Dale had to move from his parents as it was being targeted by revenge mobs.

'They were planning to come to the house, set fire to it, kidnap me and my brother,' Dale says. He stayed with his grandparents.

During this time, he lost his job and ended up in court. He received a twelve-week suspended sentence after admitting the public order offence of intentionally causing harassment, alarm or distress. He was ordered to do two hundred hours of unpaid work.

The judge said he accepted the attack was impulsive but the fact he had not meant to hurt the Lowery family was little mitigation.

I asked Dale if he'd ever apologised to the Lowery family and he said he had sent a letter and given it to his probation officer. He wasn't sure if the family got it.

'I just hope she got it, just to see I'm not that person.'

'What type of person are you?'

'I've grown up a bit – but I've always been loyal. I've never backstabbed anyone. I'm hoping I've still got my personality.'

Dale says he had been taking cocaine most weekends, but after what happened, he went to drug support groups for a time. Then he started a railway training 'boot camp' and has worked there ever since.

'It gives me some purpose,' he says.

Dale is still nervous when he goes out – in shopping centres, in pubs – convinced others are talking about him. People point and whisper. But overall, he says, he's been supported by friends and family.

'I've had a lot of support, to be fair,' he says. 'Because. . .'

He stops.

'I'm not a bad person . . .'

He trails off.

'What I did was a terrible mistake.'

He tells me about his friendship with Kallum. Since everything broke, Kallum has visited him regularly, called him every day – mentoring him, checking in – despite knowing that his football coaching business could be damaged simply by association.

'Having Kal has meant the world to me.'

He pauses. For a moment I can barely see him through the vapour. Then he reappears.

'It's just meant the world to me.'

The strength of their relationship stays with me. In a culture quick to shame, loyalty – especially when reputations are at stake – is often the first thing to disappear.

I bring up Nick Walker, the friend who died outside school when he was fifteen.

He witnessed him being hit and still has the phone with the text Nick sent him, arranging to meet at the gates seconds before crossing the road.

'Fucking hell,' he says, shaking his head. 'It was horrible.'

Despite his own sense of unravelling after the tragedy, Dale tells me it was Kallum who held the group together.

I ask him if he still misses Nick.

'Every day,' he says.

He's quick to add that it doesn't excuse what he did.

I tell him that's exactly what I'm getting at – that he understood, at least in part, what Gemma's loss must have felt like.

His eyes fill. 'That's what's hurt me the most. Knowing I've added to someone's pain. Knowing they'd already lost someone close.'

The camera wobbles as he shifts in his seat, grounding himself.

I ask if he's okay.

'I wanted to do this,' he says, his voice shaking. 'I really did. I want something good to come out of it.'

I ask how he's doing now. He leans forward.

'It was such a mistake,' he says. 'I need her to know I'm sorry.'

I thought about the WhatsApp messages that Dale had sent in the aftermath of the attack. They came across cold and callous. But from my own experience, I know that when I'm accused of doing something awful – especially by people I love – expressing remorse is not the first thing that surfaces.

To truly acknowledge what I've done to hurt someone else means opening myself up to shame – the possibility that the story I tell about myself being kind and thoughtful is not the full truth, and that's painful. Instead, I'll justify myself and dig my heels in. It's not a great strategy, but it's human.

I was conscious that he was still in his car, and I'd slipped into therapy mode. I've worked with many perpetrators before; helping them come to terms with terrible things they have done, what is known as *moral injury*. But with Dale, I must be careful. He's not my patient and I won't see him again.

'Hey, listen – you look like you're doing okay,' I say. I can see how easy it is for Dale to bring out the paternal qualities in Kallum.

'Like I say,' Dale shrugs, 'I just plod along now. Just concentrate on work.'

I ask if he'll ever go back to watch football.

'I still love Wednesday,' he says. 'That'll never change. But I need to get some confidence back before I go to Hillsborough. There were a lot of Wednesday fans that got rightly pissed off with it.'

Maybe, one day, he'll return with his grandfather, who is now eighty-five. That would be his dream. He wipes his eyes and regains composure. We come to the end of our time.

'Take care, pal,' he says.

* * *

Gemma tells me she initially asked the police not to pursue Dale any further, recognising that he'd been caught in the heat of the moment.

'It was disgusting but I'm a football fan myself,' Gemma says. 'It doesn't matter who you are, you've probably said or done something you're not proud of.'

Being drunk and high like Dale no doubt amplified his mindless cruelty. But it was what happened after Dale was caught that Gemma still struggles to accept. Police showed her WhatsApp messages Dale had sent afterwards, where he apparently attempts to justify himself. One said something like, 'What about all the other kids with cancer?' Police maintained he was remorseless.

Gemma asks me whether Dale showed any remorse to me. I tell her he did. I ask her whether that makes any difference to her.

She takes a moment, weighing it.

'It does, yeah,' she says softly.

There's a short silence.

'Thank you,' Gemma says.

I describe my experience of him, and how the tears in his eyes felt genuine.

Gemma nods.

'Dale seemed like a child, really . . .'

But before I can finish, she cuts in again.

'He's *not* a child, Damien. He's a grown adult.'

The sharpness lasts only a second. She exhales, then smiles when she sees the look on my face.

I press on, slightly defensive. I tell her I write forensic court reports – I can usually tell when someone is putting it on. And he wasn't, if that helps at all.

'It does,' Gemma says. She hesitates, her voice softening. 'I did feel sorry for him. I kept saying to Carl that I felt for his family, for what they're going through. But there have to be consequences, don't there? He's not a child. He's a grown man.'

Gemma never received Dale's letter. I think that's a shame because I believed him when he said he'd written it. I wondered whether it was somewhere lost among the thousands of cards she received for Bradley.

I couldn't shake what Gemma had told me – that Dale told police there was nothing *special* about Bradley. That's what hurt her the most. I wondered if, beneath the cruelty, there was envy, resentment at the attention her grief received. He'd lost his own childhood friend in brutal circumstances, and he hadn't worked through it. Now someone else's pain was being witnessed, tended to, even televised. I wondered whether showing that picture wasn't just cruelty but a kind of distorted revenge, a punishment for what he perceived as the world's selective compassion. I wish I'd asked Dale more about the WhatsApp messages, but I didn't.

I ask Gemma whether she would ever meet him if he wanted to apologise.

'Probably not,' she says. 'I don't know if I could hold myself together face to face.'

I nod. She tells me she thinks he's already been punished.

'I appreciate that he's sorry now,' Gemma says quietly. 'But what am I supposed to say? That I forgive you?'

She looks away, then turns back. We sit in silence for a while.

'I probably do forgive him,' she says at last. 'But I'll never forget.'

24

Bradley's Legacy

I'm always hesitant to suggest forgiveness when I'm not the one who's been wronged. Who am I to tell Gemma to forgive Dale. But she raised it first – and it was clear that holding on to hatred wasn't part of her plan. James, the revenge expert, told me that forgiveness was a 'miracle drug' when you have been wronged. He was careful to say that it was not for the benefit of the perpetrator but for the person who has suffered the grievance.

Just imagining forgiveness, he explains, deactivates the pain networks in the brain and reactivates the prefrontal cortex, restoring self-control and perspective. Unlike dopamine, which only masks the hurt, forgiveness eliminates it. In his book he has a strategy called 'The Miracle Court', to help people work through injustice.

Gemma's willingness to forgive Dale, even if she did not trust herself to meet him, meant she could focus on more important things than hating him. A new GoFundMe page was set up and Sheffield Wednesday fans poured thousands into it. More than £40,000 was raised, mostly by Wednesday supporters, to help build a holiday home in Scarborough for sick children who spend weeks or months in hospital.

She also continued her mission to bring football fans from different clubs together under the banner of Cancer Has No Colours. Gemma tells me how Sunderland-supporting Bradley was once asked to be a mascot at a Newcastle game and he had

'Thank you NUFC' printed on the back of one of his Sunderland tops. Meanwhile, her brother David, a lifelong Newcastle fan, had a Sunderland badge tattooed on his calf to raise £1,000 for Bradley's charity. Above it, it reads: Just For Brad. Gemma takes football rivalry seriously, but she instinctively sees fandom as a rare opportunity to play with our innate tribalism, rather than surrender to it.

She's telling me about Cancer Has No Colours when, in the background, I hear Carl calling something out. 'All right, all right,' Gemma says, rolling her eyes. 'I know – you came up with it, didn't you?' She laughs. 'Carl came up with it. We even got it trademarked.'

The Bradley Lowery Foundation has raised more than £1 million.

Cancer Has No Colours struck me as a reminder of how tribal boundaries are not set in stone. How football fans can work together for good. Carl's brilliant idea is a perfect example of this. Give rival tribes a bigger monster to fight – in this case childhood sickness – and they become one tribe. Social psychologists call it the Common Enemy Effect.

* * *

In the weeks and months before his death, Paul Mitchell became a small celebrity in his own right. Ever since he hit Grealish, fans had wanted photographs with him. He would pose with them as he worked behind the bar. Debbie told me it wasn't just Blues fans, but fans of other teams too, including Villa.

Sometimes, as he walked home, he would be spotted by Blues fans and encouraged to extend his evening with the promise of free drinks. It happened so often that he ended up staying in just to get some peace. His mum Debbie says he liked the validation at first, but he eventually got sick of people wanting pictures with him. He moved into Clydesdale Tower in central Birmingham, beneath the Radisson Hotel. His girlfriend left, taking the children to Scotland. Paul was bereft.

Debbie told me the attack on Grealish was used in the family courts as evidence that Paul was an unfit father. He was barred from seeing his children, and his mental health worsened. There had been accusations and counter-accusations in court; Paul claiming she was an unfit mother; while she claimed he was violent and unstable.

Whatever the truth, it's clear Paul had a softer side. He kept working in pubs and kitchens but was known locally for his kindness to young people with special needs. He had time for them and would sit and talk with them if they looked lonely. Several young protégés turned up at his funeral.

Hayley says just days before his death, Paul had seen a video of Grealish with an eleven-year-old boy called Finlay Fisher. Finlay had cerebral palsy, like Grealish's younger sister Hollie. Finlay had written to Grealish asking to see him and the pair met at the Manchester City training ground. Finlay was speechless as he collapsed into the player's arms. Finlay then asked him if he would do a worm celebration the next time he scored. Grealish said he would. And he kept his promise: Finlay watched in amazement as his hero performed the breakdance move after coming on to score in England's 6-2 demolition of Iran at the Qatar World Cup.

Paul had been so touched by this that one day he took Hayley aside and told her something in secret. He told his sister he had stopped hating Grealish and that he wished he hadn't punched him. While they were very different characters from very different worlds, Paul had, in some strange way, recognised himself in the player he had attacked. In Paul's mind, the pair now had a common mission – to address the prejudice and challenges faced by disabled children.

* * *

Needless to say, the capacity for tribal boundaries to change has been tested in the lab – and scientists have used football fans as guinea pigs.

Professor Mark Levine, a social psychologist, tested how easy it would be to interfere with one of football's most hostile rivalries, by introducing a common cause. He recruited Manchester United fans and asked them to complete a survey about their love for their club. The survey was designed to prime allegiance to their beloved team.

They were then told they had to complete another task in another building on the Lancaster University campus. Meanwhile, Levine had secretly arranged for a bogus jogger, splattered in mud, to run down a bank towards the United fan as he made his way across the car park to the other place. The jogger wore either a Manchester United shirt or a Liverpool shirt. Three observers were hidden nearby. As the fake jogger scampered down the bank, he tripped and fell about fifteen feet away, clutching his ankle and groaning in pain.

The observers watched to see whether the United fan helped. Twelve out of thirteen United fans helped the United jogger, kneeling beside him and yelling for help. But only three helped the Liverpool jogger. The rest walked on by. Some later claimed not to have seen the accident, though observers clearly saw them look.

The researchers then conducted a second study to see if they could manipulate the tribal boundaries. They repeated the experiment – with different United fans – but this time they were told the research was about how football fans in general were unfairly cast in a negative light. Their identity as members of the broader football tribe was primed, instead of United.

Again, the jogger tumbled down the slope – this time in either a United shirt, a Liverpool shirt, or a plain sports top. Now, the United fans helped the jogger in both the Liverpool and United shirts. The non-football fan was left to suffer. He was the Common Enemy. The new larger football tribe was the salient one.

Notwithstanding the poor non-football fan, Levine showed how easy it is to widen tribal loyalty.

Harvey Whitehouse, the anthropologist we met earlier, believes that it's a big mistake to deny our tribalism. I had arranged to meet with him to speak about one of his studies and while I had him, I was going to ask if he had any tips on how I might detach myself from Wolves given the 250 days or so since they'd won a game. But then I got flu and had to cancel.

Harvey was still kind enough to send me an email instead. He had good news and bad news for me. The bad news was that he didn't really have any tips on how I could extricate myself from Wolves. It might be possible if I committed an act so heinous against the Wolves tribe that I was myself booted out and had to fix myself to another target. Or, if Wolves, as an institution, did something so unforgivably bad – something of genocidal proportions – that I had to distance myself.

It looked like I was doomed to suffer on.

The good news was that Harvey believes I need not be too ashamed of my tribal brain. In fact, he thinks we may need *more* tribalism, not less. We need to harness it.

Just as Levine had primed the larger football tribe, and Gemma (and Carl) had brought fans together with the Cancer Has No Colours project, Harvey thinks we can use our evolved tribal psychology to make the world a better place.

He believes football fans worldwide could form a very powerful band of brothers and sisters to tackle some of the world's most serious issues. He and Martha Newson have worked in prisons to bond inmates to the football tribe, helping them to peel away from the gang life that led to their incarceration.

While many world leaders have used their primitive human brains to take us to the cliff edge, tribalism might be the only force powerful enough to pull us back. Harvey says that in the past, tribes were often very small – hunter-gatherer groups that rarely saw each other. Then the tribes expanded to bigger groups, then states and continents. He believes we are on the cusp of expanding our tribe to a global one, able to meet existential challenges like disease, pandemics and climate change.

With the right leadership, he thinks we can prime our global identities, recognise our shared vulnerability and fuse ourselves to what he calls a Teratribe.

Tribalism could easily destroy us.

But it might just save us too.

* * *

Back in Oklahoma at Robbers Cave in 1954, where the two sets of boys – Eagles and Rattlers – turned on each other in a real-life *Lord of the Flies,* there was an optimistic note too. Sherif was determined to see whether he could get the boys to like each other. After his failed attempts to get the boys to eat meals together and watch movies, he decided to sabotage the camp itself, breaking the water pipe supply and stranding a food truck. It forced co-operation, the boys coming together to mend the pipe and hauling the truck with a tug-of-war rope. By the end, the boys were singing together around a campfire and chose to ride the same bus home.

PART V

Nightmares in Nairobi

25

The Terrible Tale of Suleiman Omondi

I slide into the back seat of a custard-yellow taxi in Nairobi at 1 a.m. I catch the eye of my driver in the rear-view mirror. His name is Stephen. The roads out of Jomo Kenyatta Airport are flanked by cracked concrete and billboards plastered with Arsenal players, grinning above endorsements for aftershave, betting apps and televisions. I waste no time trying to bond over football. He grimaces. He says he hates the game and prefers rugby, which is more civilised.

I slump back, disappointed. I'd flown four thousand miles to investigate just how profoundly football can impact our moods, and been met by a unicorn, the only man in the country uninterested in the beautiful game. I quietly hope the conversation will fizzle out. I'm running on instant coffee and very little sleep, too tired to make small talk. The easy conversational currency of football is all I'm good for at this moment. I don't want to explain what I do and I can't pretend to want to know more about Kenyan rugby. I'll talk about football, or we can sit in silence.

But Stephen keeps talking, skilfully using the football-shaped hole I'd offered. And slowly, I realise he does have a relationship with the game, one that has its own kind of complexity. It is a relationship that will end up distorting the shape of my brief trip.

We turn on to the main highway leading into central Nairobi and Stephen explains that the problem with not following football here is that it makes him feel like an outcast. He forces himself to watch certain matches, especially towards the tail end of major tournaments like the World Cup. 'At least I have something to say to people,' he says. 'If you don't watch, you don't feel like a *human*.'

I tell him a little bit about why I'm here – how I wanted to find out more about what happened to a young Kenyan football fan called Suleiman Alphonso Omondi in Nairobi's infamous Pipeline Estate. Stephen lets out a long sigh and shakes his head. He seems to be familiar with the tale.

He tells me about football fans in Nairobi, the blood-and-thunder devotion that splits the city along tribal fault lines, Arsenal and Manchester United. Thousands of miles away from the Emirates and Old Trafford, the rivalry is raging, and the consequences can be devastating.

Stephen explains, with genuine disbelief, that he's seen pictures of Kenyan men crying in football stadiums. He bangs the steering wheel as he laughs at the absurdity of it. In Kenya, he says, nothing makes a man shed tears.

'But football . . .' He trails off.

'Is it true Kenyan men don't cry?' I ask. He nods, almost offended at the question. 'They're raised that way,' he explains. 'As a boy, you're beaten and expected to stay dry-eyed; tears mark you out as a girl.' He claims he hasn't cried since childhood.

'But football . . .' He shrugs again. He seems utterly bewildered by the sport.

He glances at me in the mirror. 'Your research needs to be published. People here need to know what's going on in their brains.'

The city rises around us in glass and steel, and we're about ten minutes from my hotel in central Nairobi when Stephen starts telling me a story. He says that on 9 March 2025, he was at home in Utawala, on the eastern edge of the city, when he heard screaming outside. It was late, maybe 11 p.m., and a couple of hours earlier Arsenal had drawn with Manchester United, effectively ending the London team's title hopes.

There was a man's voice and a woman's scream. He recognised the voices. They were his neighbours, Emmanuel and Asunta. When he stepped outside, Emmanuel, an Arsenal fan, was beating Asunta, a Manchester United fan, in the middle of the dusty road. She was half-naked, yelling something about Arsenal. He wouldn't stop hitting her. Stephen pulled them apart and pleaded with Emmanuel to stop.

Stephen slaps the steering wheel again, as if trying to eradicate the memory. I lean forward between the seats as he gathers himself. He explains that he'd warned Asunta to keep quiet, that Emmanuel was 'no longer joking', that something in him had snapped. Emmanuel, he insists, is usually gentle – 'a very chilled guy,' he says – but that night, everything changed.

Stephen shrugs helplessly.

'Was she hurt?' I ask.

He nods. 'I thought he was going to kill her.'

We turn off the main road, the hotel just ahead.

After things had calmed between the neighbours, Stephen went home.

'I told my wife,' he says, decisively, 'that if I was ever a football fan and it made me beat you, I'd stop being a fan.'

'That sounds sensible,' I say.

Just before I get out of the car, I ask whether his neighbours might be willing to speak to me. Stephen pauses. 'I'll try,' he says. We exchange numbers and he promises to let me know tomorrow if he hears anything.

* * *

I walk into the Serena Hotel – my trackies are sagging like wet bunting and my eyelids are at half-mast. The concierge smiles at me, a little unsure. There's football playing on the giant screen in the hotel sports bar.

The receptionist, barely stifling laughter, gently takes the mickey out of me for only having hand luggage. I tell her I'm writing a book about football, and she bursts out laughing, scuttling into the back to fetch a colleague. He comes out beaming and tells me that the great midfielder Bastian Schweinsteiger brought the Champions League trophy to the hotel a few weeks ago. The popular Arsenal fans' platform AFTV – fronted by Robbie Lyle – also filmed a broadcast from the hotel.

I head to bed. Tomorrow I'm meeting the Kenyan photojournalist Peterson Githaiga. He was my only lead while researching Suleiman's story. His byline had appeared beneath one of the photos from the aftermath. Peterson had warned me that the Pipeline Estate wasn't safe for us to visit alone, and he said he'd try to organise security, someone who knew the area to come with us.

The next morning, I draw the curtains to reveal Land Rovers with blacked-out windows gliding through electronic gates draped in the black, red and green of the Kenyan flag, waved in by men in purple bibs. Skyscrapers rise from chaotic roads. Palms sway in the fumes, above green-and-white buses and a swarm of mopeds. From up here, Nairobi doesn't look like a pretty city, but it hums with intent.

My wife texts to say she loves me and sends a photo of the dog, looking mournful. Apparently, he's been squealing more than usual but still launched himself up our Corten steel steps in the back garden – the expensive ones that resemble rusty death traps – to chase off a fox. She thinks he's probably fine.

I eat breakfast in a quiet courtyard next to a large pool where green umbrellas shade a scattering of sunbathers. A woman in full-body Lycra and a highlighter-yellow beanie frolics in the water with a bendy float and birds with tangerine bellies whistle away in the trees. It would be peaceful, but a nearby table of locals in baseball caps have voices like megaphones and laughs to match. They discuss tomorrow's Champions League final between Inter Milan and Paris Saint-Germain. A woman in braids sitting with them bellows 'Football?' and collapses into hysteria.

I eat yellow lentils and a couple of hash browns with mango juice and coffee. Around me, waiters in crimson waistcoats and crisp white shirts glide between tables with polite smiles. Pilots flash gold stripes on their cuffs as they pass. There's a fair bit of showboating here.

Peterson texts to say he'll be late – there's been an accident on the road. I decide to use the time to dig deeper into stories about Kenyan football fans. There are wild tales everywhere.

I watch a video of a man called KK Mwenyewe, a live stream he filmed after losing a bet that Manchester United would beat Chelsea on 5 April 2024. Chelsea won 4-3. KK, dressed in his United shirt, proceeds to eat a full kilogram of chilli peppers as penance. He's sweating and scampering around the kitchen in agony, yelping and pacing like he's covered in ants. Later, there are photos of him in a hospital bed, attached to a drip. On Instagram he posts a photo and writes: 'It's been a long day. I'm good. I quit football.'

There's another story that catches my eye. It's a story about the Pipeline Estate itself. The headline describes the estate as the 'laughing stock of Nairobi'.

Peterson arrives at reception, looking sharp. He's dressed in a green-and-white Bermuda shirt, black trousers and black shoes.

He's fifty-six but looks younger, tall, handsome, with a lean frame and piercing eyes. He doesn't smile much but, when he does, he means it.

He looks tired though. He'd been in hospital most of the night with his five-year-old son, Rodney, but assures me he's fine.

We head off in his car. He's phoned one of his contacts, someone who knows the Pipeline Estate, and arranged for him to meet us on the road there, arriving by motorbike. He'll be our security. The plan is for him to lead us into the estate and towards the bar where Suleiman's story transpired on 5 May 2009.

The road out of the city centre is thick with traffic, and we roll the windows down. I can feel the smog in my lungs. The modern business district fades quickly into roads flanked on both sides by corrugated-iron stalls selling fruit, bras, jeans, sandals, signs reading Wape Wape Lounge, handbags, mobile phones – and many replica football shirts.

Flames curl out of roadside bins and pallets lean against walls. A stream of people walk down the central reservation as if it's meant for pedestrians. Most of the replica tops are Manchester United or Arsenal, but I spot the odd Chelsea one too. They hang along fences by the railway track, under barbed wire.

We slow to a stop and I spot a young man on an old blue Honda motorbike in the rear-view mirror. I get out and walk over to the railing of the raised highway. Below it twists and turns like a concrete serpent, coiling towards a slum settlement stretching out beneath.

Next to a vast rubbish dump – cows milling through the filth – there's a single football goal. A group of children are chasing a ball – some of them can't be older than four, most of them in United shirts. Around them, iron shacks and makeshift tents sag in the heat. People sleep in the dust, under bushes, some of them wearing football tops. In the distance, I spot a dilapidated red-and-white painted shack with a faded sign above it that reads 'The Emirates'. A young man sits outside with a cola. A makeshift bar, so I'm guessing it will be showing the Champions League final tomorrow.

I walk over to meet our guide, Pineas Mokhara. He tells Peterson that Pipeline has changed a lot since 2009. Many new blocks of flats have gone up. He'll take us to where he thinks Suleiman was watching the Champions League semi-final between Arsenal and Manchester United with his friends back then. It's a bar called Bamba 70.

The first leg at Old Trafford had ended 1-0 to the hosts. Arsenal had everything to play for. But Cristiano Ronaldo had other ideas. Bamba 70 was packed that night, a blaze of red shirts – some Arsenal, some United – jostling for space in the heavy heat. Suleiman, in his Arsenal top, was drinking like everyone else, watching the game streamed live on a massive screen. He was hopeful Arsenal would claw it back.

Eight minutes in, Ronaldo crosses, Kieran Gibbs slips, and Park Ji-sung slots home. Three minutes later, Ronaldo stands over a free kick so far out the Arsenal players don't even form a wall. The commentator says: 'It's thirty-five yards or more away – too far for Ronaldo to think about it . . .' But Ronaldo strikes it. And it thunders past the hapless, bleach-haired Manuel Almunia and into the net.

'Oooooohhhhh . . . that is absolutely sensational.'

Ronaldo wheels away, arms outstretched, then stops, points to his chest with both hands, rocks gently, lips pursed into a tight, triumphant knot, as if to say *I told you I was better than Messi.* Alex Ferguson hops up and down like a man trapped on a bouncy castle.

Suleiman is slowly unravelling.

United fans start teasing him and he lashes out, grabbing one man around the neck. The bar staff step in and the row fizzles out for a while. But when Suleiman isn't raging, he's in tears.

At half-time, with Arsenal two down, friends try to console him. Stay strong, they say. It's only a game. But some are also mocking and teasing him. Then, in the 61st minute, it's over. An exquisite back flick from Ronaldo triggers a lightning break. Rooney picks it up, sprints into space, crosses, and Ronaldo – speeding like a missile – meets it with precision for United's third.

'United can pack their bags for the final in Rome,' the commentator says.

Suleiman is weeping. He leaves the bar, unable to take any more. He is raging at the same time. His friends hope he'll cool off. He lives with his parents metres away, in one of the matchbox flats. But his parents are out and the next morning, a caretaker glancing up at a nearby balcony, sees something terrible.

* * *

As Pineas leads us off the main Mombasa-bound highway into the Pipeline Estate, Peterson tells me how his byline ended up on the newspaper photograph I'd spotted back in the UK. The original story only had a few paragraphs, all with the same police source.

The photograph shows a group of young men and women gathered inside a small turquoise flat, washed in the stark glow of a strip light. They look stunned and upset. The photo doesn't show that Suleiman's body lies just outside the frame. He has hanged himself.

'I wanted to know why,' Peterson says. 'Why would someone do that over a football match?'

He explains that the scene was chaotic when he arrived there. People were crying and others sitting in small groups, gesticulating. Suleiman's body was there, still in his Arsenal strip. His parents were wailing, 'We have lost our son over nothing.'

Peterson adds that Suleiman had left a note asking for his mobile phone to be given to a particular friend. Neighbours described him as respectful and kind. No one had expected this.

Police later confirmed it was suicide. They could find no evidence it was linked to gambling and used the case to urge fans to support local teams – clubs like AFC Leopards or Gor Mahia.

Peterson told us that Suleiman was buried later that day in accordance with his family's Muslim faith. And that was as much as journalists could know.

'In Kenya,' Peterson says, 'when we do a story, that's the end of it. We just moved on.' My call, so many years later, took him by surprise. 'Everything had been forgotten,' he said.

* * *

Pineas guides us into the Pipeline Estate on his Honda. Before I can get out of the car, his face appears at the window and he gestures for me to wind it down. 'Put your phone away,' he says. 'It's not safe. Stay close to me.'

The news article I read about Pipeline at the hotel described it as 'Nairobi's wildest corner where if you are not sharp, you will either get lost or go mad'. It spoke of robbers and thieves and brothels and hawkers. And it's not hard to see how you could go mad or get lost here.

It is a warren of dusty lanes, flanked by concrete blocks stacked like Tetris pieces. Thousands of flats, all the same height – nine floors – balconies drooping with laundry, including countless replica football shirts. The roads are so narrow and the buildings so close to the roadside they seem to lean inward, contriving to shut out the sky.

The buildings are vaguely post-apocalyptic, but there's a jarring abundance of life. Barrows of sugar cane creak through the dust. Music blares. Church bells clang. Neon-lit wine and spirit shops sit shoulder to shoulder with hand-painted gospel signs. Apparently, the higher you live in these blocks, the cheaper the rent.

Peterson admits he has no recollection of his whereabouts among all this concrete chaos sixteen years ago. But Pineas leads us to where he thinks we'll find Bamba 70. He asks a shoe seller something, then stops to talk with Peterson. 'It's gone,' Peterson explains. Bamba 70 has been replaced by new flats.

My guides keep asking around; they wonder aloud if they might find the caretaker who discovered Suleiman's body – maybe he remembers something, maybe he knows where the family went. Since it is not looking hopeful, we slowly drift back towards the car.

Then, from the blur of movement, a young man jogs over and taps me on the shoulder. He points across the lane to a woman hunched over a hotplate, frying chapatis under one of the towering blocks. Her hands flick and fold through the steam as the oil spatters and the dough turns gold. Her name is Elizabeth Ngongo.

Elizabeth has lived in the area for most of her life and she starts telling Peterson what happened. He translates it to me directly, sentence by sentence. Yes, she says, it's true – he'd been teased and had stormed off, and then he'd killed himself. She waves her arms around frantically, stares at the ground in front of her chapati stand and demonstrates how she wept at the time. Then she jumps up, points at the flats above her and looks up and then down.

Peterson turns to me and looks a bit confused. He explains that Elizabeth is not talking about Suleiman Omondi. The man she's describing didn't hang himself – he jumped from the seventh floor flat directly above our heads.

I'd known there'd been another football-related death, a 28-year-old Manchester United fan, but I hadn't followed it up. I'd decided to focus on Suleiman, because Peterson was my only way in. But by accident, we'd stumbled across Elizabeth, an eyewitness to the death of another young Kenyan man, John 'Jimmy' Macharia, four years later.

Elizabeth grabs Peterson's arm to steady herself as she continues the story. Her voice wavers, and as she speaks, a group of young men start to gather around us, all of them wearing Arsenal tops. I don't feel particularly intimidated. If anything, it feels like we're all bound together by the story. The young men shake their heads, sigh and sip from plastic cups. Pineas is nearby, sitting on his Honda like a guard dog in repose. He looks like he could handle himself. Elizabeth tells us more about John's death. It wasn't clear whether John had also been at the Bamba 70 bar, but she says he'd been watching Manchester United-Newcastle on 7 December 2013. Alex Ferguson was gone, the new boss David Moyes was floundering, and United were ninth.

John had watched them lose midweek to Everton. Before that, there were two draws. It was part of their monumental fall from grace. United had won five of the last seven titles and finished second in the others. Their decline was a crisis of identity.

Elizabeth says John was a lovely, humble boy. But that night he was full of rage. United lost 1-0, their second home defeat in four days. His friends chased after him after he became upset, worried about what he might do. They followed him up the seven floors of his block, but John was too quick. He stormed on to the balcony, his friends just metres behind, and jumped.

Elizabeth had seen him fall to the ground, right there, in front of her stall.

She weeps as she remembers. She says the main problem is the teasing between rival fans. They think they're just bantering, but some receive it as brutal humiliation. Many of the young men are also betting on the game and losing money amplifies the shame.

She lifts her hands in a helpless arc. 'They're overwhelmed,' she tells Peterson. 'They can't cope. They collapse.'

She knows boys who go home and wreck their flats, beat their wives, beat their friends. John jumped. Elizabeth is still crying and she looks down and pinches off a ball of dough. She rolls it between her palms and drops it on to the flour-dusted table. Her rolling pin moves like a piston; back and forth, then a turn, then back again, coaxing the dough into something roundish. She doesn't look up again, not even when I thank her and say goodbye.

'It's time to go,' Pineas says, noticing more people in the crowd. But the same boy who introduced us to Elizabeth has now recruited someone else. I glance at Pineas. He nods, as if to say, go on then, but be quick. He knows things can change fast around here. And Elizabeth looked shaken.

The new man is in his forties. His name is Peter and he knew John, but not Suleiman.

'He was happy the season before,' Peter says. 'He was a champion. He kept saying Rooney was his friend, Van Persie was his friend. But then Ferguson left. He was getting more and more down. He was getting so angry. He was not in his right mind. All the United fans thought they mattered the year before. They were the best. Better than Arsenal, better than Chelsea.'

Pineas and Peterson tug me gently by the elbow, and I climb back into the car. I hand Pineas some money for being our guide, about £20. He guides us back on to the highway and shoots off down a side road.

* * *

Back at the hotel, I feel ambivalent about the trip to Pipeline. I feel like I've caught a glimpse of what it might be like to live there. And something about what Peter said stuck with me – John's fantasy that he was part of the team, a friend of the players, basking in borrowed glory. But it was the anger and impulsivity of these men in the moments before they died that shocked me most. They weren't slumped and collapsed; they were raging.

I was disappointed too. I hadn't learned much more about Suleiman. He seemed to have been swallowed by the estate and forgotten. I look up what happened in the game after John took his life. The next match – Sunday, 15 December – Manchester United beat Aston Villa 3-0 at Villa Park. I think of John and what might have happened if he could just have hung on.

A text buzzes in. It's Stephen, the taxi driver. His neighbours are willing to talk to me. He'll pick me up tomorrow, after lunch, take me to see his neighbours, then drop me at the airport for my return trip.

26

Asunta's story

Stephen picks me up outside the hotel at 4 p.m. in the custard-yellow Toyota. The receptionist is still chuckling about my solitary bag. 'I hope you got what you needed from your stay,' she says, waving me off with the same mischievous smile she gave me at check-in.

I feel charming and slightly tragic.

On the way to see his neighbours in Utawala, Stephen tells me that, in his twenties, he had lived on the Pipeline Estate, where Suleiman and John died. His block of flats was called Aston Villa and he paid the equivalent of £15 a month. He's keen to stress that Pipeline, which I'd imagined was almost as bad as it gets, is actually aspirational for many young Kenyans. It is a considerable step up from the vast slums, where people live under corrugated-iron shelters.

'Why did you leave then?' I ask.

'The parking,' he says.

He tells me about the couple we are about to see, Emmanuel and Asunta. They met as young children on the Mathare slum, not far from Nairobi's business centre. Emmanuel was six years older than Asunta, and he kept her under his wing as they hustled for survival. The pair played football together on the dusty, grassless pitches, alongside smouldering rubbish dumps, threading battered old balls between wandering cows. Survivors of slum life often speak of it as a place ruled by jungle logic. Older kids bully the younger ones. Strength dominates weakness.

Their life trajectory changed one day when talent spotters from a football project noticed fourteen-year-old Emmanuel playing in an Arsenal shirt and thought he had potential. They agreed to sponsor him through his education. He begged them to bring Asunta, who was eight, and they agreed. Emmanuel was aware of the fate that awaited many girls in slums.

Stephen knew the Mathare slum well. He visited regularly to teach the children piano. As well as being a taxi driver he is a jazz musician. Some of the kids Stephen taught on electronic keyboards in cramped community rooms are now professional pianists.

He tells me about a boy he once taught named Robert. Robert would show up to lessons either drunk or high. He was maybe thirteen or fourteen. Eventually Robert asked Stephen to teach him properly. Stephen agreed on the condition that he turned up sober. And he did. Again and again, Robert turned up. Now he lives in Germany, performing professionally. He's built a house for his mother.

'People had given up on Robert,' Stephen repeats, shaking his head. 'I tell you; people had given up on him.' From all our conversations, it's clear, Stephen is a strong believer in the power of redemption. A story he tells me later will make this very clear.

Emmanuel went to college and studied masonry, while Asunta learned IT skills.

We rattle along the potholed road towards Stephen's house. The taxi jolts like a kettledrum with every crater. Chickens scatter in front of us.

Asunta and Emmanuel's home is a low-slung one-storey building with a front door painted sky blue – cheery, almost defiant against the grey breeze blocks and corrugated iron roof. Asunta appears. For a second, I think she might be one of their children – she looks so young. Her hair is braided close to the scalp. When she smiles, she tilts her head slightly.

She's barefoot, dressed in a grey hoodie and a green, knee-length skirt. She is smiling but has bad news for us. Emmanuel has been called out to a masonry job and so won't be back in time. I suspect there's more to it than that.

'Welcome to our small home,' Asunta says, ushering me into the single room. A large double bed with a red sheet takes most of the space. I perch on a stool and tell her I prefer Utawala to Pipeline.

We all hoot with laughter.

Asunta explains her two children – Brahman, five, and Jewel, two, are being looked after elsewhere. She wastes no time telling me about how football rescued her.

'I hear you're a Manchester United fan,' I say. She giggles, slapping the bedsheets.

'Yep,' she says, raising an eyebrow.

'Why?' I ask. She grins.

'I LOVE Rooney,' she shrieks, practically bouncing on the bed.

'Rooney?'

'I LOVE Rooney.'

She tells me her obsession with Manchester United started after Rooney's outrageous overhead goal against Man City on 12 February 2011, when she was fourteen. Until then she had been neutral. But she was aware that her best friend, her future husband-to-be, Emmanuel, was a diehard Arsenal fan.

She tells me what happened a couple of months earlier, on 9 March 2025. Asunta had been watching United against Arsenal with her sons at home, while Emmanuel was at a sports bar called Wallet in the city. The match ended 1-1 but Arsenal's failure to win had likely sounded the death knell for their title hopes.

Asunta was thrilled. Her beloved United had sucker-punched their rivals, and the schadenfreude warmed her soul. She decided to cook a celebratory meal, a fish and wheat dish. It was partly because she was pleased for herself, but also because she wanted to cheer her husband up.

When he got home, she rushed to greet him and wrapped her arms around him. He didn't respond. His arms stayed limp by his sides. Maybe she sensed some rejection from him and maybe that's what prompted her to tease him about another Arsenal capitulation.

'He was staring at me like this,' Asunta says, twisting her face into a mask, eyes wild, jaw locked. 'And I was like, what is wrong? It's just a match.'

Feeling rejected and, on the defensive, she stepped up the teasing.

She taunted him about Manchester United's 8-2 demolition of Arsenal on 28 August 2011. Rooney had scored a hat-trick that day. Emmanuel snapped. He grabbed Asunta and threw her out of the house.

'Then he pushed me back inside,' she says. 'And started beating me. Beating me, beating . . .

'He was punching me, slamming me against the wall. My sons were watching.

'He took my phone and hurled it at me. He threw the fish dish. He was throwing anything he could grab.'

She points to a mark on her head, then picks up a pair of plastic sandals from the floor. She cracks them together, demonstrating the sound of the blows.

He tore off her clothes, leaving her naked.

'I said, "It's just a match," and he said, "Why don't you go marry Rooney? You're mocking me. Go get him. Go get his money."'

She pauses for breath.

'I thought, this guy is going to kill me.'

She lifts her arm and the hem of her top to show me more bruises. 'He was biting me. Biting me like an animal.'

I ask if he'd been drinking or had ever done this before. She shakes her head.

The children were screaming. 'The bigger one, he's five – he was shouting, "Mommy, come back home." I was outside, naked. And Emmanuel had gone out to find a big stick.'

Asunta ran naked up the dirt track to Stephen's house.

Emmanuel pursued her like a zombie. Stephen rushed out with his wife after hearing the screams. They took Asunta in, and she called her mum, who lives about ninety minutes away by car. She and the kids went to stay there.

Although Asunta wanted to stay away, she had to return because she depended on Emmanuel's wage to feed the children and pay school fees.

We pause. Stephen has been sitting beside her on the bed the whole time, head bowed.

'I'm still trying to figure out what happened with my husband that night,' she says softly.

'We've been married five years – and there was a personality I never knew.'

Asunta tells me she tried to get Emmanuel to speak to the pastor, to help him make sense of the attack, but he refused.

'He told me, "Go get married to that pastor. Go tell him you're a fan of Rooney. I'm praising Rooney over him, right? Praising another man over him."'

Now they sleep head to toe in the same bed, the children curled up beside them.

Then Asunta smiles.

'I don't think Rooney has ever come to Kenya,' she says, half-asking for confirmation.

I smile back.

I wonder how the children are, after what happened. She tells me that Brahman, the older boy, pleaded with her not to discuss football with his dad any more.

'Is he a fan?'

Asunta reaches for a small football she had bought for him. Brahman hates it.

Asunta looks sad now. She tells me that Emmanuel used to be a 'calm, kind person'. He was quiet. He mostly just spoke to Stephen and her. It reminded me of the way people in Pipeline described Suleiman and John, quiet boys, polite, who kept everything in. Inside, they were burning with rage.

Of course, I worry about Asunta. But I worry about Emmanuel too and about what shame can do to someone.

Asunta's smile has gone, but she holds my gaze.

'I told him, "Remember we were brought up with this football. This is what made us. Remember we were in the football field together. Remember we were playing together, in the slums."'

And then she puts her head in her hands and weeps. Stephen consoles her, but she can't stop.

* * *

I say goodbye to Asunta and climb back into Stephen's taxi. We sit there for a while, the engine off, neither of us speaking. I wasn't sure what I was expecting, but I wasn't prepared for the savagery of the attack. I felt helpless and guilty that Asunta had poured out her trauma and was now alone again.

Part of me felt I'd cracked Asunta open and then simply left her, raw and exposed.

I was also conscious that Emmanuel hadn't been there. It bothered me because I wanted to understand him more. Stephen reassures me that he will look after Asunta and that he hopes he can act as a mediator between them. He says he will continue to try to persuade Emmanuel to talk to me but warns me that he was in a 'very bad state' the night before.

As we drive to the airport, I can tell that Stephen has been deep in thought, then he catches me off guard.

'If you hit a woman, it has to be for the right reasons,' he says.

'Right reasons?'

'Like if you find your woman with another man . . . if I hit you over that, that's okay.'

'Okay?'

'It's *very* okay,' he replies. 'If they allow a woman to do that, it teaches the other ladies they can do that too. It teaches the kids.'

He shakes his head.

'But that's the first couple I've ever seen fight over football.'

He outlines the acceptable justifications for hitting; adultery, verbal disrespect, mistreating the children.

'We just call it spanking. You're not supposed to use your fist against your wife, right?'

Stephen tells me there's a protocol after a woman is attacked. First, the wife goes back to her family with the kids. Then the man reports the violence to *his* family. If he wants her back, the men of both families meet at her house and decide on a way forward. If the man is considered at fault, some kind of recompense is expected – several goats, perhaps.

'So, it's tedious,' Stephen says. 'It's a lot of work. You're better off just talking things through, rather than beating her.'

I ask if he's ever hit his wife. Her name is Mercy.

'No,' he says. 'I've never done that. My father never did. My grandfather never did.'

'What do you think about hitting women?' I ask.

Stephen goes quiet.

'I condemn it. In my sober mind, I condemn it so much.'

The contrast between what he is saying now, and the misogyny he appeared to condone a moment earlier is confusing. Later, I checked the law on domestic violence in Kenya. It was criminalised back in 2015 under the Protection Against Domestic Violence Act. But from everything I read – and hear – it's clear that enforcement is often more theoretical than real. Survivors are still shamed or silenced or told to sort it out 'within the family' – a euphemism for the patriarchal system of elders and clan hierarchies Stephen described.

Stephen and I talk about anger, and how to work with it. He tells me he's been full of rage with his wife Mercy countless times, but they have an arrangement. When he gets angry, he tells her to leave and then calls her back when he is calm.

'Do you think that's fair?' I ask.

'It works,' Stephen says. 'If I go, I might go to drink, I might seek comfort in the wrong place. But because she is not angry, she is okay.

'We've been married eight years now and I've never hit her. I think these are the conversations you need to have *before* you get angry.'

* * *

We talk about therapy for men and emotions. He says it's deeply unpopular.

He shrugs. 'We have our *masculinity*, right?' he says in a self-mockingly growling voice.

'In Africa, we don't go for therapy. It's weakness. We don't cry off to a therapist in Kenya.'

I can't tell how much Stephen actually believes this, or whether he's simply reporting the ideas he grew up with. We sit in silence for a moment. 'But that kills us,' he says, picking up again. 'Because if you just talk to another person – an expert – it might help you see something you didn't see, right?'

I ask him what he'd do if one of his male friends told him he was seeing a therapist.

'I would laugh,' he says. 'I'd tell him he was stupid. Why are you going to see a therapist? You're wasting your money.'

He says it almost angrily, but you can feel the fault line running through him; one part repeating what he's always been told a man should be, the other acknowledging that this is how men end up dying from the inside.

'You sit with a therapist and he just sits there in silence, going *ahem, ahem, ahem*. What's the point?'

We laugh. Stephen says that instead of paying for it, men should be encouraged to talk to each other. We agree that in Kenya, as in the UK, football is a way for men to share intimate moments, moments where they show their emotions to each other.

We park up in the airport drop-off area, and I make sure all the pockets are zipped up on my solitary bag before I say goodbye. Then he pauses. I already sensed there'd been something building up in him during the last part of the journey. He concedes that if there was ever a time he might have needed therapy, it was three years ago.

His brother Robert was returning from work as a bus driver when he noticed a woman screaming in the dark. She started pointing at him and he was confused. A mob gathered. And then they began to beat him with rocks.

Stephen was in his taxi at the airport – right here, where we're sitting talking – when a friend called from the scene.

'Your brother is being beaten,' the friend said. 'Come quickly.' By the time Stephen arrived, Robert was barely alive. He died soon after.

Stephen later found out that a woman had falsely identified Robert as the man who'd robbed and threatened to rape her in the street in Utawala. The actual perpetrator was eventually caught and convicted.

Stephen tells me he went to visit the woman, who was devastated.

They are close friends now.

'Forgiving her helped me heal . . .' he shakes his head, '. . . without therapy.'

There's a big smirk on his face.

Then he turns to me. 'Out of interest – how would you have approached me if I came to you for therapy after this?'

I told him I would have first assessed him and checked whether he had post-traumatic stress disorder (PTSD).

He nods.

I ask if he still saw images of his brother dying in the street.

He goes quiet.

'In my dreams,' he says.

I get out of his car and go to shake his hand. He grabs me and hugs me.

I walk towards the terminal.

I'm four hours early for my flight. I don't mind too much because it means I can watch the whole of the Champions League final on my laptop.

27

Life and Death in Sunderland

At the airport bar, I'm caught between watching the actual game and live YouTube streams of fans watching the game. The latter feels like research for this book. As Inter sink towards a 5-0 capitulation, there's despair everywhere – but most of all rage.

One live fan stream features an Inter Milan fan who calls himself Footy Judge Mo. He's wearing headphones and a black T-shirt. On the wall behind him, a framed Inter shirt – number five, Dejan Stanković.

Mo's commentating: 'Fabián Ruiz, Vitinha . . . 1-0, 1-0. Oh for – fuck off. FUCK OFF.' He screams and throws something down. His face twists with rage. He doesn't appear to be acting. He's so intense and furious I'm not sure I want to absorb all of it, so I skip stream.

Now there are two Inter fans and two PSG fans watching together. One of the Inter fans is strapped to a heart monitor, rising and falling with the game like a storm-tossed buoy. When PSG pull ahead, it spikes: 'Disgusting, disgusting,' he yells, shaking with fury. His heart rate jumps from 88 to 115. Earlier he'd torn a fluorescent blue wig off another supporter's head and hurled it to the floor.

I switch back to Footy Judge Mo. He's still there, but the rage has drained out of him. The energy's been sucked clean away. His shoulders slump, his head dips. But then, out of nowhere, a spark of anger flares again, jerking him back to life. He turns on the manager.

'It's 5-0. We are the worst team in the history of the Champions League final.' He's oscillating between rage and hopelessness, like a man possessed by radically shifting sub-personalities.

Live comments from viewers are pouring in. 'Is the first guy all right? 😂😂 can somebody check on him? Pretty sure he had a heart attack during that game 😂'

There are thousands of Inter fans flooding out of the stadium early, with twenty minutes left. I have half an hour till my flight is called. I turn the stream off and take a sedative ahead of the journey.

The laptop is silent now, but the chaos still loops in my mind. I can hear Footy Judge Mo howling inside my head and see the heart rate monitor flashing and pulsating. People may have been joking, but the concerns about cardiac arrests make me wonder what all this frustration and rage does to the human body. Can it really do you physical damage? It feels like the right moment to bring in Bill Kirkup.

* * *

It's the autumn of 2002. Bill, a medical doctor, sits in his office in the North East chatting football with his colleague David Merrick. Bill supports Newcastle, David, Leeds. By the time he retires, Bill will have helped lead major inquiries into Hillsborough, Jimmy Savile at Broadmoor, and NHS scandals, collecting a CBE along the way.

But on this particular afternoon, long before all that, he and David are batting around a question inspired by the Bill Shankly quip:

Some people think football is a matter of life and death. I assure you, it's much more serious than that.

They decide to test Shankly's assertion out – empirically. Can fandom kill you?

By chance, Bill and I spoke on 15 January 2025 – six hours before Newcastle hosted Wolves.

He appears on screen: bald, bespectacled, in a black sweater. 'How are you feeling about tonight?' I ask.

'Hard to say,' he says, his Geordie accent unmistakable. 'Always had a soft spot for Wolves, though. First football annual I ever owned had Billy Wright in it.'

'Some clubs just feel . . . proper?' I say, fishing for solidarity.

'Aye. Unlike those new outfits . . . down the south coast.' He waves a hand, dismissing an entire region. 'Never quite felt like real teams, did they?'

I laugh. Just like that, we've drawn new tribal lines – a Common Enemy coalition of northern lifers versus southern upstarts. I tell him about the book and ask if he gets the violent mood swings too.

'God, yes,' he says. 'If we lose badly, I'm done for the weekend. No Sky. No *Match of the Day*. Nothing. But if we win and play well? I'll watch every game going.'

He tells me he prefers live matches to television. He needs to feel part of the crowd or else he starts kicking things about in his house.

For a moment I picture this CBE-winning doctor side-footing a coffee table, and it makes my stand-off with the dog feel less embarrassing.

Bill tells me about his research. He and David analysed 1,094 matches played by Newcastle, Sunderland, Middlesbrough and Leeds between 1994 and 1999. They cross-referenced the scores with cardiovascular deaths. Was there a correlation?

The answer was an alarming *yes.* When teams lost, the number of men dying from heart attacks and strokes shot up.

Sunderland supporters posed a big problem for the study though. Not because they were immune, but for the opposite reason. The death rate in Sunderland after losses shot up by a remarkable sixty-six per cent. They were dying much more than anyone else. Scientific journal editors baulked – what if the Sunderland deaths had skewed the whole study?

So, Bill and David reran the data without Sunderland. The effect still held. Losses by Newcastle, Middlesbrough and Leeds raised death rates by thirty per cent. Football heartbreak, it turned out, wasn't just metaphor.

It's not that emotion causes coronary disease, Bill explains. But in someone already vulnerable, it can tip them over the edge. The combination of adrenaline, blood pressure spikes and inflammation can rupture plaques in the arteries. That's what causes the heart attack.

Anger in response to defeat is particularly risky, Bill explains. One study found that you're up to nine times more likely to have a heart attack in the hour after an angry outburst.

What about delirious joy? I ask. Bill shakes his head. Positive emotions aren't associated with triggering heart disease or stroke.

Bill told me none of the clubs wanted to talk about his study and they had to do a press conference from Croft Park, the ground of Blyth Spartans, who weren't even involved. The other clubs didn't want their fans to think they were at risk of death.

I was curious about Sunderland though; why were so many people dying there after football losses? I looked through their results at the time of the study. It was emotional carnage; two relegations, a famous 4-4 play-off final with Charlton, then losing

7-6 on penalties. Meanwhile, Newcastle were, relatively speaking, soaring.

And these seasons of emotional carnage for Sunderland came after a longer period of chronic stress. The city had been hit harder than its neighbours by the miners' strike and by the closure of its last pit – Wearmouth Colliery – in 1993. Four years later, the club's new stadium – the Stadium of Light – rose on the same ground. By the river, a winding wheel still stands, a memorial to what used to be.

* * *

A few hours after our conversation, Bill heads to St James' Park. Meanwhile, I'm in my upstairs office watching our teams on the computer. I'm slouched like a broken marionette in my swivel chair, while my wife is sprawled out on the sofa, watching *The Traitors*, in front of a crackling fire in the lounge.

It's not often that I abandon watching Wolves, no matter how dire the situation. I have a deep-seated disdain for fans who leave early. What kind of supporters are they? Fair-weather fools, the lot of them. Support is most crucial when it's grim, when your team is being battered at the coalface. That's when you dig in, lift your spirits and stand by them.

But here I am, seventy-four minutes into the game, bashing my mouse against the desk, my hands shaking, but somehow, I guide the little arrow to the tiny red dot at the corner of the browser and switch the damn stream off.

'Huh,' I mutter. 'I'm done this time.'

The office plunges into darkness as I flick the lights off in a huff. There are a few scented candles on my desk which I blow out dramatically, scattering Christmas cards sent to me by patients. The cards flutter to the floor, and I curse them too.

I stomp downstairs, but the act of quitting the game torments me. It's the same regret you feel after storming out of a social gathering in a moment of self-righteous fury, expecting everyone to beg you to come back. Only as the door closes behind you, the cold air hits, and the horrible realisation dawns; you've made yourself look like a complete tit. This is that feeling, except multiplied, because this time I've broken the sacred, unspoken code. I've abandoned the game. I'm plastic.

Downstairs, my wife tentatively asks, 'How's it going?' Her tone makes me flinch. Is she afraid of me? *For God's sake,* I think, scowling. *Please don't be frightened of me. I'm not a monster.*

'It's not even over,' I grunt, barely meeting her eye. 'We're 3-0 down.'

'Aww, babe, come here and watch *The Traitors* with me,' she says.

I slump on to the sofa. She reaches out her hand and while I don't pull it away, it doesn't feel comforting.

Claudia Winkleman is looking very serious and explaining something to the contestants around the circular table in the Great Hall. Their faces contort with overblown shock as if she's just informed them that an airborne version of the Ebola virus has been released in the castle. The camera pans from one stupid face to another. My own face twists with contempt. My wife notices but quickly looks away, pretending she didn't.

'Look at these idiots,' I snap, 'It's a joke.'

She ignores me. I check my phone. I'm desperate for something to validate the fact I've stormed off in a raging huff. Hopefully it will be 4-0, or even 5. At least that would justify my dramatic exit. I could let out a sarcastic, self-vindicating laugh: HA! HA! HAAAH! – and be done with it. But no. Wolves have scored. My app says Santiago Bueno has made it 3-1 with twelve minutes to go.

'Right,' I announce, springing to my feet. 'I'm going back up. There might be a comeback.'

'Oh, that's good,' my wife pretends.

I scramble upstairs and thump on the keys on my keypad. The screen comes on, but I must sign in again and something wants to send a code to my phone for extra verification. I sprint down the stairs to get my phone. It could be 3-2 by now – the lads could be staging a remarkable comeback. I tap the code numbers in and the stream reappears. But what's this – there must be a mistake or a terrible lag? The score still says 3-0.

It dawns on me painfully that VAR has ruled the goal out.

What do I do now? Turn it off again and storm back downstairs with my tail between my legs, and sit beside my wife, who will undoubtedly glance at me with that blend of concern and exasperation she has perfected over years of these tantrums? I can already hear her voice, trying to tread the line between supportive and amused: 'That bad, huh?'

No, I can't do it. It's not just about loyalty to Wolves any more; it's about loyalty to my own integrity. I've made the choice to come back and rejoin this doomed shitshow, and now I'm trapped. If I abandon the game again, I will look ridiculous.

So, I just sit there, seething.

The game ticks on and I manage to convince myself that abandoning it was just a blip and now I'm showing my true colours. Loyalty, I tell myself again, is important. It's what separates the diehard fans from the deserters.

In the stadium, Wolves fans begin to trickle out with five minutes left.

And as I watch them, I do the only thing left to make myself feel better. I project every ounce of my self-disgust at my own disloyalty into the fans leaving the ground. Those people, those weak, fickle losers, slinking out before the final whistle. I imagine them, shuffling down the steps, muttering excuses to themselves: *Beat the traffic, no point watching this, it's only a game.*

Traitors.

28

'Real Fans'

Later, I'm on one of the Wolves Facebook pages with tens of thousands of members. I'm hoping it might make me feel better after the Newcastle defeat. But I was mistaken. I'd asked what I thought was a reasonable question relating to our previous home match against Nottingham Forest: why did Wolves fans seem to hate Morgan Gibbs-White so much?

To me, it seemed odd. He was a home-grown player, after all. He was from Stafford, just up the A449. But after he signed for Forest, we'd boo him with every touch of the ball. The likes of Mexico-born Raúl Jiménez, on the other hand, was welcomed back to Molineux like a returning war hero. Many of the replies are helpful and thoughtful and fill me in politely on my ignorance. Some point out Gibbs-White's attitude during Covid; others reference his girlfriend's alleged social media outbursts. Some acknowledge that he felt more of a traitor precisely because he was a local lad. That felt unforgivable. I didn't agree but it was helpful to understand.

Then a bloke called Steve replies.

'Really!!!!!' he screeches.

'Your [*sic*] clearly not a proper fan or your [*sic*] out of touch with everything.'

It properly bothers me. I feel the gut punch of inadequacy first, but within seconds that transforms into anger.

How fucking dare he? Who is this cunt? I am about to type something to that effect.

While I wonder what to write, the doubt creeps in. Maybe Steve is right. Who the hell am I to think I can write a book about football? I know nothing compared with some fans.

Within minutes, I am spiralling in my head, picturing sports journalists like Miguel Delaney or Barry Glendenning dismantling my book in the public square, exposing it for the dilettante nonsense it is. Next, I am live on talkSPORT, being eviscerated by Simon Jordan, flailing under his forensic jabs, caught out as a fraud in front of a national radio audience.

'It's "you're", not "your", Steve,' I write back.

Then, unable to help myself, I add, 'Otherwise you end up looking a little bit stupid.'

To my immense and disreputable delight, others begin piling in. Someone demands he explain himself. Someone else posts a meme of a medal fashioned out of a tin can lid.

My sister, a fellow member of the group, jumps in with a thumbs up, like a proud parent watching their child win a fight behind the bike sheds.

Steve doesn't reply. Not to my follow-up either, where I gently suggest he seeks help for all that bottled-up hatred.

I leave a 'praying hands' emoji. It is my attempt at transcendence, to show I am above it all.

After a few hours, he still hasn't responded and so I decide to check his Facebook profile.

He looks like a Wolves fan through and through. There are pictures of him at Molineux, grinning with a blonde-haired woman I take to be his partner.

He has one of those England/Wolves hybrid badges as his profile motif, Wolves overlaid on the St George's Cross. He is, to my surprise, an ambassador for a well-known UK charity.

And there he is in Rome, smiling in front of the Trevi Fountain, announcing some major life milestone, greeted with hearts and likes and a cascade of gushing comments.

A few more hours pass. I've calmed down. But his page is still open on my laptop when I notice something; he is now listed as a *former* member of the Wolves Facebook group.

Has he been kicked out? Because of me?

I message the group admin, a man named Ian Davis, and ask him what's happened to Steve. 'He was blocked,' Ian replies, booted out for being unpleasant.

Empathy is a strange thing. At first, there is a surge of vindication that Steve has been exiled. It is justice served, sweet revenge. But then comes the comedown and a feeling of deflation. The realisation that, in the end, nobody has really won. He is a fellow Wolves fan after all.

I picture Steve, somewhere out there, staring at his screen, newly excommunicated. No longer the smiling man at the Trevi Fountain. No longer firing off aggressive comments under Wolves matchday posts. He has been banished from the tribe. A black sheep.

And how close was I? One misjudged 'fuck you, you cunt' away from joining him in the digital wilderness.

These casual insults seem to happen all the time in these groups. It's toxic. One fan recently posted that the abuse he was getting from fellow fans was making him mentally unwell. 'The worst part of losing is these social groups and people self-destructing and tearing into each other,' he lamented.

I reach out to John Price, who moderates a Facebook group called Dingles Ay We, home to more than 25,000 Wolves fans.

John appears in the group as Jack Sparra, a name left over from a bar he once ran in Spain called the Jolly Pirate. He's bald, heavily tattooed, and wearing the green and red Wolves third kit from 2019/20. He's not wearing spectacles.

John's been a moderator on the Dingles page for ten years.

He's astounded how fast fans of the same team turn on each other, especially when the tribe is wobbling. Like Ian Davis banning Steve and a platoon of others on the other group, John has also dished out numerous red cards. The 'real fan' thing crops up constantly; scraps of evidence waved around to prove authenticity – being at that game, that loss, that night on the ropes.

John mentions a female fan in her fifties or sixties who's been banned from every Wolves group going. She posted relentlessly negative criticism of everyone and anyone, especially after a loss. I find her profile on another site. The pages are a shrine to Wolves. She's at the centre of endless debates about what to do with her. 'Just block the silly fucker,' one man demands. 'Or scroll by and laugh at some of the shite the troll posts!!'

And yet every year she still gets a dozen 'Happy Birthday' messages from fellow fans.

I message her. She never replies. I feel sorry for her. I can't shake the thought that the birthday wishes, and the arguments, might be her only crumbs of connection.

Occasionally she applies to rejoin, and the six Dingles moderators gather like tribal elders to decide her fate. The elders always say no. Members get a yellow card for a first offence; after that it's a red. No way back. She's become a black sheep. 'Putting your psychologist hat on, John,' I ask, 'what do you think motivates those who get nasty?'

He pauses.

'Knowing what I know about people,' he says, 'I wonder if it's loneliness. It's almost like . . . "look at me." You know? "Look at me, I exist."'

I liked John's compassionate analysis. Insecurity seemed to run beneath all of this.

I began to wonder whether turning your back on the team by leaving early, and turning on fellow fans online, might be connected by the same psychological thread. I decided to dig a little deeper.

In some respects, I wish I hadn't.

29

A Narcissist, Moi?

In the autumn of 1973, the American psychologist Robert Cialdini was working as a visiting associate professor at Ohio State University. His office was inside the university's American football stadium. At the time, his research had nothing to do with sports fandom. But one Saturday, while attending a game, he witnessed the winning crowd erupting with what struck him as a wildly excessive display of joy.

A few days later, walking through campus, he noticed an unusual number of students wearing red Ohio State jackets. The local newspaper had just reported that Ohio State were now top of the league. Cialdini sensed there was a social and psychological phenomenon at play. He decided to investigate. He and his researchers began covertly observing students at seven universities to see whether the outcome of a Saturday football game influenced how many students wore their team's colours the following Monday.

They confirmed that students were significantly more likely to wear team apparel after a win than after a loss. Cialdini hypothesised that students believed their association with a winning team would boost their perceived status among peers.

To test this further, he ran a second experiment. This time, he called students from a single university. Half were asked to describe a game in which their team had won; the other half described a game they had lost. As he expected, those who recalled a win were far more likely to use the word 'we'. Those who described a loss switched to 'they'.

Then he added a bit extra. Before asking the students about the football games, the researchers gave some a multiple-choice quiz on university life – decoy questions like 'What percentage of students at your school are married? 20% or 35%?' After the quiz, half were told they had done extremely well, while the other half were told they had performed poorly.

The students who were told they had failed the quiz were even more likely to use 'we' when talking about a past victory. In other words, when their self-esteem took a knock, they clung to their team's success even more tightly. The victory served as compensation for their sense of failure. Cialdini called this phenomenon *Basking in Reflected Glory,* or *BIRGing*. The basic idea is that people associate themselves with the success of others to enhance their own self-image.

In the 1980s, other researchers introduced a companion term: *Cutting Off Reflected Failure* or *CORFing*. This describes the opposite behaviour – when people distance themselves from a failing group to protect their own sense of worth and deflect from shame.

BIRGing and CORFing were tested decades later with England football fans during the 2018 World Cup. In a study of 47,268 tweets during England's match against Colombia on 3 July, researchers analysed shifts in pronoun use – specifically looking at when fans used 'we', 'us' or 'our' versus 'they', 'them' or 'their'.

When Harry Kane scored a penalty in the fifty-seventh minute, the tweets were flooded with inclusive, celebratory language – 'we' this, x happened to 'us' – classic BIRGing. But when Yerry Mina equalised in the ninety-third, many fans abruptly shifted to CORFing mode. 'They've bottled it.' 'They never hold on.'

Remarkably, the BIRG–CORF cycle persists beyond the grave. Researchers analysed obituaries across four sports and found that a person was far more likely to be described as a passionate supporter if their team had performed well the previous season. When the team had a bad season, mentions of fandom curiously disappeared. Even after death, we cannot bear the pain of being tied to a loser. Loved ones (or the person themselves if they write their own eulogy) redact the evidence. Our social status and sensitivity to rank still counts after death. The obituary becomes a final defensive manoeuvre against humiliation.

* * *

Ben Larkin is a softly spoken associate professor based in Massachusetts who has spent years studying the psychology of 'CORF-ing' fans who turn their backs on their team after defeat. He's not convinced they should be dismissed as 'fair-weather' supporters though. Fair-weather, he argues, implies a lack of deep investment.

That came as a relief to me – especially after the Newcastle debacle and my brief but intense desire to call Steve, the Wolves fan on Facebook, a cunt.

Then came the blow.

The real driver, he said, isn't indifference. It's narcissism.

Generally speaking, narcissists present with an over-inflated sense of self-importance, entitlement and grandiosity. But it's typically a façade. Beneath it sits an unbearably painful sense of inadequacy. Most narcissists are deeply wounded people

– exquisitely sensitive to loss and criticism.* Often the damage began early, and they survive by constructing a false self: one that must dominate, deny weakness and lash out to stay intact.

Some fans project their narcissism on to the team. It's called collective narcissism. When the team loses – when the collective false self fails – the narcissistic fan may drop the club instantly to avoid collapsing into shame.

Ben tells me his research indicates that narcissism doesn't just account for the fans leaving the stadium, but also the ones most likely to turn on other fellow fans after games. In doing so they prop up their fragile egos – and make the forums a toxic nightmare for the rest of us.

I say 'us' as if I'm innocent. But I'm not immune from responding like this myself. Plus, I had other disturbing evidence too.

I thought back to the moment my own therapist had casually referred to my 'narcissistic wound'. It wasn't an attack – it was a passing comment, offered almost kindly, in the middle of a completely different conversation. But I heard it like a slap.

A narcissist? Me?

My first instinct was to sack him on the spot. To storm out, like I had during the Newcastle game. But my reaction proved his point. Narcissists lash out when their self-image is threatened. If I quit therapy, I'd be proving I couldn't tolerate the truth. But, if I stayed, I'd be trying to win him over and manipulate. Straight out of a narcissist's playbook. I was stuck in a terrible psychodynamic Catch-22.

And then there were the grandiose daydreams that appeared to prop my therapist's assertion up. The imaginary blurbs for this

* Not all narcissists are insecure. There's another breed who have been made to feel so special that they feel entitled (See Terry Real's distinction).

book. The glowing endorsements from Stephen Fry, Gary Lineker and David Nicholls. The mental rehearsals of *Desert Island Discs*. (Luxury item: a Firestick, so I could stream matches illegally from my tropical exile. 'Oh, I think we can allow that,' Lauren Laverne would say with a wink.) And don't get me started on my *Loose Women* appearance.

Eventually, I took an online quiz based on the Narcissistic Personality Inventory. I scored fifteen out of forty – about average for the population. It was a relief, though as my book editor kindly pointed out, this was an online test and hardly conclusive or reliable. I embraced the results nonetheless. My results showed I was low on entitlement and exploitative behaviour, but slightly higher than average on vanity. That made sense to me. After years of being bullied – for my buck teeth, my skinniness, my massive curly blond hair – I'd clung to appearance like a life raft. I got a Nik Kershaw haircut. I started bodybuilding. It was vanity as self-protection.

30

Emmanuel's Story

Some days after my return flight from Kenya, I hear from Stephen, the taxi driver. He has managed to set up an interview with Emmanuel.

A few hours before the interview is due to start, I get a text; things are unravelling in Nairobi. Stephen tells me Emmanuel is uncertain about talking.

Asunta has taken all her belongings and left with the children. She's gone to stay with her uncle, fifty miles away in a town called Murang'a – formerly Fort Hall, a colonial trading post.

Emmanuel is nowhere to be found in Utawala. Stephen suspects he's gone after Asunta to plead with her to return. He says he'll try to track him down.

'My foot is on the gas, bro,' he adds, as he speeds towards Murang'a.

A couple of hours later I get an update. He's tracked down Emmanuel and they are waiting in a car ready to talk to me. Emmanuel looks much older than Asunta, though he's only six years her senior. His face is worn, eyes ringed with fatigue. He wears a black cap and a red-and-white lumberjack shirt and worries at his teeth with a wooden toothpick.

I ask how he is. He says he's nervous about the interview, still unsure whether he should have agreed at all. He's worried that talking to me will 'bring that picture back'.

He means Asunta's battered body.

'It's horrible,' he continues. 'But it's a book. It will be read. My history will be read. What I did will be read. And maybe others will never do the same.'

He tells me the story of how he became an Arsenal fan. Thierry Henry pulled him in, but it was bigger than one player. Football, he says, gave him purpose in a place where purpose was scarce. He talks about growing up in the slum, watching neighbours claw their way to national fame – footballers like McDonald Mariga and Victor Wanyama – men who made it out by sheer insistence on belief.

'No one sees people from the slum as human beings,' he says.

He looks down, searching for the right phrasing. 'One thing I know. You have to believe. You have to believe something good will happen.'

He links this optimism to the anticipation he feels before football matches. He starts predicting the future. He can fantasise and dream of something big, borrow status from the team. But he admits that this hope, when left unchecked, can lead men like him astray. They start bragging before the match has even begun. They taunt their rivals. They bet on wins they've already imagined; with wages they can't afford to lose. Football becomes a kind of oracle.

It reminds me of shamans – figures who are often marginal and disregarded, who break through status barriers when they are reimagined as powerful minds with access to hidden knowledge. When conventional routes to status are blocked, people look elsewhere. They invent new ladders to climb up.

He says he feels like a failure after Arsenal lose and what is worse is being belittled and mocked by rival fans.

He tells me about his relationship with Asunta and football. He says he coached her to be a fan and was disappointed she chose Manchester United based on Wayne Rooney's success.

On the night of the attack he had bragged before he had left about Arsenal winning. When he returned, Asunta teased him and he says he remembers nothing of the initial attack.

'All I know . . .'

He trails off. His voice falls into a whisper.

'. . . I just saw her down.'

It goes quiet. There's a look in someone's eyes that I have become very familiar with while working with traumatised people. It is the look when someone is reliving an old experience as if it's happening in the present. For victims of crime, like Asunta, it often looks like terror. And for perpetrators too, for those who have done terrible things that they are deeply ashamed of, you often get the same look. Emmanuel had this look now.

'You just saw her down?'

'I don't know what happened,' he says. 'I don't have CCTV in my house to see how it happened, but I just saw her down.'

He pulls his cap down further. He says he felt like he had become 'possessed'.

'You don't remember beating her?'

'If I said I did, I'd be lying to you,' Emmanuel insists.

He says that if Asunta went to the police he would go to jail and he knows he deserves it. He shakes his head. 'It's bad. It's bad. It's bad.'

'And what's the reason to be in jail – for people I have never seen play in real life? Destroying a family for people I only know by their names?'

He takes a breath and then looks at me, perhaps seeing me as an ally for a moment. 'I have to figure this out.'

Emmanuel says the worst part is remembering the look of horror on his children's faces afterwards.

'For children, memory never fades.'

He breaks down. I wonder whether he's thinking about something from his own childhood now.

'That was not self. That was not me,' he continues.

'Who did it then?' I ask.

'The anger. Because me, me? No, I can't do it. No one can believe I can do it. No one thinks it can happen, so . . .' He trails off.

I ask him whether he's tried to repair things with Asunta but he says things are too volatile at the moment.

Either a policeman or security guard knocks on the car window and tells them they have to move because they are illegally parked.

I speak with Stephen briefly to thank him for setting up the interview and for all the effort he has gone to, racing to Murang'a, even if we only had thirty minutes.

'I had to,' he says. 'I told you, I'm crazy about this book.'

'You are,' I say.

'I've driven for 170 kilometres.'

Emmanuel has his head bowed.

PART VI

Why Does Football Affect My Mood So Badly?

31

Tricky Brain

I needed to make sense of all of this. How could something as seemingly trivial as winning and losing in a game of football exert such force over mood and behaviour? A theme that kept surfacing was the idea of being mocked or belittled. Emmanuel used the word 'mockery' repeatedly. Elizabeth mentioned it in relation to John Macharia. I recognised it immediately in myself – that sinking, belittled feeling, that sense I was being looked down on by my brother.

Emmanuel's extreme reactions to being teased by Asunta made me think of an adage adapted from Margaret Atwood: men are afraid women will laugh at them, while women are afraid men will kill them. I wondered whether it pointed to something deeper about shame, status and what humiliation does to men in particular.

I meet with Professor Paul Gilbert, one of the world's leading evolutionary psychologists and expert on how social status impacts mood and behaviour. Paul Gilbert pioneered social rank theory, then created compassion-focused therapy, a psychological approach which helps us understand and work with the primitive architecture of what he describes as our 'tricky human brains'. Human brains are very badly cobbled together, he says, and we are 'potentially one of the cruellest and nastiest species that have ever walked on this planet'.

Paul is an early riser and we meet at 5.30 a.m. He appears on the screen at his home, against a backdrop of lush potted plants. Two guitars rest casually against the wall. He tells me he once dreamed of being a musician, but psychology won out.

His grey moustache glows faintly in the artificial light, and his eyes carry the reassuring, weathered quality of someone who's stared into darkness and come back softer.

Paul tells me he became interested in depression and its relationship to competition through painful personal experience. He was born to traumatised parents and was sent to boarding school at a young age. He came to associate self-worth with academic achievement and when his PhD faltered and a job fell through concurrently, he felt like a failure. He was suicidal.

He started to develop panic attacks and would wake in the morning at 4 a.m. to take cold baths, to calm himself down. He couldn't travel on public transport and had to take taxis everywhere. He had thoughts of throwing himself in front of a train, like Alfie Perkins.

Paul had reached out to the eminent psychiatrist John Price, who believed mental disorders might have an evolutionarily adaptive function. (There are two John Prices in this book, lots of Pauls – five at last count, along with two Alfies, two Jennys, two Bills, and a Sara and a Sarah. There is also an abundance of bald and bespectacled men. I promise they are all distinct individuals.) Price was intrigued, for example, by reports of unusual patterns of schizophrenia in far-northern populations, and by speculative theories that voice-hearing might have helped Arctic hunters endure long, silent hours at seal holes – keeping them alert through isolation and fatigue.

While working as a senior lecturer in psychological medicine in Newcastle, Price kept a vervet monkey in his lab. Vervets have patches of bright blue skin, most of it hidden under fur, but the male scrotum is hairless and vividly coloured. In the wild, other monkeys watch this display with near-religious attention. What fascinated Price was what happened when a male vervet lost a fight or slipped in social rank: the scrotum turned white. The shift was physiological – water flooding the tissue – and it came with reduced energy and behavioural retreat. A low-status monkey with a white scrotum – one who was signalling defeat – was left alone. He faced little interest from others and wasn't challenged or threatened.

Price began to wonder if this was the point: depression and withdrawal were evolved mechanisms for signalling submission and avoiding further attack. He called it the 'yielding subroutine of ritual agonistic behaviour' – more pithily known as *defeat depression.*

Paul told John how suicidal he felt as he competed – and failed – in the world of academia. John listened, then let out a sympathetic sigh.

You've got defeat depression.

As Paul tells me this, he leans back, almost amused by the memory.

* * *

I press on like I'm confessing my sins. I tell him about what happened in Kenya and then I show him what happens when Wolves lose, shaking my head, cupping my hands, dragging them upwards over my face, in a gesture so melodramatic, I'm sure I see Paul recoil.

'It doesn't end at the final whistle,' I exclaim. 'It carries on all weekend. I'm irritable. I'm hostile to my wife. I'm still feeling low on Tuesday.'

I mimic myself collapsing like a crumpled heap of laundry.

'Why is this happening to me?' I ask.

He takes a sip of his coffee. I'm sure this is not what Paul thought he was signing up for. He was hoping for an intellectual conversation about his latest research in neurobiology and compassion, and here I am, pouring my heart out about Wolves for free before breakfast.

But he nods, smiling, as if to say, *carry on mate, I've heard worse.*

'The first thing to notice,' he says, 'is that you're describing your reactions as if they say something shameful about you: why aren't I more mature, why am I like this? That isn't curiosity. That's blaming yourself for the feelings themselves.'

Of course I shouldn't be like this, I think to myself. I'm acting like a lunatic, and everyone in my house – from my dog to my nephew to my poor wife – knows it.

'Then why shouldn't you be like this?' Paul insists, as if reading my mind. 'Let's start off with that question.'

I mutter something about my level of despair but also the rage, how it feels grotesque, how ashamed I am of my scrunched, contorted face when I'm jabbing at the TV. I demonstrate the face. Paul's eyes widen.

'That might be true,' he interrupts sternly, 'but like having to have a shit in the morning – people don't necessarily like that.'

I blink. The scatological pivot catches me off guard.

'You must be careful because it carries diseases. But why shouldn't you shit?'

My face is blank. I have no answer.

'Because you have to, right?'

'I suppose so,' I say.

'Because it's part of your *design*.'

He leans in close. This, he says, is the point; if you judge your despair and rage from a place of self-loathing, you lose twice. First you experience the despair and the rage, then you beat yourself up about it and feel ashamed.

If I wanted to understand the moods and extreme behaviours of football fans, I needed to get my head around the different pressures that have made my badly designed human brain especially sensitive to winning and losing. We start with evolution and our cousins, baboons. There's lots of research on baboons.

Male baboons live in dominance hierarchies. They are acutely sensitive to where they rank in the hierarchy. High-status male baboons get access to resources, mates and lots of grooming opportunities. Status is a matter of life and death. Low-ranking male baboons are picked on and bullied. They are targets of displacement aggression from other male baboons who pass bullying from above down the hierarchy. Being a low-ranking male baboon is very stressful and many of them get ill and even die. Their cortisol levels are through the roof. Status in these dominance hierarchies is achieved through aggression and control. Threat to status is very stressful and defended vigorously. Female baboons are attuned to status too, but they achieve it, less through aggression, and more through demonstrating their nurturing capacities and social and emotional intelligence.

Testosterone regulates and responds to status. In dominance hierarchies, like the baboons, it is linked to aggression, because aggression and power are rewarded by status. When status is threatened, *testosterone surges*. When you win, testosterone remains high (along with dopamine), and when you lose, it plummets. This energises winning baboons to reap the benefits of their success and losers to mope into obscurity, where they try to avoid further challenges.

Animals signal defeat by withdrawing from threat. This is called the Involuntary Defeat Strategy. We've seen what happens to the balls of vervet monkeys. In fish it's even more obvious. Cichlids, some of the small, belligerent residents of our domestic aquariums, are great examples. Winners blaze. They patrol the tank in neon technicolour, electric with dominance. Losers, meanwhile, lose all their colour with astonishing speed, turning to grey in moments, hiding away in sunken pirate ships.

These colour changes have nothing to do with pigment. They are driven by abrupt shifts in internal chemistry: testosterone and dopamine rising and falling with status. What's even more amazing – and relevant to football fans – is that the female cichlids watching from the sidelines also change colour depending on whether their partners win or lose. Their hormonal profiles are in sync, tracking social rank.

The unfortunate defeated male cichlids also see their gonads shrink by ninety per cent. Mercifully, I couldn't find any evidence that this happens in human football fans, though as we are about to see, losing and winning might disturb your sex life.

Males have a lot more testosterone than females (in humans about 10–20 times more). But testosterone is misunderstood. It is not all about aggression. In groups that are not about control and dominance, testosterone is linked to whatever qualities are rewarded with status in that particular society. The great anthropologist Robert Sapolsky jokes that if you burst into a monastery and inject one hundred monks with testosterone, they will become *obsessed* with who can carry out the most random acts of kindness. In the Andaman Islands, east of mainland India, ethnographic accounts in the early twentieth century described a society in which the most respected men were not the most aggressive but those known for generosity and calm temperaments. Losing one's temper reduced standing; kindness and steadiness enhanced it. What counts as 'high rank' is not fixed – it is culturally constructed. Testosterone reflects rank, not aggression.

Football is nothing like being in a monastery or on the Andaman Islands. It is an unforgiving, remorseless and brutal dominance hierarchy. Status is achieved by dominating and beating your opponents. And the problem is – just like the cichlid fish spectating from the sidelines – the status of fused football fans rises and falls with the teams.

* * *

In 1994, Professor Paul Bernhardt demonstrated just how much football fans resemble the fishy spectators. He tested testosterone levels in Brazilian and Italian fans watching the World Cup final, held in the USA. The Brazilians watched it from a sports bar, the Italians from a pizza restaurant, both in Atlanta. He paid them $10 to take part. It was a tense, nail-biting contest – nil-nil after extra time and the game went to penalties. Roberto Baggio steps up, needing to score to keep Italy in the game. He takes a ridiculously long run-up and blazes it over the bar.

Researchers had asked the fans to chew gum before the game, after the game, and then again the next morning so that saliva samples could be taken. Unsurprisingly, researchers at the venues observed a 'striking difference in mood between the two groups' after the result; Brazilian fans were euphoric; Italian fans despondent. In fact, some of the Italians were so pissed off they fled with their $10, refusing to return their salivary testosterone samples. I imagine them hurling their gum on to the pavement and flinging their tricolore napkins behind them in disgust, bolting into the Atlanta sunset. For a delicious moment, it made me feel better about my sulking after Wolves lose.

Yet despite a depleted sample, the results were clear: winning fans saw testosterone surge, while the losing Italians saw it plummet.

All of these fans were male, but another researcher, Dr Christian Burk, ran a similar study during the 2014 World Cup and observed that while the spikes in testosterone were larger in males, the *shape* of the hormonal response in female fans was the same.

At the same 2014 World Cup, Martha Newson, the anthropologist we met earlier, showed that levels of the stress hormone cortisol also tracked wins and losses. Cortisol makes us irritable, sensitive and has been linked to an increased risk of cardiovascular disease, including heart attacks. Martha found that psychologically fused fans showed much stronger, mood-altering cortisol responses than casual supporters. Many of her participants – Brazilians who had witnessed their side's 7-1 drubbing by Germany – buggered off before returning their samples too, even refusing a free buffet, complete with beers.

These hormonal changes – heightened testosterone and dopamine, and reduced cortisol in winners, with the opposite pattern in losers – are automatic and have a profound impact on mood and behaviour. Together, they make up what's known as the winner–loser effect: a cascade of physiological shifts that boost confidence and dominance in winners, while flattening the motivation and draining the confidence of losers, encouraging withdrawal from threat.

* * *

Which brings us back to the matter of shrinking or colour-changing gonads. Do the hormonal shifts that follow watching your side win or lose actually translate into behaviour – specifically, into seeking out mating opportunities, as anthropologists would have us believe? Does winning make us hornier? (When I think about this, I'm forced to revisit my own behaviour at the church carol service shortly after Wolves beat Leicester 3-0.)

The first study I found wasn't about football at all. It was about Barack Obama, democracy and people masturbating more than usual. Psychologists Patrick and Charlotte Markey tracked the frequency of pornography-related Google searches after the 2008 US elections. They discovered that those living in states who voted for the winning party – Obama's Democrats – watched more pornography in the minutes and hours after the result was announced than those in states that voted for McCain's Republicans. Their suggestion was that even a symbolic win can push us towards mating behaviour.

Football fans, though?

My first piece of evidence came from an unexpected source.

32

The Scientist Who Lost His Mojo

Dr Alex Jordan is one of the world's leading marine scientists and had told me about the cichlid fish that change colour with status. But he also told me a more personal, humiliating story.

He sits in his home office in Germany. He's forty-four, South African, clearly very fit, with perfect stubble and what he fully concedes is 'Jack Grealish hair'. Behind him there is a luminous diving watch curled like a sea creature and scuba gear wedged into a cubby hole. There are sketches of crabs and an octopus pinned to the wall.

He hesitates about whether to tell me his personal story about the hormonal impact of defeat.

He scratches his jaw and glances off-screen. Then he turns back to me and grins; 'Ah, fuck it. Why not.'

He tells me he used to play in football tournaments and was the sort of player that would often get into rucks on the pitch. One afternoon in South Korea he collided with a US military guy who 'flew off the handle', threatening to fetch a gun from base and 'shoot up the place'.

Alex was petrified.

'WOOOOOOOFF,' he exhales. 'An all-American experience, right?'

He finished the tournament and even reached the final, scoring a headed goal. He should have been buzzing. But his body disagreed. A girl at the afterparty made her interest known and his physiology made its own announcement.

'I couldn't perform,' he says. 'I couldn't get it up.' He shrugs.

He was fascinated because it mapped perfectly on to the winner–loser effect he was studying in animals. 'I'd effectively, physiologically, lost a fight,' he says. 'Even though no punches were thrown.'

The mere threat of a gun had tripped his hormonal wiring into a defeated profile, where there would have been *no point* in mating.

* * *

It was a fascinating story. But was there anything a little more scientifically controlled? A year after the 2008 elections, which saw Obama fans pleasuring themselves with abandon, one of the greatest footballers of all time, Andrés Iniesta, scored a last-minute winner for Barcelona against Chelsea. It meant the Spanish giants reached the final of the Champions League. There were wild celebrations across Catalonia. Car horns echoed through the night. But nine months later there were echoes of the goal in maternity wards too.

Anecdotal reports began to surface – hospitals in the region were seeing a spike in births. Scientists were sceptical. But a researcher called Jesús Montesinos checked it out. He looked at birth rates at two hospitals in the Bages area of central Catalonia and discovered there was indeed a birth spike nine months after the Iniesta goal was scored. The number of births rose by sixteen per cent on what was expected.

So, it appears that winners really have it good. And it gets worse for losers. Because while winners saunter off looking to pull someone or masturbate, losers compound their losses by getting fatter and generally unhealthier. Elevated cortisol signals uncertainty or threat and uncertain environments favour energy storage. Calorie-dense foods – like Doritos – increase survival odds.

In one study, forty-seven football fans were told to write about a team victory or defeat. They were then asked to complete an unrelated task; finding random words hidden in a matrix.

While they worked, they were sneakily offered snacks in four bowls: crisps, chocolate, grapes and cherry tomatoes. Fans who wrote about defeats reached for crisps and chocolate. Those who wrote about victories munched on grapes and tomatoes.

Even remembering defeat sends you into a delusional calorie deficit where you unconsciously feel compelled to eat crap food. No wonder I couldn't stomach my sister-in-law's beautifully prepared salmon dish.

33

The Bipolar Mind of a Football Fan

There are at least a couple of critical differences between baboon hierarchies and football ones. In my opinion, they make being a football fan even more stressful than being a baboon.

The first is that most baboon hierarchies are relatively stable. A baboon does *not* wake up *every* Saturday wondering if he's about to be publicly demoted. In most troops, the hierarchy doesn't shift much from week to week. Alphas maintain top spot for several months to years. When it does change, it's hugely stressful – but it doesn't happen often. Fans, by contrast, are asked to process status threat on a weekly basis, apart from the brief mercy of the summer.

Baboons also don't have televisions or mobile phones, unless they nick the latter from visitors to safari parks. When a defeated male wanders glumly on the edge of the troop, he doesn't receive a magnanimous message from his Liverpool-supporting brother reminding him how useless he is. He isn't forced to listen to Gary Neville explaining, in forensic detail, why the collapse was inevitable, systemic and down to his own mentality issue. And he doesn't have to watch his mauling replayed on a loop on giant jungle screens. Football culture drops us into an amped-up dominance hierarchy our nervous systems were never designed to inhabit this often. Our bodies never get the memo that it's only a game.

Paul leans forward again, locking eyes with me.

'So,' he says, 'your rank system as a football fan is a bit . . .'

He pauses. I detect genuine compassion for me in his eyes.

'. . . unstable.'

'Right,' I say. We both take a long sip of coffee.

To underline how profoundly status threats in football fans impact our moods and behaviours, Paul makes a comparison I'm absolutely not expecting.

'Let me see if I can find something,' he says, already scrolling. He pulls up a research paper with a diagram and talks me through it.

'What you're experiencing as a football fan,' he says, 'is a kind of bipolar disorder.'

He explains how, in the manic phase of bipolar, people feel superior, confident and assertive. Individuals often feel creative, sexually impulsive and appear grandiose and gregarious. They are in an extremely positive mood. But in the depressive state, they feel inferior, accompanied by low mood and avoidance.

I glance at his diagram. The manic descriptors: uplifts in social comparison, assertiveness, libido, positive mood, grandiosity, impulsivity – then back to the depressive ones: inferiority, submission, low mood, avoidance. The contrast is stark and extreme, and disturbingly close to the violent swings I feel when Wolves win or lose.

'That sounds like me,' I squeak before I can stop myself.

Paul's point is that we get knocked into bipolar-like brain states on a weekly basis – and it's not our fault. Our hormones are playing havoc with our mental health. Of course, he is not suggesting that football fans suffer as much as individuals with bipolar, just that the brain state switches are remarkably similar.

* * *

Football fans have another big problem which distinguishes them from baboons and fish. Not only do our nervous systems respond to status threat on a weekly basis, but we also have an unrivalled capacity to ruminate about how shit we are in comparison with everyone else. In other words, the primitive winner–loser response is amplified and maintained by our evolved human capacity to *reflect* endlessly on our social status.

Paul gears up for a demonstration.

'And you can share this in your book, right?'

'Yes,' I say.

'So, how are you right now?' he asks. 'Take a moment to notice what brain state you are in.'

'I'm fine, maybe a little anxious,' I say.

'So okay, just let that go now, and now recall something that made you feel defeated or angry . . .'

For some reason, I don't immediately think of football but I'm back in the kitchen a few days ago, battling with the toaster. I picture the scene unfolding frame by frame. The soothing cello strains of Classic FM fade into obscurity as my brain redirects every ounce of its attention to the toast that had wedged itself in the toaster slot.

I try the finger method first. Then a knife. And with each failed attempt, I can hear the echo of my wife's voice warning, 'Don't do that, you'll electrocute yourself. Use something wooden!' Which, of course, makes me angrier.

I grab the wooden tongs, trying to claw the toast out. But it doesn't budge. I'm now a caveman armed with tongs, convinced that sheer brute force will prevail. I jab at the toast, harder and harder, until it breaks into three jagged bits. It's impossible to get the fuckers now. My frustration spills over – Paul can see it etched on my face.

'Keep going,' Paul urges. 'Keep thinking.'

I spiral further, now dredging up every other domestic failure of my adult life. Why am I so useless at *anything* that requires even an iota of practical nous? My brain gleefully plays a highlight reel: the dishwasher I loaded wrong, the brown Amazon package I shredded instead of opening like a functioning human, the IKEA chair I assembled heroically and incorrectly.

I decide I deserve to be electrocuted and, in a dramatic flourish, tilt the toaster sideways and spear the largest toast fragment with a metal knife. Victory.

I can feel my heart hammering. My face is screwed up, my body rigid. 'Okay,' he says, surprised at how seriously I'm taking it. 'Suppose you're lying in bed, and you have a sexual fantasy. What happens?'

'Erm,' I mutter vaguely. Does he want an answer? I begin to close my eyes.

He stops me just in time. 'You know the old line; what's the lightest thing in the world? The male penis – because it can be raised by thought alone.'

Paul is demonstrating that, unlike most other animals, we can shift into winner or loser brain states simply by thinking about them. This is why I'm still suffering on Wednesday, days after the match ended. Just as I think I'm free, an intrusive thought about Yerson Mosquera's own goal against Arsenal in the ninety-fourth minute pops back into my head. Before I know it, I'm trying to solve the problem: 'Why are we so shit?', 'Why did the whistle not go thirty seconds earlier?', 'Why does my brother think he is better than me?' I'm stuck in a loop which triggers massive changes to my nervous system, like in the toaster example.

'None of us chose our bodies or our brains,' Paul carries on. 'You didn't request two arms or two legs, did you?'

'No,' I say.

'You didn't choose a visual system that sees a pathetic sliver of the light spectrum. A mantis shrimp sees twenty-five more colours than you do.'

'No,' I grumble.

Our brains, he says, were shaped entirely for survival and reproduction. Happiness never came into the design spec.

'We've got a brain that was *designed for us, not by us*.' He rocks back in his chair.

* * *

We talk about what I found out about John Macharia, the young man who jumped from a balcony after Manchester United lost in the Champions League. I told him how his friends mocked him and reduced him to 'the loser' and how he was flipping between slumped despair and aggression.

Paul doesn't even blink. 'That,' he says, 'is raging depression. Not the head-in-hands, "oh I feel so sad" kind. It's the *fuck this, I'm out* kind.'

He explains that when the rage that is fired up by status threat cannot easily be displaced elsewhere, it can turn inwards. One of the pathways to suicide is precisely this sense of impotent rage – when you feel utterly trapped and the fury has nowhere to go. He recognises that a lot of his own depression was rage he was not able to express and process in his childhood.

'If you're getting depressed,' he says, leaning forward again, 'you've also got to work out how you're going to deal with your rage. Because your rage can kill you.'

He tells me that sometimes, with suicidal patients, therapists ask: *If this were the last minute of your life, and you knew it, what would you want to say to the world?*

'Some people say, "Why didn't you care for me?"' he says.

Then he leans even closer to the camera, eyes widening in mock fury, raising his middle finger so it eclipses the entire screen.

'But others?' he says. 'Others just go . . .' He shrieks into the lens: 'FUCK YOU. Just FUCK YOU.'

He sits back, breath steadying.

34

Bicycle Locks and Broadmoor

I'm on a video call with forensic psychiatrist Gwen Adshead – known for her work with murderers and other violent offenders in Broadmoor Hospital. Paul Mitchell's attack on Grealish is playing on a loop on our shared screen.

I'm with her because, after my return from Kenya, a friend sent me a link to the BBC Reith lectures she gave in 2024. Each year the lectures are delivered by a prestigious thinker in a particular field.

Contributors have included Professor Stephen Hawking, the novelist Hilary Mantel and theoretical physicist Robert Oppenheimer.

Gwen gave a series of four lectures called 'Four Questions About Violence' and the reason my friend sent me the link was that she mentions football.

She references a study written in 2014 looking at domestic violence attacks in Lancashire during the World Cup tournaments in 2002, 2006 and 2010. The authors discovered that when England lost, violence against women by men went up by thirty-eight per cent and it was at its highest when England were knocked out.

When they won it went up by twenty-six per cent.

The authors – academics at Lancaster University – suggested different factors might contribute to the figures, including alcohol consumption, testosterone levels and heightened tensions over who had control over the TV during the month-long tournaments.

I wondered whether Gwen might help me to understand Emmanuel, and some of the other individuals in this book, including me.

Gwen spent years at Broadmoor working with some of the country's most dangerous offenders. In her first week, she noticed a man with a big white beard who looked oddly like Father Christmas.

A colleague leaned over and whispered, 'That's Peter Sutcliffe.'

What struck Gwen was how ordinary he looked – hardly monstrous, just a normal-looking man. She later described the people she met there as 'not mad or bad, but sad'.

In 2021, she and a colleague published *The Devil You Know*, a book about her encounters with killers, arsonists, a child abuser and a teenage girl who killed an elderly man. It is part memoir and part psychological excavation, containing the uncomfortable idea that evil isn't an alien force but a human potential in all of us.

I speak to her at her home, where she sits in a yellow hoodie. Before we talk about Emmanuel, she tells me that even in Broadmoor, football mattered.

In her therapy groups, football was the icebreaker. The running joke was that Gwen knew nothing about it, so the men had to explain everything to her. It cracked the room open. Football became a way in – a tunnel beneath the walls of shame.

Extreme violence, Gwen explained, gets you expelled from the social world. You are monstered and exiled from every tribe. But sitting in a group of others like you, talking about football, offered a route back towards belonging, towards being human again. It reminded me of Stephen, the taxi driver, telling me he didn't feel fully human unless he could talk about football. Even in Broadmoor, the game functioned as a currency for connection.

I tell Gwen about Emmanuel and Asunta. She responds with an analogy – a bicycle lock.

For an act of violence to happen, she says, all the numbers on someone's bicycle lock have to line up. Some numbers are rooted in our genes and biology, such as our hormonal profiles and temperament. Some numbers are cultural – the scripts we learn about what it means to be a man or a woman, about dominance and honour. Others are shaped in childhood – the humiliation, chronic fear and adversity that leave people with threadbare tyres, meaning emotional regulation is more difficult.

Many of the numbers can sit there for years, aligned. But the lock remains unopened. It's waiting for the final twist.

'It's the final number that opens it,' Gwen says. 'And that number can be tiny – an eye roll, a smile, one phrase that hits the wrong nerve.'

Often, she explains, that final number is the perpetrator's sense of being belittled – even if that isn't what the other person intended.

She's lost count of the number of murders that follow something *said* by a victim.

She tells me about a teenage boy who murdered an elderly man in a lift after being criticised. The boy stood over the old man, kicking him to death, screaming, 'What you *saying* now? What you *saying* now?'

'Something the victim had said had just been intolerable,' Gwen continues, 'so, he just had to be wiped out.'

She pauses and looks sad for a moment. 'What an appalling thing to happen – two lives gone because of a complete inability to manage that rage.' It's not hard to see how many of Emmanuel's numbers were already aligned that night. The masculine script he absorbed in a Kenyan slum where women are often treated as inferior. His belief that he was Asunta's protector and provider – benevolent on the surface, hierarchical underneath. The chronic stress that primes a nervous system for ignition.

And then the final number: Asunta teasing him, invoking Rooney – everything Emmanuel wasn't and could never be.

'He experiences her not just as a threat, but a belittler,' she says. 'And the perception of being belittled – even if you later realise you were wrong – is enough to release a very destructive kind of rage.'

She pauses. 'When you feel anger towards the person you think you're supposed to protect,' Gwen says softly, 'what do you do with that?'

She explains how unbearable shame sometimes gets projected outwards.

'If you can't bear these horrible feelings, you get rid of them by evacuating them into someone else's body.'

She echoes something she said in her first Reith lecture, when she said England fans may have been expelling their frustration and disappointment on to the physical forms of their victims, and destroying it.

We turn to the footage of Paul punching Grealish.

'He's really going for it isn't he,' she says.

Now, Paul is being herded away, blowing kisses like a conquering hero. I tell her about Paul's death and she sighs.

'I'm sure he felt on top of the world when he hit him and as he walked off the pitch,' she says. 'But it doesn't last.'

We pause. The crowd is cheering and clapping.

'Within hours the headline is calling him a wanker,' Gwen continues. 'Men I work with often say – after a lot of therapy

– that for a moment they felt triumphant. "This time I get to dish it out." But it's a very short-lived high.'

I tell Gwen about something Paul's sister Hayley had told me that only comes to mind because we have been talking about the bicycle lock analogy. At the time I hadn't given it much thought.

Hayley was telling me about the moments before Paul ran on to the pitch. Paul's mum Debbie was unaware.

Hayley says her father noticed Paul's phone light up during the game. He saw him take a brief call. Paul seemed excited and unsettled. Then he disappeared.

A few minutes later, Paul Sr. watched in disbelief as his son stormed on to the pitch.

'Whatshisface phoned him,' Hayley told us.

'Who?' Debbie snapped back.

Hayley explained that one of Paul's old employees from a pub he helped run – a place in Atherstone called Sweeties – had rung him just before the pitch invasion and dared him to do it.

'Are you sure?' I asked. It sounded a little like an excuse.

'Yes,' Hayley said, naming the friend.

Debbie turned to me, eyes wide. A crucial piece of a long-unsolved puzzle seemed to slot into place.

'He rang Paul after Grealish got another foul and said, "Go on, do it,"' Hayley repeated. 'And Paul . . . well, Paul being Paul . . .'

'I know he had his own mind,' Debbie says, 'but . . .'

She doesn't finish the sentence.

I tell Gwen this part of the story and she nods. It's an example of the final number clicking into place.

'If someone had rung him and said, "Come round later, we'll rewatch it and count how many times that bastard dives," it would have been different,' Gwen says.

'But instead, someone winds him up further. Gives him permission.'

Gwen says we need to be curious about violence, so we can work out how to prevent it.

It's a simple idea, but it runs through almost every story in this book. People need to be seen. They need to feel that they matter to someone. When no one tends to their wounds, when their stories are dismissed, when their pain goes unrecognised and unnamed, it doesn't fade away. It finds somewhere else to go. And when it does, things tend to go wrong.

35

Confessions of a Nine-Year-Old Loser

There's a guy on our six-a-side team called Mick. He's a decent player and once the whistle goes, he's as competitive as the rest of us, snapping into tackles, sprinting after lost causes, shouting at us to 'switch on'. But there's a difference. The moment he loses, he becomes bafflingly cheerful. It's like watching a man stroll out of a burning building smiling because the flames made his skin feel warm.

When he's on my team and we lose, I can't help but notice him. The lights go out at 9 p.m. and there he is, instantly transformed into this post-match Labrador, tail wagging, tongue out, delighted simply to have participated in sport.

Meanwhile, the rest of us on the losing side are fuming. I want to grab Mick by the shoulders, point at the phone pinned to the fence showing the score on the screen, and say: *What is wrong with you? Look. Here. We've lost. Why aren't you vibrating with self-hatred like me? Why aren't you experiencing the appropriate level of masculine despair?*

But Mick just doesn't seem to experience competitive failure like the rest of us.

This is Paul Gilbert's last point. How we experience winning and losing is not just biologically determined, nor the result of human brains that have a natural tendency to ruminate over past events. Our dispositions for competitiveness and the meaning we give status are shaped by our social environment, and, of course, it starts with childhood.

Is this why Mick and I are so different? Two competitive men with completely different reactions to loss.

I decided to meet with Dr Derek Farrell, one of the world's most respected trauma therapists. Maybe he can help me understand what happened in my childhood that turned me into such a bad loser. Derek has helped establish trauma-based projects in Iraq, Cambodia and elsewhere, and is President of Trauma Aid Europe. In 2020 he was awarded an MBE for services to psychology and trauma. He's also a global authority on EMDR – Eye Movement Desensitisation and Reprocessing – a trauma therapy I use in my own clinical work. Derek fits me in between international projects – he's just returned from Iraq – and today he's in his private practice in Bridgnorth, Shropshire, about fourteen miles from Wolverhampton, talking to me about football. Like most trauma-informed approaches, EMDR starts by identifying what's going wrong in the present, then traces back to a traumatic or humiliating memory that is the root of the problem. For example, war veterans who are spooked by fireworks can trace their disproportionate response back to the explosions and gunfire of the battlefield. The old experience is held in the nervous system and when something matches in the present, the visceral feelings and old beliefs are relived as if they are happening here and now.

The healing process comes from revisiting the trauma in a safe therapeutic space. Memories contain different pieces of information. They contain emotion. They contain sensory data like images and sounds. They contain bodily sensations. They also contain beliefs, like 'I'm in danger', 'I am powerless', or 'I am worthless'. Most experiences are processed as they happen, but traumatic ones often bypass normal processing and remain in raw unprocessed form, ready to spill out when there is a present trigger. We re-experience the whole visceral experience of the original event. We relive it in the here and now.

The good news is that memories are plastic. They can be accessed and updated with more adaptive information. Emotions associated with memories can be processed. Beliefs like 'I am in danger' can be changed to 'I survived'. The memory can then be popped back into storage, fully processed. It means that when something happens in the present that resembles the old experience in some way, the old material does not completely hijack the nervous system. People doing EMDR will typically move their eyes from side to side following a therapist's fingers while thinking of the old memory. This is thought to aid the reprocessing.

So, I'm in a Zoom session with Derek trying to work out why I react so intensely to Wolves losing. Derek asks me to focus on the worst bit of the Wolves vs Liverpool game that started this book. I tell him I see a clear image of Jürgen Klopp's beaming face, with his fist pump after the third Liverpool goal. He asks me to imagine and notice where I feel it in my body then to close my eyes and float back to an earlier memory where I felt the same.

'Just go way, way back to an earlier time,' Derek says calmly. 'Way, way back.'

* * *

The Lawn Tennis and Squash Club in Wolverhampton is usually a picture of calm. The courts sit beside the Black Country canal, and just beyond them lie the football pitches of my old Catholic comprehensive. They've since been swallowed up by Wolves, my school bulldozed and reborn as the club's state-of-the-art training ground. The old 713 bus stop, where we used to pile off in Patrick cagoules, untucked shirts and Farah trousers, now sees a steady roll call of Range Rovers, F-Pace Jaguars and Audi Q8s, all purring in with tinted windows and personalised plates.

Derek's prompt lands me back on a tennis court in 1979. I am nine years old. To my left and right, doubles matches unfold with the hushed decorum of a National Trust gift shop. 'Great shot, Sue.' 'Unlucky, Tom.' Everyone is tanned, middle-aged and moisturised. The men are comfortably overweight and wear sun visors. The women are all tennis whites and calibrated politeness, their hair helmeted into perfect, honey-lacquered submission. Even then, I suspected the civility masked years of seething marital contempt.

And there I am, amidst the calm, feral and molten with rage, gouging a divot into the pristine lawn with my racket. My dad is beating me 5-0 in the first set. I've just served a double fault and handed him a 30-0 lead. I chastise myself – something about me being a fucking useless dickhead. I am a little John McEnroe, with even bigger hair and a worse temper. Games grind to a halt around us. Onlookers glance over. Is this kid playing his dad or his court-appointed social worker?

My dad, meanwhile, is unfazed. He ambles to the back of the court to collect stray balls like a monarch inspecting his orchard. He sprays them back to my side as if I wasn't there.

I want to tear the sun from the sky and hurl it at the smug, unbothered man across the net who somehow shares my surname. I want to smash his fucking head in with my wooden Slazenger racket. I imagine it; a pint-sized psychopath vaulting the net, sweeping his legs with a scissor kick, and reducing his head to a fine pink mulch. Then I'd march off victorious, racket hoisted aloft like a tribal sceptre, leaving the posh wankers to clear up the carnage with tea towels and discreet murmurs of, 'well, it was bound to happen.'

But really, I want to cry. Because in this moment, I feel useless. An unmitigated disappointment to everyone, but most of all my dad.

Derek spots I've landed somewhere important and asks me to stay with the scene. He urges me to settle on the worst part of the memory. It's my dad's look of disappointment and contempt. Derek asks what I believed about myself in that moment. 'I'm a disappointment,' I tell him. He asks where I feel it in my body. *Behind my eyes. In my stomach.* He tells me to hold the scene in mind and begin to move my eyes from side to side.

And now I'm travelling through time.

Other memories surge forward. Being cast as an ox in the school nativity play. Forgetting my only three words – 'Come sir, away' – in a Year 9 performance of *Twelfth Night.* Being picked last in PE. Failing to get into Oxford, my dad's university. Then a highlight reel of being bullied for being posh, skinny, buck-toothed, spotty. Everything was thrown at me for a couple of years – from eleven to thirteen. I felt a complete misfit, and as I sit here with Derek, the memories come at me like one of those Facebook montage summaries, except these aren't clips of holidays and dog purchases, they show me being kicked and spat at and followed home from school and pinned down. It is unbelievable that all of this was coming up uninvited, sprouting initially from Jürgen Klopp's smug fist pump.

It's like my mind is an overzealous librarian. Whenever Wolves lose, the librarian sprints through the corridors of memory, flinging open drawers and lobbing every file marked 'loser' on to my desk. 'Here you go – everything we've got on you being shit. Enjoy.'

And I don't even read them. I'm largely unaware that any of this relates to the past. I just feel the pain coursing through my nervous system as shame, as self-loathing, as heat in my cheeks and a stone in my gut.

But then, as I continue to reminisce about my loserhood, something unexpected happens.

A new memory rises. It's more positive. It's a boy called Jimmy Duffy, the school football legend, telling me I played well after a game. I remember his arm slung around my shoulder, the pride in his voice. Then another: my dad telling me he was proud after I played in a five-a-side final at Molineux. For the first time in the session, I feel some relief. The processing is enabling my mind to *access* more balanced information on the whole 'I'm a disappointment' condemnation.

It's as if that bitter, red-eyed librarian has paused, sighed and returned with a second folder. This one is much dustier, but it's filled with evidence that I'm not a total failure after all. The librarian looks vaguely surprised, as if these positive memories haven't been requested in decades. Maybe ever. But I'm weaving them into a more holistic narrative of who I am. More positive memories surface now as we carry on.

Derek asks me to return to the original scene on the tennis court. Has anything changed?

Somehow, the scene has lost its emotional intensity. The tightness behind my eyes and the churn in my stomach have gone. I'm watching it now from above – a bird's-eye view – and I see a boy who's really struggling, raging and ashamed. I feel compassion for him. My heart opens, instead of contracting with anger.

I no longer see the look of disappointment on my dad's face. I just see a boy and a man – one overwhelmed, the other unable, for whatever reason, to keep his competitive instincts in check.

The blame shifts. It moves away from me – from the shame of my tantrum and the awkwardness of not being good enough at tennis – and lands, more rightly, on my dad. He was the adult. He should have known better. And with that shift, the shame begins to lift.

Derek asks what I'd *rather* believe about myself in that moment, instead of *I'm a disappointment*. Something that feels like it fits better with the scene of the boy on the court with his dad.

'I *am* good enough,' I say.

Not good enough to beat my dad at tennis aged nine. But as I look at that little boy – humiliated, raging, sweaty, trying to hold it together on the baseline – I know now that he *is* good enough. There's nothing inadequate about him. He's just a child doing his best, playing against a father who needed to win.

The librarian, now reluctantly invested, merges the two files – the good and the bad, the adaptive and the maladaptive – into a single, updated record. The label is changed from *Disappointment* to *Good Enough*, and it's filed carefully back into the archive.

* * *

My trip to Kenya, and the people I have spoken to, have helped me get a better sense of my dramatic mood shifts. Winning and the associated biology is designed to keep us in an excited state. Our energised predecessors celebrated victories with tribal dances around fires. Players celebrate with choreographed goal celebrations: the archer's mime, imaginary arrows fired into skies; the cradle-rocking; the chest-beating. They are signals of virility, dominance and triumph. Fans feel it too because we are fused. My tribal dance is pacing between the window and office chair, shirtless, muttering, 'Get in, lad!' at a slab of pixels, or strutting through a church clutching a small fluffy dog like a shamanic drum. Losing leaves us in the opposite state and ruminating about why we are losers turns what should be a temporary brain state into a long-lasting mood.

How we experience winning and losing is also shaped by our own histories. If our experiences of losing or failing brought embarrassment or teasing in childhood, those memories lodge as shame. Over time, they shape how much we dread losing later on.

Men have historically been funnelled into dominance hierarchies where winning and aggression have been rewarded. It might partly explain why men appear to be most affected by football results. But most people would agree that the pattern is changing. Today, women are increasingly exposed to the same kinds of status competitions once filled by men. Men and women compete on the same corporate ladders, and girls are being socialised into football fandom at pace.

In fact, women and girls, perhaps even more than men and boys, are relentlessly exposed to the brutal rankings of social media. In my day job, I am deluged by referrals from the parents of girls who are suffering at the hands of ruthless online bullies (other girls), jostling for rank on the various social media platforms.

I reflect once more on Emmanuel and Asunta. I think of Asunta with her head bowed, weeping, and how she'll probably never get the support she needs to move through the trauma of the attack. Nor will her children. And I imagine where Emmanuel would land if Derek asked him to float back from those terrible scenes on the night of the attack. I'm guessing he would travel way back, beyond the match, beyond the living room, before his injury, back to the slum where he grew up. Back to the bullying older kids and the desperate scavenging. Back to the places where he was mocked, kicked, forgotten and where he learned what it felt like to be nothing.

* * *

Despite our 'tricky brains', Paul Gilbert remains hopeful. Once we are aware of how they work, we can start to work *with* them. Mindfulness gets a bad press sometimes, but this is because, like the word trauma, it gets used for everything. Paul is quite clear about what we need to develop mindfulness for. We need to train ourselves to notice when we get knocked into a particular mental state and then to turn towards it with curiosity and compassion, rather than letting it grab the steering wheel. He leads me back to Wolves and suggests a script for when we next lose.

I'm upset. I'm dealing with a brain creating a lot of pain. Deep pain. That's not my fault . . . Do I really want to stay a puppet to these genetic programmes? Yes, I'm angry. Yes, I'd quite like to go and kick the dog – but I'm going to slow it down. Does this really matter? I'm more than this. These are biological programmes running through me. It's not my fault it feels so painful.

For Paul, being mindful means being aware, moment to moment, that you have a *tricky brain* that you wouldn't have designed this way.

Not in a million years.

PART VII

Addicted

36

I'm Never Ever Watching Again

It's coming up to a year since we were all sitting in our living room on Boxing Day watching Wolves beat Manchester United. That blissful afternoon when Matheus Cunha scored directly from a corner, and we got the added festive schadenfreude of watching Bruno Fernandes sent off. But football is cruel, and the universe punishes smugness with remarkable efficiency.

We've invited Rich, our builder, round. We haven't seen him properly for about six months, not since he put the finishing touches to our Wolves-themed bathroom upstairs, complete with old-gold wallpaper.

We have asked him round for a pre-Christmas dinner followed by Wolves vs United on Sky's *Monday Night Football.* Rich is a United fan.

Wolves are currently the laughing stock of the league. With two points from fourteen games, we are on track to become the worst Premier League side ever recorded. By the time Rich arrives, we haven't won a league game in 227 days. We haven't scored a goal for 500 minutes.

It's good to see him, but the evening arrives preloaded with danger. My wife has insisted on baked gnocchi and sweet potato with basil and pine nut sauce. I love it. So do the friends who come to our Ottolenghi nights with their salads and legumes and boutique oils. But I have fed Rich lunch for three years and he hates anything without crunch, or anything that does not clearly announce sugar. Smooth textures alarm him – eggs, avocado, soft cheeses.

Gnocchi will repulse him, I'm sure of it. And after six months apart, having to refuse it will put him in an etiquette quandary no builder should ever have to navigate. My wife waves this away. 'Rich loves potatoes,' she says, citing his fondness for crisps.

'But gnocchi and sweet potato are—' I want to say 'soft', but my wife cuts in.

'It'll be fine,' she says, sliding the tray into the oven.

Rich has become part of the family. For three years he practically lived with us, arriving at 8 a.m. each morning as the house was slowly dismantled and rebuilt. He looks after Crackle when we're out. He's small, wiry and looks like a man a strong breeze could knock over, yet he lifts steel beams like they're baguettes.

Our friendship started with football – cheap shots about United and Wolves, him winding me up about whichever player United were about to pinch next. It was a safe, neutral language that let us skip past the fact that our biographies had little in common. Most mornings I'd be ferrying bits of timber back and forth like Stan Laurel after a mild concussion, never quite sure which piece he meant, him gently correcting me without ever saying the words *for the love of God*. Other times I'd be holding a metal bracket in place while he drilled within millimetres of my fingers, trying to look calm as masonry dust sprinkled into my eyes. We'd talk about football the whole time – revealing almost nothing of ourselves and yet still feeling connected.

Like the scaffolding around the house though, football gave us room to build something sturdier. A workaround for intimacy. And eventually we risked something else. I remember the two of us perched on the pitched roof after fitting the wood-burner flue, backs leaning against opposite sides of the chimney. Drinking tea, we talked about our dads and our childhoods. Up there, slightly removed from the world, we could risk being honest. And we both knew that once our boots were back on the ground, we could always drop back into the safety of football banter again. My wife loves Rich too, but she says she is envious about our shared passion.

As for the gnocchi–sweet potato affair, he musters only a token degree of hesitation. He makes one brave effort – a mouthful chased with juice – and I can practically see him retch. He abandons the effort and starts pushing the soft, pale lumps around his plate and hiding them behind garlic bread. I swipe his plate away with a grin.

'Here,' I say, 'have a couple of mince pies,' burying them in cream. Rich's shoulders loosen instantly. We take our plates through into the living room. The pundits are already discussing how terrible Wolves are with the bright cheerfulness of people who won't suffer the consequences of what they're describing. They mention how thousands of fans plan to protest by entering the stadium fifteen minutes late. The forums are full of talk about 'scabs'. It's getting ugly. Some people are openly wondering whether to ditch the team altogether. They are asking who they should support when we inevitably suffer back-to-back relegations and go bankrupt. Hednesford? Chasetown?

Even the podcasters are cracking up. After the recent Villa defeat, one of the Wolves 77 Club podcasters went on a drunken tweeting spree instead of turning up for the show, forcing the others to apologise and change the password to their socials.

Rich and I sit on the sofa with our trays and mince pies. The dog is tucked between us. My wife is upstairs listening to a Stephen King audiobook. United score after twenty-five minutes and I hardly flinch. In fact, I laugh sarcastically. This is what defeat feels like when you pre-grieve properly. I'm detached and a little numb. Free, in a way. Hope has left the building and all that's left is grim acceptance and the freedom to mock our own decay. 'Hahahahahaha – go on then, score as many as you like. See if I care.' I have also been thinking more about Paul Gilbert and his compassionate scripts to support my football pain. Every now and then I discreetly move my hand to my heart, soothing the sad defeated creature inside, the boy who felt so useless on the tennis court, the one still trying to understand why losing always feels like annihilation.

Then, one minute into first-half stoppage time, God commits a clerical error. Jean-Ricner Bellegarde hooks in a goal.

What did you go and do that for, man?

My nervous system boots back up with a violent jolt. It's obscene how fast it happens. One second, I'm half-conscious; the next my heart is pounding and my leg has begun its familiar tremor. I'd assumed that months of exposure therapy to misery had built some kind of immunity. But I was wrong. Hope surges straight back into my bloodstream. Bellegarde's ridiculous goal has destroyed my hard-won state of dependable misery. And now some desperate little part of me – against all lived experience – dares to imagine we might turn the season around by beating United.

Seven minutes into the second half, United score again. Bellegarde limps off. Our only impactful footballer gone. The equaliser feels unnecessary. All that emotional turbulence, for nothing.

Rich doesn't even celebrate. Maybe he's close enough to me on the sofa that he's picking up on my despair. He's glancing at me nervously, fearing the hand on my heart is something more worrying than self-soothing. The dog defected a while ago, clambering over Rich and wedging himself safely against the armrest. So, it's just me at my end of the sofa now.

The Sky commentators begin itemising our disgrace, leafing through football's Book of Shame with breezy gusto. Southampton! Derby! Come marvel at the ruins! Do they understand Wolves fans are watching this in actual houses, clutching actual chests with actual cardiovascular frailty? Their tone stays infuriatingly chirpy.

'The Premier League – you've got to love it!' one of them trills.

Mason Mount scores a third.

I suspect that Rich would have preferred United not to score again. For a man who rarely stops talking, the silence is worse than a thousand soft-boiled eggs.

Rich isn't usually a tactile man. He reacts to hugs the way most people react to flies. But as I sink further into myself, I feel the unexpected squeeze of his hand on my arm.

My wife comes down and sits in the rocking chair beside him. The dog changes sides yet again, curling into the warm folds of her dressing gown, fixing me with a soft, pitying stare from her lap.

Wolves are not me. I'm loved. This is biology, not truth. I'm trying. The warmth of my hand on my heart does feel soothing. I remember what Paul said – it's not necessarily about feeling better, it's about acknowledging that this is hard for me. *The point is not to feel better, it's to get better at feeling.*

United get a penalty. And of course it's Bruno Fernandes, the man my family cheered off the pitch with wanker signs and imaginary red cards last Boxing Day. He dispatches it perfectly. I see him and Cunha – our former hero – hugging. Wolves fans begin to leave in waves. Nine minutes of added time are announced to an almost empty stadium. Some who remain turn away from the pitch entirely in protest. All colour is drained.

* * *

'I am never watching them again,' I announce, springing into the bedroom.

'Hmm,' my wife says, turning a page in her book.

'I hate them. It's pointless. What a waste of my fucking time.'

'Yes,' she says, calmly.

United beat us 4-1, Rich left fifteen minutes ago, and I can feel the insomnia settling in like fog.

'And now I'm not going to sleep, am I?' I continue, expecting some sort of solution from her. 'I never sleep after watching this rubbish in the week.'

Ever since games started kicking off at 8 p.m., it's been like this. My arousal levels spike, meaning my poor pineal gland – the ancient, shrivelled thing that's supposed to drip melatonin into my bloodstream like bedtime syrup – just gives up.

'Do we have any Nytol?' I mutter.

I march to the bathroom and start rifling through the wicker basket where we keep all the medications. There are blister packs, half-empty bottles, everything but what I'm looking for.

'Have you checked the actual cupboard on the wall where we keep that sort of stuff?' she murmurs from bed.

I narrow my eyes. Actual = her gentle way of saying, *you really are helpless, aren't you?*

I try to squeeze the basket back in place, but it jams, so I curse it and leave it half-protruding like a herniated drawer. I open the wall cabinet and immediately knock a bottle of Olbas oil off its perch – it crashes into the porcelain sink.

'Aaaaggh,' I yell.

I sense my wife bolt upright in bed. *Please don't come and help me,* I think. There's barely room for one person in here, let alone two. She comes in anyway, tugging her dressing gown around her, eyes bleary.

'Here it is,' she says, pointing to a shelf that's just slightly too high to reach comfortably.

'Typical,' I say.

I grab the box.

'Herbal?' My voice goes up an octave. 'How the hell am I supposed to sleep with herbal stuff?' I won't be fooled by a placebo.

'All right, all right,' she says, backing out gently.

I return to the basket, digging like a raccoon.

'There's some melatonin in there, right at the back, same top shelf,' she calls, 'from that flight from America.'

Her tone conveys: *I love you, but my God.*

'Yes, that's what I'm looking for,' I snap, more irritated with myself than her. 'Thanks, babe, you go back to bed – I'm on my own from here.'

I join her and the dog in bed.

'I'm serious this time,' I say. 'I'm not watching the Arsenal game on Saturday. Please don't let me watch it.'

'Good,' my wife says, cautiously.

I pull the duvet around me and hover on the edge of the bed where the dog lies starfished across my zone.

She strokes my shoulder. 'It's good you're not watching. We could do something nice on Saturday.'

'Hmm,' I say. 'Just don't let me do it. Please.'

* * *

Tuesday arrives, and I am doing brilliantly. Football is dead to me. I am a man reborn. Sky Sports remains untouched. Champions League fixtures pass me by like clouds in the sky.

My family WhatsApp group is buzzing. My brother is wittering on about Liverpool's game against Inter. A mate from six-a-side is rallying troops to watch Villa vs Basel down the pub. I mute them both.

Wednesday is the same. No league table checking. No post-match analysis videos with those local paper journalists and YouTube pundits I usually live for. Liam Keen, Harry Mansell, Dave Azzopardi? Not today, lads. You can fuck off with the rest of them.

I am still holding strong on Thursday. I refuse to wear any of my Wolves shirts to our six-a-side game. Not the red Portugal-style away strip, nor the purple and pink monstrosity, not even the less vulgar grey training top. I am a dignified man. A man of principle. I will wear something age appropriate.

On Friday, my wife makes a suggestion.

'Maybe we could go for a nice walk on Saturday? Visit some antique shops? Burwash is lovely this time of year.'

She knows I have a soft spot for shuffling through antique shops, pretending I understand mid-century furniture. 'Then, in the evening we could go out for dinner?'

'Absolutely,' I declare. 'No game for me this weekend. I've moved on.'

* * *

But then Saturday morning arrives. And with it, the voices.

It's not my wife's voice suggesting a bracing seaside stroll in St Leonards before Burwash. No, this is something more sinister.

37

The Most Compulsive Sport in the World

The maddening question of why I keep going back followed me to Manchester for the case of Alfie Holt. He was the second fan to attack Grealish, the man who slapped him at the end of the derby and jeopardised this book's narrative arc.

My days in Manchester were strange and disorienting. I came away with a clearer sense of why Alfie did what he did. But I also came away with something I didn't expect; a sharper understanding of why watching Wolves feels like an *addiction*. Beyond loyalty and fusion, there is compulsion. Something in the machinery of football specifically that keeps pulling me back.

I stay in a city centre hotel overnight. The evening before the case there's frenetic activity on my six-a-side football WhatsApp group. Chelsea are playing in the Club World Cup final. A couple of Chelsea fans in the WhatsApp group are incredulous that their team are 3-0 up at half-time. But there's a deeper concern about one of the 'pundits'. I switch on the hotel TV. Wait. Is that Donald Trump?

At first, I assume it's some budget Rory Bremner impression, a parody. Or maybe I've made a mistake – maybe I've turned the TV on halfway through an episode of *Black Mirror*. But no, this isn't satire; this is the actual broadcast. Trump is really here, at half-time, praising football for being 'great', with the same tone he once used to promote bleach and hydroxychloroquine during Covid.

Emily Austin, interviewing Trump, for the sports broadcaster DAZN, nods along, as if this is all completely normal. There doesn't seem to be a whiff of irony. It's like we're all supposed to swallow this as part of the half-time package. Trump weaves in a party political broadcast and panders to Austin's suggestion that he make an executive order to change the name of the game in the States from soccer to football.

What next, I think? J.D. Vance introducing *Match of the Day*? Elon Musk refereeing? At this point I wouldn't blink if the stadium burst into flames and Andrew Mountbatten-Windsor descended from the roof shouting, 'It's coming home!'

Half-time lasts twenty-four minutes. TWENTY-FOUR. This blatantly breaches one of the foundational rules of the game* which cap the interval at fifteen minutes.

Chelsea are victorious, maintaining their 3-0 lead. Now, Trump is on the pitch presenting the trophy. He's booed relentlessly by the crowd as his orange face fills the jumbotron. It's the communal sound of football fans, screaming: *What the fuck is happening to our game?*

Reece James looks shocked as the American president refuses to leave the stage so Chelsea can raise the trophy. But there are no police sirens. No one rushes on to the pitch with a tranquiliser dart. Cole Palmer – man of the match with two goals and an assist – looks bewildered. Trump lingers beside the team, blocking the camera shot. Cole's head peeks out from behind the president's shoulder – a shy nephew forced to pose for a family photo. And still, no one pulls the plug.

---

* Rule 7:2 of the International Football Association Board's laws of the game, to be specific.

And me? I just sit there, trying to remember whether I actually like football any more.

* * *

Watching Trump turn up as a pundit on DAZN only underlines how radically football consumption has shifted in the past half-century. It's easy to forget that no top-flight English football matches were shown live on television until 1983. *Match of the Day* – launched on BBC2 in 1964 – became the go-to highlights show, but for its first decade, the title was to be taken literally – it only featured one match. The first game shown was Liverpool-Arsenal at Anfield. To be fair, it was a belter – Shankly's Liverpool went 2-0 up through Roger Hunt and Gordon Wallace; Arsenal, managed by Billy Wright, came back in the second half with goals from Geoff Strong and Joe Baker. Then Wallace nicked it for Liverpool in the 87th minute.

There were 47,620 people in the ground and just 20,000 watching on TV at home. Despite the low TV audience, many clubs were hostile to the programme, worried it would damage attendances. A compromise was reached; the BBC wouldn't reveal which match had been filmed until after all the games had finished. *Match of the Day* only moved to BBC1 after England's 1966 World Cup win.

ITV's *The Big Match* launched in 1968 as a Sunday highlights alternative, but live coverage remained taboo. That changed on 16 December 1983, when ITV aired the first live league game: Manchester United vs Tottenham. It was shown at 7.15 p.m. on Saturday with Jimmy Hill both presenting and rushing off to be co-commentator, alongside John Motson. It was another brilliant game – United winning 4-2.

But it wasn't until the Premier League's launch in 1992, and its exclusive deal with Sky Sports, that live coverage took off. Sky began with just one live match per weekend, then gradually expanded. The rest is history.

Back in 1964, there were more than twice as many people at Anfield as there were watching the highlights on TV. Today, when Liverpool play at home, there are just over 60,000 in the stadium. But globally, more than 12 million fans tune in via TV and streaming. That's more than two hundred times the number of people inside the ground. According to media research company Nielsen, Liverpool are now the most-watched football club in the world.

Millions of people in the UK are watching football on illegal streams. A YouGov poll last year suggested that at least ten per cent of the population watch such streams. The majority of these people – perhaps millions a week – are watching on their own.

* * *

The next morning, I head to court for the Alfie Holt case. I expect a scrum of journalists outside. There's only one. A lone Sky Sports cameraman named, yet again, Paul. He has that unfair genetic combo of dark Mediterranean hair and glacial blue eyes. Like me, he's got the time wrong too. The case has been bumped to the afternoon. We head for a coffee.

I tell him about the book and he seems interested. He's competed in a lot of sport to a decent level – football, rugby, boxing – and his son plays for a Premier League academy. He's curious why football, more than any other sport, exerts such an addictive pull on fans. I tell him it's a question I've wrestled with too. I take a sip of my oat cortado and tell him all about a conversation I'd had with one of the world's leading experts on behavioural addiction. Did football even qualify as one?

Professor Adam Alter has spent years researching behavioural addictions. Born in South Africa in 1980, he moved to Australia when he was still a kid and began obsessing over the great Liverpool sides of the '80s: Grobbelaar, Hansen, Mølby, Rush, Dalglish.

I'd recently read his brilliant book about addictions to things like smartphones, gambling and pornography. Adam defines a behavioural addiction as something you feel compelled to do repeatedly, even though – on balance – it harms you. Listening to music while making dinner might be a nightly ritual, but it's unlikely to do damage. For Adam, a true behavioural addiction involves harm in at least one of four areas: financial, social, psychological or physical. So, I wondered: what about football fandom? Did he think fandom could become a behavioural addiction? Was this why I couldn't resist watching Wolves even after their worst run in their history?

Before talking to him I had researched whether psychiatry already had a proper diagnostic label for the emotional and behavioural turmoil of football fandom. Surely, buried somewhere in the vast catalogue of mental disorders, there'd be a mention of the beautiful game?

I started digging through the two bibles of medical classification: *The Diagnostic and Statistical Manual of Mental Disorders, Fifth Edition* (DSM-5) and the *International Classification of Diseases, 11th Revision* (ICD-11). They list pretty much every form of human distress you can imagine.

The DSM-5 is published by the American Psychiatric Association and lists 297 disorders, depending on how you count them. The ICD-11, published by the World Health Organization, contains thousands of physical and mental health conditions.

I trawled through them as best I could. There were plenty of obscure diagnoses I'd never heard of:

Apotemnophilia (now known as body integrity dysphoria): the overwhelming desire to amputate a healthy limb or become paralysed. ICD-11 code: 6C21.

Ganser syndrome: the compulsive giving of wrong-but-close answers to basic questions. How many legs does a dog have? Three. What colour's the grass? Blue. I figured a lot of politicians could be diagnosed with this.

I couldn't find anything on football. Yet, I wasn't the only one asking the question.

Dr Massimo Lanzaro, an Italian consultant psychiatrist, argued that extreme football fandom might qualify as a legitimate addiction. He laid out the DSM criteria for behavioural addiction and matched them, symptom by symptom, to the most extreme football fans.

- Repetitive engagement that leads to dysfunction
- Obsession, withdrawal, cravings
- Failed attempts to stop
- Neglect of other life domains
- Continued use despite harm
- Using it to self-soothe
- Risking relationships

The symptoms sounded suspiciously familiar. As well as the obsession and failure to stop, there was the damage to relationships. I had also recently been on forums and discovered that some fans were in financial difficulty after taking out interest loans to pay for season tickets.

I gave Adam my usual spiel about the premise for this book. He says he's been studying behavioural addictions for years and still suffers the emotional fallout of football. He pushes up the sleeves of his grey sweatshirt, like he is about to get serious.

Football, he says, has at least two inherent qualities that make it uniquely, mind-bendingly compelling. The first is the scarcity of goals. The second is the sheer unpredictability of results. Together, they hack into the brain's reward systems like a slot machine.

In football, goals are relatively rare things. It is a feature that sets it apart from sports like rugby, cricket or basketball, where the scoreboard is constantly ticking over. And when something is limited in supply, people tend to value it more. We prize a diamond over a bottle of water, even though one keeps us alive and the other doesn't. We ignore the beauty of things that are abundant. Marketers exploit the scarcity principle to sell us their products all the time; limited offers like 'only two left in stock' and 24-hour flash sales. Research shows that when people are presented with jars – one full to the brim with chocolate cookies and the other with just a couple left inside, they rate the cookies in the emptier jar as tastier, even though the biscuits are identical.

Scientists have shown how powerful this scarcity effect is in the brains of football fans too. In one study, nine Rangers supporters were put into brain scanners and shown four-second clips of their team either scoring, narrowly missing or just passing the ball harmlessly in midfield. When Rangers scored, the researchers saw an 'intense pleasure response' in the anterior cingulate cortex – akin to cocaine use. Football gives you long, barren stretches of nothing, and then – suddenly – a goal. Each rare goal feels thrilling precisely because they are few and unexpected.

Linked to this – and also differentiating football from some other sports – is the unpredictability of results. If you give pigeons a choice – peck a button that delivers food consistently at fifty per cent of the time or one that pays out more randomly at only twenty per cent of the time – logic says they should go for the better odds. But that's not the case. They keep hammering the unreliable one.

Humans look similar. In a study by Gregory Berns and colleagues, participants lay in brain scanners while receiving squirts of juice and water through tubes in their mouths. In one condition, the squirts were perfectly predictable. Water, juice, water, juice, water, juice, and so on. In the other, the timing and sequencing was chaotic – juice after juice, water after juice, water after water. There was no pattern at all.

Subjectively, the volunteers said they preferred the taste of the juice and said they didn't care about the sequencing. But their brains told a different story. The dopamine-linked reward regions of their brain lit up far more for unpredictability than for flavour. It wasn't the juice that was compelling. It was the surprise, just like the pigeons.

Slot machines work the same way. Most spins, you lose. But every so often – bang – three cherries, and your reward circuits light up. That kind of unpredictable reinforcement is what makes gambling addictive. If you won with every spin, you'd be rich but bored.

Psychologists call this a variable ratio schedule – rewards delivered after an unpredictable number of actions. It is the most powerful form of reinforcement we know. For most of our history, food, water and mates were variable; hunting trips paid off sometimes, but often they didn't. Like other animals, humans who kept sampling uncertain 'patches' rather than quitting or just returning to the same patch every time, gathered more total resources over time. That bias towards sticking with variable payoffs still runs in us.

Football seems to exploit this predilection for variability mercilessly. Even if we get thumped most weeks, the odd win is enough to keep us hooked. There is evidence that results in Europe's top leagues, including the Premier League, are becoming more predictable as foreign money floods into the ultra-elite clubs, widening the gap between teams. But shocks and surprises still happen often enough to qualify as a variable ratio schedule. Even the top six clubs lose or draw in roughly half their games, which means the system keeps offering just enough uncertainty to pull us back in.

The FA Cup is football's purest tribute to the chaotic joy of unpredictability. Sutton United – then of the Conference – beating top-flight Coventry 2-1 in 1989. Wrexham dumping out Arsenal in 1992. Bradford City turning Chelsea over 4-2 at Stamford Bridge in 2015. Grimsby Town beating Manchester United in the EFL Cup. And now, Macclesfield beating FA Cup holders Crystal Palace. It is harder to see this happening in rugby; I'd bet my Steve Bull-signed Wolves top that Tonga will never beat the All Blacks at rugby (games in the last decade have included 102-0 and 92-7 obliterations). And in the equivalent of the FA Cup for rugby, the lowest-tier sides have never beaten a Super League side (a recent example is Wests Warriors losing 92-0 to Leeds Rhinos in the Betfred Challenge Cup in 2025).

The Bradford vs Chelsea game mentioned above might be one of the most unpredictable results of all time. Chelsea were at home and they'd gone 2-0 up. The fourth round looked done and dusted. But the Bantams stormed back with four unanswered goals.

'This is the beauty of football,' Chelsea boss Jose Mourinho said, through gritted teeth, after the game.

But what if you never win? What if you're the shittest team in the world? Or what if you're so good you never lose? Do those teams blow the unpredictability theory out of the water?

First, I started thinking about the teams who never seem to lose. The ones so dominant they make Man City look like part-timers. Al Ahly, in Egypt, for example – forty-three league titles in sixty-three seasons.

Do their fans even feel anything? I messaged a few on a fan forum. 'Is it boring supporting your team?'

Some of the replies were in Egyptian Arabic, which I translated through Google. Several involved my mother, a donkey, a pig and a shoe.

But others were helpful. A few fans pointed out that while Al Ahly win a lot, nothing's guaranteed. During the 2024/25 season, their win rate was a mortal sixty-five per cent. At the time of writing, they weren't even top – second place, behind the gloriously named Pyramids FC.

But then I thought about San Marino.

They are officially ranked the world's shittest team. They have no competitive wins since the thirteenth century, or thereabouts. Their fans have formed a Facebook group called 'Brigata Mai Una Gioia' – roughly translated as 'Supporting This Lot Is Constant Suffering'. And there are nearly five thousand members.

Their home attendances average around 2,200. Are they all masochists?

Because if the unpredictability theory holds – that what keeps us coming back is the unbearable tension, but at least some reward – then why are they still turning up? Why aren't they all watching darts or gardening or putting pins in their eyes?

Even the stadium DJ has given up, as far as I can see. Before a recent Euro 2024 qualifier against Slovenia, he kicked things off with AC/DC's 'Highway to Hell'.

Yet, on their fan page, I found many jubilant threads. There were photos from a 5-1 loss to Romania: fans roaring with joy, shirts over heads, beer spraying like confetti. You'd think they'd won the quadruple. They were celebrating a 67th-minute consolation goal by Samuele Zannoni like it was the second coming.

The more I looked, the more I saw something else, something related to a third quality of football that motivates us to come back, again and again, even if we are constantly losing. It's a psychological phenomenon called the 'near-miss effect', and it relates to the compulsive pull of gambling machines. Because while San Marino fans (and let's face it Wolves fans for most of the 2025/26 season) don't often get the full dopamine jackpot of a goal (or a win), the counter-attacking nature of football means they're frequently in a state of maybe. And that anticipation messes with the brain's reward pathways in delightfully cruel ways.

You might assume San Marino never get into the opposition half – but it's not true. I saw their fans celebrating near misses, free kicks, corners, even saves. The stats back them up, to a point. Take 11 June 2024. They played Cyprus, ranked nearly one hundred places higher. They lost 4-1, but managed five corners, four shots on target and two off.

And this matters. Because in the Rangers fan study, where brain reward centres lit up after a goal, Professor Dave Wyper and colleagues found something else that was intriguing. They looked at what happened in the brain when there was a near miss. They discovered that when a goal feels possible, a separate region of the brain's reward centre called the putamen kicks in.

The putamen, the researchers argue, plays a crucial role in anticipating emotional events. The goal is the high, of course. But it's the flickers of maybe – a break, a set piece, a penalty awarded – that keep the dopamine flowing. It's why scratchcards and slot machines leave you one symbol away from a payout all the time.

The goal feels intensely pleasurable. But the craving is also addictive. In other words, anticipation itself registers as meaningful. The brain tags it as something worth repeating – even if the ball ends up the wrong side of the post, or Dean Henderson saves your penalty. Football's magic lies in the tease of what might happen, not just in what does. The brain has to reward the wanting; otherwise desire would simply switch itself off whenever resources – or goals – are scarce.

* * *

Dave Wyper sends me an email drawing an intriguing comparison between football and middle-distance running. The unique pleasure, he suggests, lies in the build-up. The slow accumulation of tension. That sense that something is about to happen.

He compares football to the tactical stalemate of an 800 or 1500-metre race, where nothing appears to be happening until suddenly everything is. I can see it immediately. Coe, Ovett, Cram in the 1980s, stalking each other, lap after lap. Or, more recently, Keely Hodgkinson in Paris in 2024 – waiting, waiting, then kicking. That stretch from the middle of the race to the end is pure anticipatory tension. Football works the same way, Dave thinks. As Adam had already said, it keeps us suspended in a state of anticipation – and that sustained tension is what hammers the brain's reward circuits.

'Other sports don't really have that,' Dave says.

Addiction researchers have known this for years. It isn't just the drug that hooks people – it's the craving and ritual of accessing it. Calling the dealer. Travelling across town. Unwrapping the foil. The dopamine surge doesn't wait for the drug itself. It starts with the cues. We're hard-wired to be motivated by the hunt too – and the hunt is rewarding in its own right. Which might explain why, after ~~11, 12, 13, 14, 15, 16, 17, 18,~~ 19 games without a win – after swearing I'll never watch again – I'm still watching.

But there must come a point, and I'm speaking as a Wolves fan here, someone who saw a game recently when we had no shots on goal, no corners, nothing, when the reward gets so scarce it's not even unpredictable any more – it's just predictably awful. It's not middle-distance running; it's like watching a bunch of penguins trying to climb an escalator.

Michael Zeiler trained pigeons to keep working for food as the rewards became thinner and thinner, and what he found was that they didn't stop the behaviour gradually. They tolerated far more frustration than seemed reasonable. And then, without ceremony, they stopped altogether. There came a point when the ratio of effort to reward was so tiny that the behaviour simply died. This is called the *extinction* phase in reinforcement training – the moment the organism decides the reward is no longer worth the effort.

A friend of mine, Steve, rang me in the middle of all this Wolves pain – the first half of the 2025/26 season – to express concern about the thesis of my book. He told me he'd stopped watching football. Wolves were so bad he'd blocked them out entirely. At first, I dismissed him as a narcissist – too wounded to tolerate the hurt, turning his back like a CORFing fair-weather fan. But then I thought, perhaps it's simpler than that. Perhaps he's just lost the will to peck.

38

Canon in D

It's a Saturday morning, and for once, we have nothing to do. Football is on international break. Even the dog only woke us twice with his scratching. A small miracle.

He is only eighteen inches long, but sleeps belly-up, paws flung four feet wide, like a child prince collapsed mid-tantrum on a bed of silks. Somehow, he takes up the vast majority of the mattress. We fold ourselves like origami so he can lie undisturbed in full corpse pose – legs outstretched, mouth half open, dreaming of chicken.

And unlike me – who, according to my wife, just squeaks and rolls over obediently when prodded mid-snore – Crackle doesn't budge. If it weren't for the fact his furry belly is so exposed you can actually see his little heart beating, you'd assume he'd been stuffed with concrete. In the wild, he'd be dead in seconds.

I pad downstairs, grind the beans, fill the coffee jug, pour the orange juice and head back up with a tray. I draw the curtains. Sun floods the room. My wife is half-awake, shielding her eyes.

I ask Alexa to shuffle our 'Super Mellow' playlist as I begin plunging the coffee. Music starts playing in the kitchen downstairs. Wrong Alexa. Crackle starts barking because he thinks we're being burgled, or that a fox is poised to enter through the bifolds.

'Shut up, you idiot,' my wife murmurs, eyes still closed.

But none of that matters today. I'm calm and curiously cheerful. My window of emotional tolerance is gloriously ajar. The international break means the compulsive tug of the match is absent. There's no craving. I am free.

The playlist is a 300-song soup of mellow folk and classical, and the first track it lands on is 'Canon in D' by Pachelbel.

It starts melancholically but still unbearably beautiful – violins layering and gliding in like a rising tide. The strings surge. The melody leans forward. I hold my breath at the sheer beauty of it.

Fully transported back to that chateau in France where we got married in 2019, I see her descending the stairs on her father's arm, my best man beside me in an old gold waistcoat and tie, orange and black balloons everywhere. It was a Wolves-themed wedding. No one objected. Not even her parents. I remember looking out and seeing all that love reflected back at me – not just from my wife, but from everyone. Our siblings, tearful, arms slung around our tiny nephews, miniature businessmen in their suits. Our parents, heads bowed or held high.

Back in our Hastings bedroom, I glance at my wife, expecting to see her caught in it with me – eyes glistening, maybe holding her breath at the memory. Perhaps one hand gently placed over her heart. A moment of connection.

But she's looking at her phone, scrolling.

Then, without even looking up, she barks at the speaker:

'ALEXA.'

The music shudders to a stop.

'VOLUME DOWN.'

The strings crumble mid-crescendo, like someone dropped our wedding cake down the stairs. Crackle opens one eye and scratches his ear. Then he goes back to sleep. I stand there in my grey fleece dressing gown, ready to pour the coffee. No one bats an eyelid as I walk out of the room and head upstairs to write this book.

* * *

Adam isn't surprised when I tell him what happened during 'Canon in D' – though from the look on his face, the level of self-disclosure catches him off guard.

Because it's not just the unpredictability and the scarcity of goals that our brains have to contend with, it's what Adam describes as the 'delivery device' for all this. It's football's equivalent of a crack pipe – the smartphone.

Adam's book *Irresistible* is basically a thesis on why smartphones are engineered to hijack our attention. Combine that with football – and, often, gambling – and the effect is exponential.

As we sit talking, my phone is on the other side of the room and won't shut up, because I've forgotten to put it on airplane mode. We both hear a cascade of notifications; Facebook groups full of Wolves fans arguing about what to do about the dire situation. There are Instagram reels of players in their mansions, tweets, club shop alerts.

In the olden days, I'd be depressed for a bit after watching *Match of the Day*, but then that would be it. There'd be no reminders until *Saint & Greavsie* the following Saturday lunchtime. Now there's no getting away. As well as all the pings, reruns and non-stop stats fed through the screen like intravenous drips, the matches themselves are spread out across the week. Monday night. Friday night. Saturday evening. All Sunday afternoon. The cues are everywhere, impossible to avoid. It's like being a recovering heroin addict and seeing billboards for needles and smack on every street corner. And while the 'Canon in D' example sticks in my mind, the truth is usually far less poetic. Most of the time, it's my wife trying to talk to *me* while I sit there, gawping into my phone, typing 'Wolves' into Google. I do this at least thirty times a day. I've now checked and tracked it. Every time I have a spare second – waiting for the kettle, queuing in a shop, in the loo, during the adverts on ITVX – I don't do what I advise my patients to do. I don't ground myself in the present moment and take 'five sacred breaths' or try to connect with whoever's nearby. I just reach for the phone like a brain-dead zombie and type: W-O-L-V-E-S, to see if there's any news.

Most of the stories are speculation at best. Some feel entirely invented. I click anyway. If goals on the pitch don't draw me in, the phone will. Then I swear when the page takes forty-five seconds to load, bloated with ads and clickbait. *You won't believe what the Milkybar Kid looks like now!* and so on.

And then – just when I think I've closed the ad by tapping the microscopic cross in the corner – I get redirected. Suddenly I'm being urged to gamble on virtual roulette or masturbate with MILFs and GILFs who live within a five-mile radius of my house. If I'm sitting with my wife, this is the moment I start to panic, in case the sound kicks in.

I tell Adam I own all the Wolves kits – including the pink and purple one. I blame my phone.

'It's not meant to be that easy,' Adam says. 'You're parting with valuable resources – there's supposed to be *friction*.'

When you combine that kind of instant gratification with the other addictive qualities of football – the unpredictability, the scarcity of goals, the near misses – the siren call becomes hard to resist. Add gambling into the mix, and some fans crash straight into the rocks. Most football apps are saturated with betting.

It brings us back to the idea of delivery devices. Some make the addictive substance more addictive. Injecting heroin hits harder and faster than smoking it, so the delivery device intensifies the high, makes it more compulsive. That's why harm reduction tries to move users towards slower, less intense forms, syringe to foil, foil to methadone.

And the same logic applies here. Watching *Match of the Day* on your telly or going to a live game might stir emotion, but it won't scramble your dopamine system in quite the same way as a smartphone constantly feeding you goals, odds, outrage, merchandise and memes. DAZN, the sports streaming giant who forced us to watch Trump at half-time, has learned how to manipulate our love of football and our primitive reward circuitry. They are using our data to personalise feeds, nudge users away from cancellation, and keep us hooked through design tweaks and dopamine-inducing cues. The platform is morphing fandom into a behavioural casino, where football is the bait.

* * *

Adam, who has kids, admits he's uneasy about what phones are doing to young people. He says he fears we have broken a generation.

'I ask people this: "Would you rather your phone broke right now – or you broke a bone in your hand?" Older adults say, "Obviously the phone." Young people hesitate. They ask, "Which bone? How long to heal?"'

He lets out an incredulous laugh.

'Older adults hear that and just stare. *Like – what have we done?*'

Phones connect us, he says, but they also corrode the relationships right in front of us. I ask him what we're supposed to do about this.

'We're up against it,' he sighs.

I'm braced for something ingenious – some breathwork protocol perhaps, or something using haptic feedback – but the solution is disarmingly simple.

'Pick three hours a day,' Adam says, 'put the phone in a drawer, and make it physically unreachable. Those three hours are phone-free. That's it.'

I just stare at him. It feels like the technological equivalent of 'eat your vegetables'.

Before we finish, I ask Adam whether he agrees with the psychiatrist Dr Lanzaro that, in some cases, football should be considered a behavioural addiction.

'It's a good question,' he says.

'There are a lot of experiences that, at the margins, can lead to psychological, social, physical or financial harms, and that people just can't stop returning to.

'I think football could be one of those experiences if you're someone who derives almost no joy from the game. For some extreme fans, it's mostly a negative experience, because the feeling of losing is so extreme.

'The pain from that is so intense that it can't compensate for the joys of winning.

'It's all about whether it satisfies the definition – if it does, then yes, it's a behavioural addiction.'

But for Adam, football matters precisely because it hurts. One of the most counter-intuitive insights in psychology, he says, is that a life lived constantly at seven or eight out of ten isn't necessarily a life well lived.

While researching his book, he interviewed wildly successful people whose lives lacked richness because they didn't suffer enough. One male movie star complained that he could walk into any bar or club and women would throw themselves at him.

'He was existentially bored,' Adam says. 'There was no chase. No tension. And he said, "Everyone thinks that's the dream. But it's awful. It drains the excitement out of life."'

What gives life meaning, Adam says, is uncertainty. It's the *maybe*. Humans naturally seek intense emotional experiences – especially those wired towards compulsion.

'Everyone has a compulsion cup that needs filling,' he says. 'And for people who tend towards obsession – which I do – the cup is bigger. It needs more.'

He admits that if he didn't fill his compulsion cup with football, he'd be a good candidate for drinking too much.

'You can fill it with football – something that's not net negative – or you can fill it with things that are genuinely destructive.'

His thinking, he says, was shaped by an article he read about teenage social media use: generally harmful, in his view, but still sometimes protective against worse behaviours, like smoking.

Addiction has always reminded me of Whac-A-Mole – bash one mole down and another pops up somewhere else, faster and more erratically each time. Better your mole is football than methamphetamine.

39

Man Seeking Football Widow

What Adam said reassured me – but only up to a point. One of the hallmarks of behavioural addiction isn't just what it does to you. It's what it does to the people around you. Damage to relationships was a major symptom.

I kept thinking about that Facebook message I'd received at the very start of this project, when I was walking near the Saxon church. It was the one from the wife of an obsessed fan who told me her marriage was on the rocks. I'd replied, offering to talk, but she never wrote back.

I'd also read that the computer game *Football Manager* had been cited in thirty-five divorce cases in 2012. But what about real-life fandom, the kind that colonises your weekends from August to May and leaves only little for everything else.

Could football be enough to break a marriage? I needed to hear from the other side.

I went on a bit of a wild goose chase, beginning by typing 'Football Widows' into Google. A football widow is 'someone, traditionally a woman, who feels neglected or abandoned during football season because their partner is entirely consumed by the game'.

One of the first things I landed on was an advert for a law firm, encouraging any football widows to contact them if they were struggling to cope during the season.

The advert – disguised as a blog – for Paradigm Family Law firm alluded to *Football Widow Syndrome* and was labelled 'Football Widows – Domestic Rivalries'.

'If you feel you may have fallen victim to the phenomenon [Football Widow Syndrome] described above,' it read, 'then please don't sit on the touchline. There is no substitute for contacting our specialist team of family lawyers for confidential and professional advice on your transfer options.'

There are plenty of similar adverts, invoking football widowhood, often backed by questionable surveys claiming men think about football more than sex.

According to Illicit Encounters, the UK's biggest extramarital affair site, female engagement spikes by seventy-seven per cent during major tournaments. Male libido, meanwhile, plummets after a bad result, with Middlesbrough fans supposedly the most affected. This was consistent with what I'd learned about testosterone and the winner–loser effect (not the Middlesborough bit, which is a bit baffling).

I contacted one of the founding senior partners at the firm whose advert I had noticed. He was a German divorce lawyer and former judge named Frank Arndt.

Frank qualified as a judge on the family circuit in Germany before moving to England. He counts Gareth Southgate as a neighbour, up near Harrogate, and has acted for several footballers, including Manchester United and England players.

Frank appears on screen, all in black, his brown hair parted neatly to one side. He's fifty-six, with three children.

I tell Frank I wanted to know whether football fandom led to divorce cases and more to the point I wanted to know whether my wife would actually have grounds to divorce me.

I've prepared a list, with my wife's help, and start reading.

'Shouting and screaming at the television. Throwing things. Refusing dinner. Storming out of the house. Refusing sex. Refusing hugs . . .'

Frank stares at the screen expressionless.

'. . . dismissing attempts to comfort me, cancelling social events, disappearing from family gatherings to watch games, refusing to walk the dog, not going to weddings . . .'

Still nothing.

I'd forgotten how long the list was. I was hoping he might at least find it amusing, but he doesn't flinch.

I may as well finish.

'. . . being depressed and snappy for several days afterwards, belittling her attempts to console me when she says things like "well they played well, didn't they?" or "they're not bottom are they?" . . .'

I pause for breath.

'. . . actually crying, shaking, telling her not to interrupt the game, hogging the main television when she wants to watch *The Traitors*.'

We share a long, uncomfortable silence.

'What was the question again?' Frank asks finally.

'What do you think of that?' I ask. 'What would you say to my wife if she came to you with that list?'

He clears his throat. 'If somebody comes with that list,' he says, 'the first question would be: have you tried marriage counselling?'

His tone is serious. Then, after a pause: 'I'm not a big fan of divorce.'

'Gosh,' I say.

'I believe it's possible to resolve things,' he continues, 'if both people are open and honest. I'm a glass half full guy – this is a list you can work with.'

The key, he says, is to accept that football is causing a relational problem, and to communicate honestly about it, without calling each other names.

Frank confirms that he sees many cases where football obsession is mentioned in divorce settlements.

He sees a particular surge in enquiries after a major tournament like the World Cup.

'You've probably heard about "D-Day" in January, when everyone comes back from Christmas?'

I shake my head.

'That's the peak for divorce petitions,' he says. 'But after the winter World Cup in Qatar, we saw an unusually high spike in January. I can't prove it was the football, but the timing was . . . interesting.'

Frank says football obsession often shows up in his work during financial settlements. He's seen many desperate wives needing advice after enduring coercively controlling, football-obsessed relationships for years and years. Savings are plundered to buy giant televisions before major tournaments, season tickets, merchandise and sometimes it's gambled away on matches.

'The wife comes to me asking how they'll pay the bills,' Frank says. 'Nothing is left for holidays or heating. That's when they say, "I've got to pull the plug. This isn't good."'

Costs of season tickets have risen significantly since Covid and are a source of continued anguish among fans. The most expensive non-hospitality season tickets for the 2025/26 season were £3,804 at Fulham. Nine clubs charged more than £1,000 for the best spots outside corporate boxes and several others come close to that mark.

Many fans buy season tickets on credit, and social media has stories of people admitting they can't keep up the payments.

Couples sit down with him to try and sort the mess before it reaches court. He combs through their accounts, tracing payments to bookies and football channels, trying to quantify the emotional cost of fandom in financial terms.

The same patterns appear in child contact disputes. 'Those cases are very emotional,' he says. 'When someone's always out watching football, or glued to the matches online, the children suffer, unless they love the game too. It's not always the case. So, it comes up there as well, not just with the money.'

As the interview goes on, I notice Frank is warmer than I'd first thought. I think I was just projecting my own embarrassment on to him as I realised how many ridiculous things on that long list were true, and perhaps that I wasn't taking it as seriously as I should.

Frank says he feels uneasy about finding me one of his clients to talk to but smiles and wishes me well in my relationship. I hang up thinking he's exactly the kind of calm, methodical man you'd want around when everything else is falling apart.

But I was still no closer to finding a football widow. I could have interviewed my wife, but that felt like a conflict of interest, at this stage. And besides, I like to believe she doesn't *really* dislike football. She'll watch the odd England match and feign a cheer at the right moment.

I decided to head to Mumsnet, the UK's largest network for parents, with about 9 million unique visitors per month. The vast majority of its community are women.

I naturally chose a username that was relatively neutral – DamPea – so I didn't stand out. But I couldn't help but feel like a creep hanging around the women's changing room. Was I allowed to view this stuff? Was there a special Mumsnet alarm somewhere deep within the server that might expose me as a dodgy interloper?

To start with, I navigated carefully through the pages, trying to sidestep any obvious tripwires. I resisted the ghoulish temptation to peek into threads that were clearly none of my business – 'He grunts like a wild boar', 'Do you wash your legs?', 'Penis Beaker', 'Yoni eggs' and so on.

No, if I was going to be here at all, I needed to resist my inner voyeur. I was looking for football-related threads. And, as it turned out, there were plenty. When I typed 'football' into the search bar, 1,323 results appeared from the past year alone.

StarryIsabella wrote:

> One thing I've noticed about some men I know is how passionate they are about football and the amount of effort they put into keeping up with players, transfers, tactics . . . The same men are often lazy when it comes to their own lives. If they put this much energy into improving themselves, what an amazing group of men we'd have . . . 🤣

Another replied:

> Example: one of my mates (who openly admits he's lazy) was talking about a player called 'Walker'. He knew every team he'd played for, every transfer fee. 🤣 I said, 'How do you know all this?' and he said, 'It's common footie knowledge.' I've never seen him this passionate about anything else! These men need to be studied by scientists. 🤣 It honestly baffles me. 🤷‍♀️

Asurprisevisit55 wrote:

> Many of these men are so emotionally expressive in football, yet so cold and withdrawn in their personal lives.

> They'll plan trips, buy shirts, maintain friendships . . . but at home, they're distant. Why is that? What is this all about?

It struck me that these women were completely baffled by how football seemed to unlock a part of their partners they rarely got access to. It provided their men with an emotional toolbox and vocabulary that was otherwise absent.

I decided to leave a cheerful, self-deprecating post inviting anyone interested to speak to me about Football Widow Syndrome for my book. I pressed 'send' but within seconds I had an unsettling sense that conversations were taking place behind the scenes about how to get rid of me.

I noticed a reply pop up. But before I could even read it, the message vanished.

This reply has been deleted by MNHQ [Mumsnet HQ] for breaking our Talk Guidelines.

Now I was worried. Despite my efforts to be inoffensive, I'd clearly enraged someone so much they had lashed out abusively. I could almost hear the keystrokes hammering LEAVE. US. ALONE. YOU. PREDATOR.

Minutes later, I received an email.

'Hi all, sorry for the mass mail – thank you for all your reports about that thread. This is just to let you know we have removed it and banned the OP [original poster]. Best wishes, MNHQ.'

I stared at the screen. I'd been banned, like Steve on the Wolves Facebook group, and worse, accidentally copied into the moderators' email about banning me. They'd discussed me. Reported me. And now I was gone.

A second email arrived almost immediately. This time, it seemed, meant for me.

'Hi there, sorry about that last email – sent in error.'

I was getting really confused and more and more anxious. I wondered whether I was even looking in the right place. After all, I learned that the founder of Mumsnet, Justine Roberts, was a massive Liverpool football fan. Maybe my conceptualisation of a football widow needed updating.

I headed for the more gender-neutral pastures of Reddit, trawling for frustrated threads, when I stumbled on a piece of prose by Umberto Eco, the author of *The Name of the Rose*.

The novel, later adapted into a film starring Sean Connery and Christian Slater, is one of the best-selling books of all time, shifting over 50 million copies. Eco's story is a historical murder mystery set in a fourteenth-century Italian monastery. He was also a professor of semiotics, the study of signs and symbols and how humans use them to create meaning.

When he wasn't teaching or writing, Eco played the recorder, those plastic or wooden flutes that make dogs howl and put most of us off playing an instrument for life.

He also hated football fans.

A fellow recorder enthusiast had posted a short essay by Eco, titled 'How Not To Talk About Soccer'. It captured the experience of living in a football-obsessed world when you couldn't care less about the sport yourself. Eco describes sitting in a taxi where the driver starts talking about players like Vialli and Van Basten, assuming he must be a football fan.

'It isn't that he doesn't care a fig that I don't care a fig. It's that he can't conceive that anyone could exist and not care a fig,' Eco writes.

To make his point, he asks us to imagine a different conversation. This time he is on a train in Italy and engages a fellow passenger by talking to him about his passion for the recorder.

'Have you heard Frans Brüggen's latest CD?'

'What? Eh?'

'I'm talking about the "Pavane Lachrymae". If you ask me, he takes the opening bars too slowly.'

'I'm afraid I don't understand.'

'I'm talking about Van Eyck, of course, [slowly and distinctly]. The *Blockflöte*.'

'Look, I'm not . . . Do you play it with a bow?'

And so on, until the fellow traveller is so exasperated he decides to make a swift exit at Parma station.

I found this amusing. Eco wasn't a football widow in the strict sense – so far as I know, he wasn't married to a fan. But it was clear he often felt excluded more broadly by a society obsessed with the game. He died in 2016, aged eighty-four. So, unable to talk to him, I reached out to the man who'd posted the piece, a fellow recorder enthusiast. Perhaps he could be my widow.

* * *

Ernesto Schmied was showing me his wooden flute. That alone was enough to make my inner child snigger. When he started talking about fingering and the size of his favourite hole, I had to dig deep.

But externally, I appeared unmoved. I have practised a neutral face for my many hundreds of patients, people who have confessed to all sorts of outlandish behaviour and intrusive thoughts. I have remained impassive.

So I was confident I could sit through a 63-year-old Argentinian man earnestly discussing the thickness of his shaft without betraying amusement. I focused on my breathing. If I gave the laughter any room to escape, even a single rogue nostril exhale, I would be finished.

Ernesto sits in his music room wearing an army-green jumper and matching combats. His neat silver hair is framed by large, black-rimmed glasses and his skin is almost the same shade as the big tufted tan leather sofa. He is surrounded by a small orchestra of synthesisers and recording equipment.

He seems a little nervous, and I don't blame him. Why would a football fan want to talk to him? Maybe he thinks I'm here to mock him; a sad, compensatory gesture from a Wolves supporter looking for someone to feel superior to after a string of recent defeats.

Ernesto lives in El Escorial, north of Madrid, where he manages world music and jazz festivals. His great passion, though, is the recorder.

He has an Instagram page. Most people's feeds are curated attempts to look refreshed or pretend they are living happy family lives. But Ernesto's page is just a shrine to the recorder. There is photo after photo of beautifully handcrafted wooden flutes. Each one is polished to perfection. The posts attract heart emojis and comments like: 'Fr. Morgan, voice flute. Such a great, graceful instrument!'

He relaxes quickly, and soon, to my immense surprise, he's swearing and swinging his arms like Kenny Everett's Cupid Stunt.

He tells me about the recorder's history in schools, how it became a staple simply because it was cheap to mass-produce. Many of the plastic ones were made in Germany and given to the Hitler Youth to play in military parades. When the war ended, they had a surplus and the industrious Germans successfully flogged them everywhere.

'So it's Hitler's fault?' I ask.

He gives a small, diplomatic tilt of the head.

'It has ruined the musical education of many children all around the planet,' he says. 'It's a real pity.'

He explains that despite its reputation, the recorder is an exceptionally difficult instrument to play. Hence the annual auditory torture of school concerts.

'It's easy to make a sound, but very difficult to make music. People should sing in schools. You don't have to be an opera singer to sing.'

'So we never stood a chance?'

'Never.'

Ernesto tells me he wasn't socialised into football by his parents like other boys and wasn't much good at playing it, so he lost interest quickly. He then discovered music.

As a young man, he talked about recorders with his friends the way others talk about football. It became a social backstop in awkward moments. And like football fandom, the obsession eventually took over.

He is divorced now with two children, aged twenty and seventeen.

I wondered whether the recorder had anything to do with the separation.

'Did your wife complain?'

'Oh yes,' he says. Then he launches into an impression of an exasperated person, flailing his arms like a man being attacked by wasps.

'IS THAT FUCKING BASTARD STILL PLAYING THE FUCKING RECORDER?' he shrieks, mimicking his family.

'Cousins would come round and say, "I wish I had a father who could play the recorder like that," and blah blah blah.'

He rolls his eyes.

'But they only saw me for half an hour,' he exclaims, ruefully.

'No wonder,' I say.

'I could play for SIX hours a day,' Ernesto explains. 'And I didn't have a soundproof room.'

He takes a breath.

'That must have been annoying for them.'

He nods.

Part of the reason he could not afford a soundproof room is that when you move beyond the cheap plastic varieties, the instruments themselves get very expensive.

He bought his best recorder from a famous Swedish recorder player called Dan Laurin. It cost him £7,500. But he justifies this by comparing it to some of the most expensive violins. Any violin by the master craftsman Giuseppe Guarneri del Gesù would cost millions, for example. Even just the bows – the high-end ones – can cost £600,000, Ernesto tells me.

I asked Ernesto about Umberto Eco's essay and his own experience of being a football outcast. He says taxi drivers are always asking about results.

'I'll say, "No, I'm not a footb—"'

'And they look at me like I'm a Martian.'

He imitates a shocked stare, as if an alien has stepped off a spaceship and asked for directions.

'They just can't process it. A man who doesn't know about football. Hahahahahahaha.'

'What's that like?' I ask.

'Normally I just go quiet,' Ernesto says, suddenly solemn. 'I don't argue. it's pointless. So I nod and say, "Oh yes, yes," even though I've no idea what I'm talking about.'

We say our goodbyes. I hope that one day in Nairobi he slips into the back of a taxi with Stephen and they talk about music to their hearts' content.

* * *

I loved speaking to Ernesto, but he wasn't really a football widow. I was close to giving up and thought my wife might have to go on the record after all. Then a Facebook message arrived. I had sent another request to the woman who had written to me months earlier on my walk, and this time she replied. She apologised for not getting back to me sooner and said things had got worse in the meantime. They were now trialling a separation.

She didn't want to speak on camera. She was worried she might cry. Instead, she asked if she could write me a short letter. This is what she sent:

> Dear Damien,
> I feel embarrassed that football has had such an effect on me and that I've hijacked your thread. The kids love football (we have a boy and a girl, eight and twelve), and I'm the only one with no interest at all.
>
> What hurts me is how unreachable he is. He's on antidepressants because he hates his job. He always looks sad and lonely. Our daughter was badly bullied last year and it destroyed him. But he just got angry and then went quiet. I found him crying once, but he wouldn't let me hug him.
>
> Football is the only thing that makes him emotional. When the team wins, he's briefly happy and sometimes we

> share that. But mostly I'm invisible. When they lose, I try to comfort him, but I just irritate him. I've got no idea how he feels. It wasn't always like this.
>
> We never have any intimate connection. TMI 😂 Sorry!!!
>
> With the kids' season tickets and everything else – travel, food, shirts – we spend more than £2,000 a year on football. We didn't even go out for my fortieth birthday. We're not going on holiday because he wants to watch the World Cup in America with his mates. I also found out he was gambling on games – not huge amounts, but £100 here and there. I only discovered it because the mortgage company flagged it when we were moving. Maybe we were drifting apart anyway. I know I can't blame it all on football. But his passion for football makes his lack of passion for me so obvious. 😔 We're spending the summer apart. I'm staying with my mum. The kids are sad. I hope this doesn't spoil your book.
>
> P.S. Please don't be offended that I didn't want to speak to you – I just get very emotional. 😔

I was moved by her letter, and I showed it to my wife. I asked whether my own football obsession was more than an inconvenience.

She said she was mostly fine with it.

Then she reflected.

Sometimes, she said, I could feel unreachable too. As if I were living in another world or had slipped behind glass. She often felt inadequate because she didn't know how to console me.

It reminded me of a conversation I'd had with the professor of philosophy Simon Critchley, a Liverpool fan living in New York.

He described standing in front of the television in his underpants, barely able to endure the final thirty-five minutes of a Liverpool match.

'Without going into too much detail,' Simon told me, 'I'm very affectionate with my wife – but never during games. I become a kind of little fortress. I will not be touched.'

The woman who wrote to me didn't think football alone was to blame. But it amplified a slow erosion of connection in her busy family life. I knew this feeling, sitting side by side, but feeling detached.

I had mixed emotions. My conversation with Ernesto had left me feeling grateful to be a football fan, not necessarily a Wolves fan, but part of the broader church of fandom. I was grateful my dad loved the game and that he took me to my first match when I was six. I was grateful that he took me to the park to show me a few tricks and woke me at ten o'clock on Saturday nights to watch *Match of the Day* when I should have been asleep, because he knew what it meant to me.

Unlike Ernesto, I belonged to one of the world's biggest tribes. Football had given me one of the greatest social advantages imaginable: the ability to talk to people, anywhere, about something meaningful.

But the honesty of that letter – and my wife's admission – left me morose. That word *unreachable* stayed with me.

Last weekend I went to an eighties fancy-dress reunion with some old school friends. I was anxious at first. Within minutes, we were talking about football. It became a bridge to everything else: children, illness, job losses, relationship challenges. By the end of the night, we were swaying arm in arm to 'She Sells Sanctuary' – middle-aged men in wigs, fishnets and eyeliner – declaring our love for one another with fierce sincerity.

I thought about all the men who can't quite say I miss you but can commune over the grief of a lost semi-final from twenty years ago. The ones who find *I love you* impossible but can say, *Same again next week*?

And I thought about the people who love them. About the quiet rooms football leaves behind. About the way it conceals loneliness and sometimes leaves more of it trailing in its wake.

40

The Slap

Paul, the Sky cameraman, and I return for the court case in the afternoon, when Alfie Holt is listed. There's a police officer standing outside the glass-fronted Magistrates' Court, speaking solemnly to everyone entering. But something's off. As well as his chequered police cap and fluorescent coat, he's wearing a bandana.

'That's John the Menace,' Paul tells me. 'He's not a real cop – he just impersonates one.'

'Why?' I ask.

'No one knows,' Paul says.

John sticks his thumbs up at me as I stare, bemused. Apparently, he just enjoys winding the cops up. He's holding a crumpled A4 sheet, a handwritten list of officers he's had 'dealings' with. There are videos of him online being confronted by real police, all of them unsure what to do with him.

Next to John the Menace, there's a young man in a navy blue and grey tracksuit, also wearing a bandana and a hood. He looks a lot more menacing than John.

'That one's got a bodycam,' Paul warns. 'He films everyone coming in and out of the court and interviews them about their convictions.'

'Why?' I ask.

'No one knows,' Paul says.

The truth is that this young man does have an incentive to film people. He has a TikTok channel, with 40,000 followers. I check it on my phone. He goes by the name of HM Exposed Media. He is presently holding a chocolate brown puppy labrador under one arm. He wanders over to us, John, the police impersonator, trailing behind.

'You here for the man who slapped Jack Grealish?' he asks.

'Yes,' I say.

'Where are you from?'

I immediately forget he might have his cam on and start banging on about my book. I realise halfway through my response that I may have given away the working title to a man on TikTok. I start to feel pasty and sweaty. I imagine my editor with her head in her hands as she watches a video of me on HM Exposed Media.

The dog is called Rolo. I give him a stroke.

'People like dogs,' HM says. 'I thought he'd be good for my channel.'

Poor Rolo, I think, a life consigned to hanging around Manchester Magistrates' Court with John the Menace and TikTok's answer to Roger Cook.

Cameraman Paul tells me no one knows what the defendant Alfie Holt looks like. There are no pictures of him on social media and door knocks have been unsuccessful. All we know is that he is a twenty-year-old. But Paul has an intuition for this. He ignores a trail of mostly young men as they go in, dressed in flecked suits that look too big and three togs too warm. Then one young man emerges from a side street. He has a swagger to him, and he heads purposely towards the court entrance flanked by a woman holding files and a man who looks like his father. He is wearing a Hugo Boss polo shirt and blue jeans and has the square jaw, broad shoulders and laser-focused eyes of Buzz Lightyear.

HM Exposed lunges forward, bundling Rolo into John the Menace's arms. John looks bewildered.

'What you up for, bro?' HM bellows. The young man swerves into him aggressively just enough so that HM backs away a little.

'Slapping Jack Grealish, is it?'

The young man gives him a fake superhero grin, brimming with real menace. The three enter the court with me following.

'Did you slap Jack Grealish?' HM yells over my head.

Alfie, his dad and solicitor sit in an interview before the case is called. I'm told there's no chance Grealish will attend. I'm having no luck tracking him down for an interview.

Inside the court I take my seat on the press bench with a young reporter from the *Manchester Evening News*, and another older hack. The younger reporter asks me where I'm from and I tell her about the book, and how there are two men who have attacked Grealish in it.

'Just so bloody good-looking, isn't he?' she says.

'Do you think?' I reply.

Alfie is called and sits in the glass-panelled dock. The bravado's gone. In front of the magistrates, he looks smaller somehow – shoulders rounded, chin low. Occasionally, he glances towards his dad. I catch his eye and he gives me a small, uncertain eyebrow raise. For some reason, I nod back, with a half-smile. I remember being there, in a similar dock, as a young man too, accused of stealing a JCB on a drunken night out.

Alfie pleads guilty to the charge of assault by beating. It turns out he had been going to games with his father since he was eight and is a United season ticket holder. He had been drinking in the city centre before the game.

No one – apart from police and legal teams – has seen footage of the attack, but now it is being played on a television in the courtroom. Grealish is heading towards the players' tunnel at Old Trafford after the game. A fuzzy image of Alfie can be seen leaning over towards the tunnel. There's no sound.

Alfie had already insulted Phil Foden – the player whose mum had been called a 'slag' by fans throughout the game – but Foden just ignored him and walked on by. Grealish walks down the tunnel and just as he's disappearing out of sight, he does a U-turn.

He walks back to where Alfie is standing, leaning in. He appears to put his hand to one ear, as if to say, *say that again, mate*. Grealish then says something to Alfie and turns to walk away, but Alfie lifts his arm and slaps him across the cheek. Grealish looks stunned and stewards intervene but Alfie darts out of the stadium.

It turns out that Alfie had called Grealish a 'knobhead' and, after looping back, Grealish had responded by calling Alfie a 'little ugly wanker'. Alfie told police he 'just flipped' at this and that's when he slapped him.

The magistrates ask to see the footage again. We all lean forward. Even the prosecution admits it's hard to make out the slap. By any measure, it's a minor assault, especially compared with Paul Mitchell's full-body charge.

What surprises me most is that Grealish turned back at all. Players get insulted all the time. It's unpleasant, but it's part of the game. When you're earning hundreds of thousands a week, it's the bile tax. You rise above it – or at least, you're meant to. It reminded me of Eric Cantona's famous kung-fu kick on Matthew Simmons in 1995.

I wondered whether he was really reacting to something else – the abuse aimed at his team-mate Foden's family. Maybe it reminded him of stuff that he's endured, including stuff about his brother. Footballers aren't immune to trauma. Sometimes it only takes the right provocation. The right number to come up on their bicycle locks.

The chairman of the bench Jill Hodges is gentle with Alfie, like a stern but caring headteacher. She speaks softly to him and tells him that drinking alcohol with his epilepsy condition is dangerous. She bans him from attending all games for three years and he must pay a fine and costs totalling £253. As he doesn't work and is on PIP, his parents will pay.

'You seem to be genuinely regretful, but to assault somebody is a very serious matter,' Hodges says. She asks Alfie if he wants to say anything.

'I did not expect Grealish to come back and speak to me,' Alfie says, barely audible. 'I heard what he said and I just reacted. I can't take back what I did but I do regret it.'

I hover outside Court 11 and slip Alfie a scrunched note with my number on it. 'I'm not a nasty journalist,' I reassure him. He gives me another polite eyebrow lift before his dad and solicitor hustle him on to the escalator.

Before he's even reached the mezzanine, I've WhatsApped Paul, the cameraman: 'He's coming out . . . NOW.'

The speed of the betrayal is athletic.

'Top man,' Paul replies, and I realise how fast I've reverted to type – the instincts kicking in before the conscience has time to raise a hand. On the way down the escalator, I overhear Alfie's dad telling him not to speak to HM Exposed outside the court.

Alfie emerges from the building and HM lunges forward, bundling Rolo into the arms of John the Menace once more.

'How did it feel to slap Jack Grealish?' the TikTok man barks.

Alfie stares straight ahead. HM shadows him across the pavement, and John the Menace lumbers after them, Rolo in tow. But

Rolo has other ideas. He plants his tiny feet into the road, because he's caught the scent of something life-altering. He may be small, but his fledgling brain has already learned the immutable law of the street: if there is an unfinished sausage roll in a discarded Greggs bag, all travel plans are cancelled.

John waits with him.

'Were you one of the ones abusing Phil Foden's mum too?' HM calls out.

Alfie's dad walks in silence behind him. His solicitor, Melanie Winstanley, turns, concerned, her hand on Alfie's shoulder, gently urging him not to respond.

'Are you a proud football hooligan?' HM yells.

Alfie swivels – the same fixed grin. He stands there staring.

'Eh, that smile on your face – looks like you are,' HM says, trying to provoke him into some action for his TikTok channel.

I can see Alfie trembling with the effort not to react.

'FOOTBALL HOOLIGAN, that's what you are!' HM screams. 'DIRTY RED SCUM.'

Alfie disappears around the corner.

* * *

The next day, I get an unexpected WhatsApp. It's from Alfie Holt. He wants to know if I'll pay him for an interview.

I tell him I can't, but it'd still be great to talk. Maybe he has a message for other young men caught up in the madness of fandom.

No reply. I call, but he doesn't answer. I'm not surprised. I don't really blame him either – why would he speak to me, for free?

It reminded me of Paul Mitchell, and how he wouldn't properly apologise to Grealish when he spoke to the *Sun*. But it also made me think of others – like Alfie Perkins, Emmanuel and Dale – those who have spoken to me. Was there a pattern?

I suspect it comes down to regret and exactly how much someone has transgressed the unwritten moral rules of the tribe. I might be wrong, but I don't think Alfie Holt regretted slapping Grealish. Nothing about the way I'd seen him act in court made me think he really felt sorry for what he'd done. I think the kindly magistrate was wrong.

Maybe he regretted the fallout – hauling his dad into court, journalists knocking at the door – but not the slap itself. Same goes for Paul Mitchell. I never got the sense he truly regretted the actual attack either. I think it's because they didn't violate the rules egregiously enough.

Yes, I'm sure plenty of Manchester United and Birmingham City fans were appalled by what Alfie Holt and Paul Mitchell did – but not everyone. Paul got GoFundMe pages, banners in support. I imagine Alfie Holt got support in some quarters too. Their actions didn't exile them from the tribe. If anything, they were celebrated by some parts of it. There's a version of the hero's journey that can just about accommodate what they did.

But no one cheered what Alfie Perkins or Dale Houghton did. No one lifts a pint for a lad who mocks a dead child. That's a line even football's chaos won't cross. And there's certainly no romantic narrative that can absorb beating your wife in front of your kids. Those acts aren't woven into the tribal story – they rupture it.

And maybe that's why Alfie Perkins, and Dale, and Emmanuel talked to me.

Because their actions couldn't be redeemed by the group, couldn't be mythologised into some pub-friendly tale of passion and rivalry. There was no neat arc available to them. Speaking to me – trying to make sense of their own hatred, shame and irrationality – gave it a semblance of meaning.

41

Paul Mitchell – RIP

Adam Alter's 'compulsion cup' makes sense to me – the idea that we all need something to fill it with. And the healthier the thing you fill it with, the safer you are. Football can do that, though as we know, it obviously has its casualties. Football kept Adam balanced; it kept him away from drinking too much alcohol.

But then I think of Paul Mitchell after his second release from prison in October 2022. Football could no longer fill his cup. Birmingham City were more vigilant, and he couldn't get into games. Neither could he find regular work, nor see his kids. But the cup was still there. And so, he filled it with things left within easy reach; cider, and eventually something even more dangerous.

By March 2023, five months after being released from jail, Paul had spiralled into a dark depression. His criminal record meant that he was struggling to find a secure job. Debbie was hours away from Birmingham at the pub near Glastonbury.

Paul had been diagnosed with an adjustment disorder, struggling to cope with life without his children and football games. He was drinking heavily – up to fifteen cans of cider a day – and was mostly staying with his gravely ill father at his flat in Solihull, south-east of Birmingham. Looking after his dad gave him some purpose. He hardly went out.

On 13 March, Paul and his sister were both staying at their father's home. The next morning, before going out, Hayley nudged

Paul, who was huddled under a blanket on the sofa, and reminded him there was a contractor coming to fix the internet. When she returned, Paul hadn't moved.

She tried to stir him but he was cold.

Hayley ran to the neighbours for help, and the paramedics came, but nothing could be done. Sometime in the hours before, after returning from a shift as a chef, he'd taken a whole bottle of his father's morphine. There was alcohol too, and the combination stopped his heart. At first, the police treated it as suspicious.

But the inquest held in August 2023 determined the cause of death to be drug toxicity and alcohol. The assistant coroner, Simon Brenchley, provided a narrative conclusion, acknowledging the ambiguity. Was it deliberate? Accidental? No one can say for sure, but Paul was certainly low in the weeks leading up to his death. The inquest was told he had attempted to kill himself once already after leaving jail for the second time.

PART VIII

Let It All Out

42

From Cradle to Grave

Paul Mitchell's coffin was carried by his two sisters, Hayley and Jodie, and his best friends from school. A Birmingham City badge lay on top. The strains of 'He Ain't Heavy, He's My Brother' belted out around St Andrew's as the procession circled the ground, where a few years earlier Paul had stormed on to the pitch. More than two hundred mourners followed the coffin, some in formal black, others in Blues colours.

Paul was cremated and his ashes placed in the Birmingham City urn. Months later, when his father Paul Sr. died, he too was put into a blue urn. They were buried together beneath a headstone inscribed 'From Cradle to Grave'. Debbie and the other mourners wept as the Blues anthem 'Keep Right On to the End of the Road', written by Harry Lauder in 1924, was played at the end of the ceremony.

Sitting with me in her Glastonbury pub, Debbie flicks through photographs of the funeral, tears rolling down her cheek. Hayley places a hand on her shoulder.

'He was loved,' Debbie says. 'Was he what you were expecting?' she asks me as I pack up to head home.

'He was more than the thug who ran on to the pitch, wasn't he?' I say.

'Yes,' Debbie replies.

She wipes away her tears and shows me more pictures – Paul on away days in Europe with his dad. She wants *her* Paul to be seen. Later I notice she's had a huge tattoo across her back: her son's name, angel wings and the words 'From Cradle to Grave'.

I say my goodbyes and head back towards Hastings, along the A303. Just 165 metres from the road, the ring of giant sarsen stones rises incongruously. Like Glastonbury, Stonehenge is full of pilgrims, circling the stones, touching them, lying beside them, photographing them. Cremated human remains have been found here, and anthropologists believe many of the dead – including children – were carried from Wales, where the inner circle of bluestones mark graves.

I think again about Debbie's photographs; mourners weeping, the slow procession. I imagine the music, the colour, the chanting. Paul's ashes in a Blues urn. Funerals have offered rare spaces for ritualised emotional catharsis. In Ancient Greece, grief was loud and visible; bodies laid out at home, families wailing and singing, dawn processions moving through the streets. Keening, meanwhile, was a traditional form of ritualised mourning practised most prominently in Ireland and parts of Scotland, in which professional mourners, often women, led funerals through improvised wailing, chanting and lamentation over the dead. It was loud and deliberately unrestrained. The aim was to externalise and share grief, helping to regulate overwhelming emotion. However, amid Victorian ideals of emotional restraint, the Catholic Church condemned keening for being uncivilised and excessive.

The Victorians derided football fandom for the same reason. I came across a blog by Matthew Klugman, an Australian professor, who has studied the role of emotion in football across history. It is called *Ridiculous Excess: The Emergence of Football Mania*.

The blog opens with a black-and-white cartoon from 1906: a football fan in a striped shirt, mid-delirium, firing two revolvers into the air like he's wandered in from a spaghetti western. Cricketers lie slumped across a bar. There's a discarded bat. Stumps toppled. A bartender ducks for cover. The caption reads: 'Give me Room; I want to Howl'.

It made me laugh. And it made me feel seen. Because isn't that what we all want? Room to howl in. A space where our feelings aren't dismissed as excessive, childish or misdirected. A place where it's acceptable to feel – and to act out.

From his author photo, Matthew looked improbably wholesome. He was in his late thirties, bright-eyed, neat brown hair, a cat draped over his shoulders. He had the air of someone who could successfully repot an orchid. When I met him, though, he was enjoying a much wilder phase – huge beard, long straggly hair. The gentle smile was still there, though.

Matthew tells me that in the mid-1800s, sport was widely seen as a solution to a perceived crisis of masculinity. Boys played sport to become courageous, disciplined and strong. Football made men. At elite schools like Eton and Harrow, it was promoted as moral training – a way to instil restraint and expunge dangerous urges like onanism . . . or worse still, homosexuality.

But there was a problem with this vision of football as rugged etiquette training for boys. The problem was the football fan. Fans were becoming unrestrained. They were hugging, shouting and, God forbid, crying. In public.

'Football was producing men who shout like brutes and cry like they're completely fragile,' Matthew explains. 'The emotions of spectators were seen as delicate, volatile.'

Rather than reinforcing restrained masculinity, football fandom appeared to be undermining it. Victorian authority figures – ministers, medics, newspaper editors – reacted with a mix of moral panic and dire health warnings. The language of illness crept in, with doctors cautioning that watching football might damage the brain.

The fear, Matthew says, was that spectatorship was turning men into something irrational and unstable – less than fully human. In other words, football wasn't civilising men at all. It was stripping away rationality and revealing something raw and tribal underneath.

'At the core of those white, imperial ideas of manliness,' Matthew says, 'was rationality and control. That's what made them "better" men.'

He pauses.

'And yet here were these supposedly superior men – screaming, crying, completely possessed by the game. And enjoying it. That terrified people. It looked like devolution.'

The viewpoint shifted, however, in the early twentieth century when the idea of fandom providing a safety valve to release suppressed emotion became popular. 'From then, watching football becomes a place to be acceptably mad,' Matthew says.

Not all sports followed. Cricket and rugby tried to hold the line, like upright Edwardian butlers fending off a rave at the garden gates.

'They did everything they could to limit the emotional engagement of the crowd,' Matthew says, referring to cricket. 'They tried to dampen excitement. The aim was restraint.'

Despite all the fearmongering, football went the other way. It leaned into chaos and welcomed the frenzy. And as we've seen, our emotions have since been monetised, scaled and optimised – until football became the most powerful sport of all.

43

The Opera Singer Who Tried to Mow Down Forest Fans

I am having lunch with Mark Glanville, an opera singer, at the Piazza restaurant in the Royal Opera House, Covent Garden. Mark has performed here, as well as the English National Opera, where he played Sarastro in *The Magic Flute*. He also reviews books for the *Times Literary Supplement*. He is sixty-six, shaved at the sides and bald on top, like Mark Strong, only with more weather in the skin. He is buzzing to tell me something.

Halfway through his first course – saffron-cured salmon with red pepper – he suddenly springs to his feet, knife and fork still in hand, and scans the room for waiting staff. Then he swivels and kicks out to the side, eyes bulging with focus.

'Is that a kung-fu kick?' I ask.

'Yes,' he says, slicing his leg through the air again. 'It's one of my favourite manoeuvres.'

'When did you last use it?'

'At a fox hunt ball,' he says.

He explains that he knocked a man flat with a kick like this after the man insulted – and then threw a drink over – his former partner, Marjorie.

'Jesus,' I say.

He swivels again – leg out, once, twice, three times. His eyes are glassy with excitement.

Mark doesn't normally deploy this combat technique at fox hunt balls – he's not into hunting at all but Marjorie was a bit 'rah'. He typically uses it when he's fighting as a Millwall football hooligan. He has been a hooligan for decades, breaking bones along the way. He once drove his Ford Sierra full throttle at a crowd of Forest hooligans near London Bridge, forcing them to dive for cover.

He was also there with nine hundred hooligans fighting police in 2002 after the game with Birmingham at The Den. Nearly fifty officers and twenty-four police horses were injured in the mayhem outside the Bramcote Arms in Bermondsey. A children's playground was ripped up for missiles. Many people were hurt. One police horse nearly died when a thunderflash went off at its feet, sending it crashing into a car and severing an artery.

He tells me a story. A few days before our lunch, he gave a talk about identity to an arts society in the genteel Suffolk village of Stoke-by-Nayland, where he lives. Afterwards, his friend, an old mate from Oxford University, was berating him for not expressing appropriate regret for all the violence he'd described to the audience. He warned Mark, a Classics scholar, he risked being hounded out of the village. No one would confront him directly, but they secretly deplored his stories – especially the one about driving at Forest fans in his Sierra.

The main course arrives – chalk stream trout salad, charred baby gem, fennel, Jersey Royals, wild garlic mayonnaise. He reaches back to something he first read in Greek at sixteen; *The Bacchae* by Euripides.

In it, there is Pentheus, King of Thebes, representing order and discipline. He is the straight-backed spine of civil authority. Then there is Dionysus, the god of wine, theatre and ecstatic release.

When Dionysus comes to Thebes, Pentheus mocks him and dresses in disguise to spy on their cathartic rituals. It ends with Pentheus being ripped apart in a frenzy, his body a warning to anyone who thinks they can cage primal instincts.

'We need laws,' Mark says, 'otherwise it's anarchy.'

He dabs the corner of his mouth with his napkin.

'But at the same time, we need outlets. We are animals. And civilisation, for all it gives us, drags us further away from that.'

Mark believes football fans are the Bacchae. We are bound together by ritual and emotion and ecstatic group identity. Meanwhile, the police, the stewards, politicians and the moralising media are all Pentheus, trying to regulate and civilise creatures who were never meant to be obedient.

We finish with cheese and then sorbet.

'People like my friend,' Mark says quietly, 'want moral systems that ignore basic human instincts.'

He spears a potato.

'The problem with my friend,' he says, fixing me with a serious look, 'is he doesn't know a thing about football.'

* * *

From Euripides to Freud, the idea that we need to find ways of expressing otherwise painful emotions abounds.

For Freud, feelings, especially aggression and sexuality, were thought to build up internal pressure and needed release. He believed that we are in a constant state of resentment at all of life's injustices. Expression of emotion in controlled therapeutic contexts was assumed to reduce the risk of more dangerous eruptions.

Then came Primal Scream Therapy, introduced by the American psychotherapist Arthur Janov in the 1960s. Like

Freud, he believed that buried childhood experiences create lifelong tension and psychological symptoms. Patients can only heal by re-experiencing the original pain through a cathartic 'primal scream'. Unprocessed early suffering becomes 'imprinted' in the nervous system and must be released somatically rather than merely talked about.

The therapy was pioneered by celebrities including John Lennon and Yoko Ono. Bands such as Tears for Fears even took their name from primal scream therapy (they were initially called History of Headaches) – and their music, including the single 'Shout', was shaped by Janov's insistence that buried emotion had to be confronted and released, not managed or civilised away.

One of Janov's leading disciples was an Englishwoman called Jenny James. She set up a commune in London before moving to a three-storey Victorian house in Burtonport, in Ireland's rural Donegal – a quiet, peaceful part of the country that the commune, soon known as Atlantis, was about to disrupt. Neighbours in the small village called them The Screamers. The house was painted in rainbow colours, with eyes around the windows and zodiac signs daubed across the walls. Up to thirty people lived there at any one time.

A documentary about the commune, *The Family*, directed by Irish film-maker Bob Quinn in 1978, was banned by Irish television for years because the footage was considered too disturbing. Cassette recordings captured women screaming as if possessed: 'You will die, because you cannot live off my energy. You CANNOT live off my energy.' Participants were encouraged – sometimes pressured – to scream for hours, often while being shouted at, insulted or physically restrained by others. They were surrounded to the point of emotional collapse. In tapes later accessed by the BBC, Jenny discussed her 'stud theory' of men – that they were only good for sex and cutting wood. Men who left the commune reported being routinely degraded and humiliated by Jenny and other women there. There were also allegations of sexual exploitation and other boundary violations.

In 1980, after unsettling the local community, the group relocated to four cottages on the nearby island of Inishfree, becoming almost completely isolated. But in 1989, amid growing concern about practices deemed abusive, they moved again – this time to Colombia – and a retreat near Icononzo in the mountainous Tolima region, seeking greater isolation and self-sufficiency. For a time, around sixty people lived there.

For years, the commune coexisted uneasily with the Revolutionary Armed Forces of Colombia (FARC). FARC was a Marxist–Leninist guerrilla group formed in 1964 by small farmers and land workers during the Colombian Civil War, after the Colombian military launched an attack on peasants in Marquetalia. At their height, they had more than 20,000 members and controlled large areas of rural territory, operating as a parallel state.

That uneasy coexistence ended in 1999–2000, when a new FARC commander, increasingly paranoid about informants and spies, expelled the commune from their farms. Jenny and her followers fled once again, this time to the outskirts of the mountain town of Pacho, around fifty-five miles from Bogotá.

In July 2000, Jenny's eighteen-year-old grandson, Tristan James – the son of her daughter Becky – decided to return to Icononzo to visit his half-brother, who was being fostered in the nearby village of Hoya Grande. After that, he planned to return to Ireland for a gap year. Despite warnings, he travelled with another young man, Javier Novoa.

Both were seized by a drunken local FARC militia patrol, accused without evidence of collaborating with right-wing paramilitaries, subjected to a crude show trial, and brutally killed – reportedly stabbed, decapitated and their bodies burned to terrorise the village. The murders destroyed any remaining illusion of safety.

Arthur Janov was long dead, and I assumed Jenny and her daughter Becky would be equally unreachable. But somewhere in a sprawl of old blogs and letters, I found an email address and, without much hope of a response, I pinged Jenny a message. I wondered what Jenny and any remaining Screamers – some of the earliest advocates of screaming your lungs out for cathartic effect – make of football fans screaming on the terraces. In their view, would this have a therapeutic effect?

Her reply arrived quickly, brisk as a slammed door.

'I really don't think we have any way of getting involved in this. We are mainly women and wouldn't have any empathy at all with the weird phenomenon of spectator sports!'

I replied, politely: Why 'weird'? Why no empathy? Did she not realise women enjoyed football too?

Jenny came back a few minutes later:

'Damien, there is a massacre going on in Palestine. Perhaps you haven't heard about it???!!!! I have hated football and all sports all my life. You're talking to the wrong person.'

I thanked her but persisted. One of the reasons I was writing this book was to understand the tribal impulses that led to hatred, from the terraces to Palestine. I said I was surprised she didn't see a connection between her primal work and football fans screaming their larynxes raw. I tried again:

'Everyone says it's interesting seeing men "express emotions" in stadiums? Could this be a deep group therapy?'

Jenny was having none of it.

'I live up a mountain,' she hammered back. 'There is no phone. I do not use WhatsApp. I have a farm to run and breakfast to make for workers arriving at 7 a.m. I do not want further contact. There are issues of huge importance round every corner in this sad and sorry world. Please look elsewhere. 6.30 a.m. jj.'

I assumed that was that. But a few minutes later, I got a follow-up referring to fans screaming on the terraces: 'Acting out is NOT deep therapy.'

And then the deluge began – not from Jenny, but from some of her followers, all now looped into the same email thread.

Becky, her daughter and Tristan's mum, introduced herself as 'a masseur and counsellor to people damaged by the criminal "VAXXine"', and informed me that football fans should know the game originated with kicking human heads around after tribal battles. As evidence, she forwarded a ChatGPT printout describing medieval soldiers booting Danish skulls across fields.

The subject line to the thread had shifted from my wording of *Emotion of Football Fandom and Your Work* to: *Present-Day Use of Heads as Footballs.*

Then someone called Ian weighed in. I think he was back in the UK. He'd been at a Gaza protest, he said, and on his way there had encountered a swarm of football fans at Charing Cross chanting so loudly it was 'deafening', a perfect example of mass delusion. From the date I could tell he was referring to Crystal Palace fans after their FA Cup final win against Manchester City at Wembley.

'Must be peaceful up your mountain,' he wrote to Jenny.

I tried to bow out gracefully – 'Sounds like you're definitely not fans. Thanks for your input. Enjoy your breakfast.'

But they weren't finished. Another notification pinged. The subject line now read: 'Top of the Weirdo List', which I assumed was referring to me.

Becky again:

'Does he not know that all SPORT is a deliberate superficial invention to keep people away from real news and issues. B.'

At this point I really was ready to pursue other avenues – Roland Orzabal? Yoko Ono? – anyone less furious about the concept of a football. And then an email arrived from someone else who had been included on Jenny's email round. His name was Robin de Brea and he had been one of the first Screamers. He had married another of Jenny's daughters, Snowy.

Unbelievably, a week before he sent his email to me he'd been to the Amex stadium in Brighton to watch them beat Wolves 2-0. He'd supported Wolves for sixty-four years.

'I am absolutely satisfied that attending football matches and screaming one's head off is a very therapeutic experience,' he said in his email. We agree to meet.

44

Robin the Screamer

It's 1963, and Robin is twelve years old and travelling alone to Molineux from Essex. He travels by a series of buses and trains, without supervision. He's escaping a home where emotions aren't allowed – certainly not from him. He's looking for a place where noise is permitted. A place where he can howl.

As he walks from the station, he hears it already – a low, distant roar. The closer he gets, the louder it becomes, waiting and ominous, until the sound is vibrating through his chest. Then he sees it, the stadium, an outrageous alien spacecraft that's crash-landed among terraced houses and bus stops.

He pushes through the turnstiles and on to the terraces, up on his toes among men packed shoulder to shoulder, shouting, swearing, swaying, grabbing each other by the neck. Beer slops. Spit flies. Some don't bother with the gents – they just turn and piss where they stand, steam rising, greeted with laughter and cheers. Nobody tells him to quieten down here. Nobody asks him to explain himself. For ninety minutes, feeling too much isn't a problem and Robin loves it.

Six decades on, a few days after my awkward exchange with Jenny, Robin appears on my screen. He's seventy-four now. He chose Wolves aged ten after being drawn to a wolf on an old cigarette card. He has wavy, shoulder-length grey hair. Fabric bracelets crowd his wrists and he's in a grey hoodie. He studied at the universities of Kent and Surrey, then drove buses for a living. Four years ago he got married.

Robin was involved with the Atlantis commune for ten years, from 1979 while it was based in Ireland. Snowy propositioned him during a retreat in Scotland. She was beautiful, fearless and unconventional. The sexual chemistry, he says, was mind-blowing. But Snowy refused monogamy from the outset, telling him she would be with whoever she wanted, whenever she wanted.

At Atlantis, sexual freedom was encouraged and, alongside the group screaming sessions and the ritualised bashing of mats, things often tipped into violence. Robin was hospitalised several times – usually after attacks by Snowy.

'How did she hurt you?' I ask.

'Chisels, fire grates. Broken bottles . . . you know.'

He looks away, as if the list might carry on without him.

Then he smiles.

'She was beautiful,' he says. 'We had the most exquisite times together.'

I tell him about my exchange with Jenny – how she loathes football – and Robin smiles again.

'Jenny is *not* a nice person,' he says, fondly. 'But she's one of the very few people I know who has the willingness to be outrageous.'

'Our relationship is good,' he adds, 'unless I provoke her.' He looks seriously into the camera.

Atlantis could be destructive – he doesn't deny that. But he also believes it woke him up. As a child, he'd been diagnosed with schizophrenia, suffering long spells of psychosis. He sees his psychotic symptoms as the natural consequence of being in an emotional straitjacket as a youngster. Atlantis, for all its chaos, loosened something and gave his emotions somewhere to go.

Like Mark, the opera-singing hooligan, Robin believes football fans need somewhere to discharge pain and emotion. Most of us move through life on autopilot, people-pleasing and placating authority.

'You've never really said yes,' he tells me, 'until you've learned how to say NO.'

Shouting and screaming at football matches are a way to voice what he calls a 'big NO'.

When we can't learn to say no for ourselves, it gets outsourced. People start looking for someone else to do it on their behalf, often loud, unsophisticated, populist figures.

What Robin seems to be suggesting is that football fandom remains one of the few remaining places to offer a sanctioned 'fuck you' to the establishment. It is a ritualised, time-limited space for cathartic mischief, where anger, grievance, identity and defiance can be expressed. Robin agrees with Mark that we may have been civilised out of our emotions – and our tribal instincts. He alludes to the maverick Scottish psychiatrist R.D. Laing, who argued that madness can sometimes be a sane response to an insane world.

Laing co-founded Kingsley Hall in East London in 1965. The solid red-brick former community centre looked municipal and austere from the outside, sitting hard against the street – but inside it was chaotic. There were mattresses scattered across bare floors, furniture was broken or dragged aside, walls were written on or smeared, and the air was heavy with the smells of cigarette smoke and unwashed bodies. There was shouting at all hours, crying, singing, long silences punctured by sudden noise; visitors described it as both mesmerising and unbearable. There were no locked doors, no compulsory medication, no hierarchy between doctors and patients. People diagnosed with mental illness lived there alongside therapists, artists and visitors. Sometimes patients were given LSD, which was kept in the fridge, and was legal at the time. Laing lived there himself, often drunk. Sean Connery, a friend and admirer of Laing's, was among celebrities who would visit to see the project and its residents. At least two people jumped off the roof and the building was raided by the drugs squad.

Laing conceded that Kingsley Hall underestimated how much containment people needed. At Kingsley there were no real bounds, unlike the ritualised chaos of a football match, with shared rules and a final whistle after ninety minutes. But Robin's basic idea is that fandom – with its licensed screaming, crying and hugging – may be one of the few remaining places where the modern world still allows us to be fully, inconveniently human.

Robin has a strong caveat though. For him we need to be conscious of what we're doing when we lose our minds on the terraces – or wherever we're watching from. We need to know that we are being *consciously* unrestrained. Without that, expression can tip into cruelty, as it did with Alfie, and Paul, and Dale, or self-harm, if you're just screaming at the TV on your own, like me. Alcohol and drugs make that line harder to see, let alone hold.

For Robin, screaming at football matches is how he gives himself permission to feel alive.

'I like to feel my body and my emotions in action,' he says.

Then he pauses.

'Just talking about it now,' he adds, 'I can feel myself lifting.' His shoulders roll back. His chest expands. His wife coasts into frame behind him, looking for something.

'YEAH,' he suddenly shrieks, starting to gyrate.

I laugh.

'YEAH,' he shrieks again, louder.

I laugh again, now slightly trapped.

'YEAH, YEAH, YEAH,' he continues, gathering momentum. At this point I'm not entirely sure what the correct response is. Should I join in?

I offer up a timid 'yeah', which is immediately drowned out by Robin.

'YEAH, YEAH, YEAH,' he screams, his arms flung wide, as if he wants me to vault into them through the laptop screen.

'I LOVE it,' Robin says, glowing. 'There's nothing wrong with enjoying mass hysteria – as long as you don't act it out on anyone else.'

* * *

The legacy of Freud and the Screamers continues to show up in the emergence of rage rooms. These are rooms where people can go in alone or with others and smash the shit out of things. Music blares loudly in the background.

But not everyone is convinced that catharsis works at all. Brad Bushman, a professor at Ohio and one of the world's leading experts on catharsis, is sceptical. He's conducted a series of studies that he argues dismantle catharsis theory altogether – and, by extension, threaten the comforting idea that football fans are getting something healthy out of shouting themselves hoarse on a Saturday afternoon.

In one experiment, he recruited around six hundred male and female participants and asked them to write a short essay about abortion – whether they were for it or against it. They were then told they'd been paired with another participant and would exchange essays to critique each other's work. In reality, there was no partner. When the essays were returned, they had been savaged by the experimenters. 'This is one of the worst essays I have read!' The aim was to make people furious.

Some of the smarting essay-writers were then handed boxing gloves and left alone in a room with a punching bag. If catharsis theory held, this should have drained off some of their aggression. Others were told to sit quietly for two minutes and do nothing at all. Afterwards, everyone was given the chance to administer a loud noise blast to the person they believed had written the brutal critique of their essay. They were told their partner was in another room. Participants could choose the volume – from 60 decibels, roughly the level of an electric toothbrush, to 105 decibels, comparable to a power saw or standing near a helicopter. Even brief exposure at the highest level can cause permanent hearing damage.

The result dealt a blow to catharsis theory. Those who had supposedly worked out their anger on the punching bag did not become less aggressive. Instead, they blasted their imaginary partners louder and for longer than those who had done nothing at all. Brad suspected that anything that raises physiological arousal is unhelpful for purging pent-up emotion, including intense physical activity like running and weight training.

So, did Brad think football fans were actually making their pent-up aggression worse? I catch him briefly before he heads out to protest Trump's cuts to university research funding. He stands up and shows me his red woolly jumper that reads STAND UP FOR SCIENCE. His white goatee frames lips pressed tight with anger. Like Professor Wilco van Dijk, he's a big Ajax fan.

I ask what he makes of fans screaming their lungs out at games, and the idea that this is somehow healthy. He takes off his glasses and rubs them.

'Well,' he says, 'it feels good. But it's actually not healthy at all.

'There's not a shred of scientific evidence that venting anger makes it go away. It just makes it worse.'

He pauses.

'How do you become good at anything?' he asks me.

'Practice?'

'Exactly,' he replies. 'It's the same with anger. When you vent, you're rehearsing aggression.'

Brad explains that anger and aggression are distinct. Anger is the feeling, which is automatic and hard to prevent. Aggression is the behaviour that follows, and that's where we still have some choice. The emotion and behaviour are difficult for us to separate because evolution instinctively links aggression to follow anger very quickly when responding to threat. But these days, we often lash out with aggression, even when we are in no real danger.

'All the yelling you vent at the players,' he says, 'they don't hear you. It's not going to change how they play. It's not very productive.'

When I tell him about Jenny, his eyes widen.

'If your therapist tells you to scream,' he growls, 'or hands you a baseball bat and tells you to start pounding a couch, find a new therapist. Fast. That person isn't familiar with the science.'

Brad believes that even speaking about anger to a friend normally backfires because the friend is just justifying aggressive impulses. Instead, Brad believes we should become as skilful as possible to notice the physiological arousal of anger in our bodies before it escalates too much. Then, instead of venting, we should do anything we can to reduce the arousal; taking deep breaths, yoga, muscle relaxation. Even distraction is helpful. Doing something that is the behavioural opposite of anger is especially helpful.

'Kiss your lover,' he says. 'Pet a puppy. Do something incompatible with aggression.'

I picture the look of horror on my wife's face, the dog rigid with fear, as I lurch across the room towards them, my lips puckered, moments after Wolves concede in extra time.

Eating sensibly is another solution because being HANGRY is a real thing, Brad says. He set up an experiment where he sent married couples home with voodoo dolls and pins. They were instructed to imagine the dolls were their partners and stick in as many pins as they felt like before bed – depending on how angry they were. Partners with low blood sugar stabbed their dolls twice as many times as those whose glucose was in good supply.

45

Synchrony

I could have dismissed Jenny's hatred of football fans – her view that we're all just acting out like lunatics – especially after speaking to Robin. But Brad's perspective threw a spanner in the works. I'd been happily thinking of fandom as a healthy release for repressed emotion, only to be told that it might actually do the opposite – making us more volatile, not less. And yet Robin's account was compelling. I had the strong sense that fandom had genuinely helped him wriggle free of his emotional straitjacket. It felt like experience set against empirical evidence.

Around this time, I was lucky enough to hear a brilliant podcast on chanting at football games by the Glasgow-based professor and sociologist Les Back – another Millwall fan. Les talked about the ritualistic power of chanting, and how songs carry memory across generations. The oldest chant still sung today is probably Norwich City's 'On the Ball, City'. It was first heard on the terraces around 1902 and is still chanted by Canaries fans more than a century later. It's a thread linking supporters to parents, grandparents even great-grandparents.

Les started following Millwall as a teenager. For him, going to the Old Den on Cold Blow Lane was one of the most visceral experiences imaginable. The ground was a place where fans communed with their dockland histories and metabolised loss. More than 80,000 dockland jobs disappeared in the 1960s after container ships replaced smaller vessels and trade moved to deeper-water ports like Tilbury and Felixstowe. The football ground became a place where that collective grief could be held.

He also loved how football, like music, offered a way to move across Millwall's racial chequerboard. It was a chance to step between black and white spaces at a time when, elsewhere in life, that kind of movement was far harder.

I wanted to ask Les whether he thought football fans were simply acting out dangerously, as Jenny and her followers were telling me and as Brad's research suggested.

But first we circled back to something I'd flagged earlier: referees.

Anthropologists say that a hallmark of ritual is that it is causally opaque. It looks purposeful, but it doesn't actually change anything.

People dance for rain, burn incense, chant to the gods, fast and offer goats – but the storm and the harvest don't care.

But what if football fandom is the exception?

What if thirty thousand people chanting and booing in unison really can influence the god on the pitch – the referee?

Les thinks it can. But is there any evidence? The answer appears to be yes.

Multiple studies show that refs give more stoppage time, more penalties and more benefit of the doubt to home teams when the crowd is loud.

In one study, forty qualified referees ranging from newcomers to veterans were shown clips of tackles and challenges from a Premier League match between hosts Liverpool and away team Leicester.

They were asked to judge whether each incident was a foul.

Half the referees watched the footage accompanied by the sound of crowd noise; the other half viewed the same clips in silence.

Those hearing the roar of the crowd awarded 15.5 per cent fewer fouls against the home team. The noise appeared to shape decision-making.

Then came the Covid-19 pandemic and what became known as 'ghost games', where all matches continued without the roar of the crowd. It turned empty, silent football stadiums into giant laboratories where researchers dug deeper into the impact of a crowd on refereeing decisions. A review of all the studies carried out at the time showed that referees became more neutral. The probability of yellow cards against away teams decreased by nearly twenty per cent in some studies and more penalties were awarded for visiting sides. Home advantage virtually collapsed. In many leagues it dropped by half.

The impact of the crowd was so profound that the authors of the review concluded that fans were indeed the 'twelfth man' and should be remunerated like the players if their team won.

More evidence came from Germany's Bundesliga, where home advantage has traditionally been lower than in the Premier League. Researchers have suggested this may be because, until relatively recently, many German stadiums featured running tracks that kept supporters at a physical distance – like moats, absorbing the crowd's intimidation before it could reach the referee.

Neuroscience suggests that referee bias is down to *fear* rather than corruption. Refs were put in brain scanners to see what happened to them when crowds boo decisions.

The researchers discovered that a wall of boos sets off an involuntary alarm in the referee's brain. It's called Error-Related Negativity (ERN). It's the brain's way of saying *you've messed up,* triggering a small drop in dopamine, the chemical that governs reward and learning. That dip hurts and the brain wants to make the feeling stop, so the referee unconsciously corrects course on the next foul. It's the brain's way of appeasing the mob. What was also interesting was that the mistake radar spiked less intensely in referees with more experience. Their brains appeared to be less reactive to disapproval, and they were therefore less likely to change behaviour. Inexperienced participants, by contrast, showed larger ERN responses and were more easily swayed – effectively seeking the dopamine 'reward' of crowd approval. Experience seems to teach referees how to stand firm, even with 30,000 people demanding otherwise.

* * *

There's one more wrinkle to home advantage. Home players tend to show higher levels of testosterone than their visitors.

In 2003, psychologists Nick Neave and Sandy Wolfson at Northumbria University took saliva samples from the men's Under-19 Sunderland team before games with Newcastle and Middlesbrough.

They found that the footballers' testosterone levels were significantly higher before home games than away ones. Players show the same biological pattern as chimpanzees preparing to defend their patch.

And while testosterone levels in Sunderland players increased before playing both Middlesbrough and Newcastle at home, they peaked during the fixture against Newcastle, their closest and fiercest rivals. It seems that defending the territory against the enemy next door comes with a heightened endocrine signature. Neave and Wolfson also noted that, on average, strikers had the highest testosterone levels, compared to other positions, wondering if this was because they were the designated hunters.

Yet there was one occasion when the Sunderland goalkeeper had the highest testosterone levels of all. It was when Sunderland were playing Newcastle at home. It led the researchers to speculate that this was because the home goalkeeper represented the last line of defence.

* * *

I tell Les about Jenny and her cronies in Colombia. He scratches his chin and fiddles with his gold-rimmed glasses. His head is shaved and he's wearing a lumberjack shirt. By the look on his face, he doesn't agree with them.

'That is *not* acting out,' Les insists. 'It's not an unregulated experience. It's contained. You're alongside others. The release happens within parameters.'

He pauses, then shakes his head, looking more offended by the second.

'It's not like being alone and thinking, "What do I do now?"' he says. 'There's both a letting go – and a standing together.'

He hugs himself. 'You're being held because you're literally alongside each other.'

Les agrees that me screaming at the TV is probably not a healthy form of catharsis. Solitary walloping of a punchbag, as in Brad's study, wouldn't do the trick either. Real catharsis, he thinks, needs other people. And it isn't confined to what happens inside the stadium – it's the aftercare too: the conversations on the bus or train home, the post-match pint, the gallows humour after defeat.

It made me wonder what would have happened if the essay writers in Brad's experiment hadn't been left alone. If they'd been surrounded by other furious essay writers, all nursing the same brutal feedback. If they'd punched bags together. What would the noise blasts have looked like then?

'We don't go to the football just to watch the game,' Les says. 'If that was all we wanted, we could sit at home with a very nice plasma screen, every camera angle, every minute detail. We go to be with others. It's a whole chain of human connectedness.'

Les tells me about a young fan who used to sit next to him at Millwall's New Den. He was blind.

'He came with his dad,' Les says. 'He wasn't watching the game. He was feeling it.'

Les's point – that football is something you feel with other people, not just see – reminded me of Andy Godfrey, a 76-year-old Brentford supporter I met earlier in the year. Andy was born blind. He's very funny. His parents were first cousins, but doctors reassured them, blindness was a one-in-a-million chance.

He grins widely, as if about to deliver a punchline.

'Five years later, my brother was born blind too.' He doesn't resent the doctors, or his parents. 'Blindness comes with many gifts,' he says.

We met at his home in Ashford and walked to Costa Coffee for a cheese and tomato toastie. Andy played football at school with a ball that rattled – 'we spent most of the time kicking the shit out of the other players' – went on to Oxford, and became a French and German teacher. Football raised his kudos amongst the kids.

'They went, "Good Lord – a blind guy talking about football."'

He's been going to Brentford for decades. He listens to the same commentator and sits in the same part of the stand every week. The repetition makes him feel contained and connected. When Brentford win, people beep their horns at him on Ashford High Street. They shout, 'Well done, Andy.'

He remembers one match above all. It was the 1995 play-off semi-final against Huddersfield, which Brentford lost on penalties.

'I could hear men crying all around me,' he says. 'People crying without shame.'

He pauses.

'The emotion was contagious. I'll never forget that.'

Les introduces me to the idea of collective effervescence, a term I hadn't come across before. It was coined by the sociologist Émile Durkheim and describes the surge of shared emotion that emerges when people gather in crowds. Individuals feel lifted out of themselves, absorbed into something larger, energised by synchronised movement, sound and attention. The boundary between self and group blurs. Durkheim believed this heightened state helped create social bonds, shared meaning and a sense of belonging.

I started to wonder whether Brad and Jenny were missing something really important. What if being swept up emotionally in a football crowd wasn't dysregulating at all, but profoundly organising? What if, rather than losing control, fans temporarily bind together – their nervous systems syncing into something larger, a single regulating, pulsating, metabolising organism?

* * *

Every 23 June, in the small Spanish village of San Pedro Manrique, a firewalking ritual takes place as part of the festival of San Juan. The village has only about six hundred residents, but on the night of the ritual, thousands gather in a purpose-built amphitheatre on the hillside. It holds up to three thousand people.

Villagers cross a bed of glowing oak embers about seven metres long, still burning at close to 700°C. The ritual was observed by the anthropologist Dimitris Xygalatas.

He and his colleagues fitted heart monitors to firewalkers and their relatives in the crowd, as well as to other spectators, to see how their bodies responded.

They were all monitored for about forty minutes – during the walk itself, as well as beforehand and in the immediate aftermath.

Each firewalker showed a distinctive pattern of heart-rate changes during the ritual, a personal rhythm. The peaks and troughs did not just depend on where the person was on the fire walk; the heart rate was unique to them.

What was extraordinary was that these distinctive heart-rate patterns were mirrored almost exactly by their close relatives who were only watching. Unrelated spectators showed no such synchrony.

It was as if the bodies of these biologically fused individuals had joined into a single system – two hearts beating to the same rhythm, even when separated by metres of space.

Xygalatas and his colleagues argue that this kind of synchrony acts as social glue. As we saw earlier, the hormone oxytocin may provide some of that stickiness. But it isn't just about bonding. When our heart rates rise and fall together, our emotional states begin to align as well. We become regulated by one another. Synchrony pulls individuals into a shared emotional field.

But would we see synchrony appear in football fans?

Xygalatas also tracked physiological arousal using heart rate monitors in fans of Atlético Mineiro in Brazil. He found significant synchrony among the fans, especially during highly charged ritualistic moments; for example, chanting as the team bus arrived, and banging drums.

Even the team's bus driver, contained safely in the vehicle as it crept through a mass of chanting fans, banging drums and setting off flares, showed the same heart-rate fluctuations as the crowd outside. His body had fallen into rhythm with theirs, because he belonged to their tribe.

I wondered whether my nervous system might also benefit from the crowd synchrony, even though I was watching the game on my own at home. At last, I would have a justification for returning again and again, even when we'd lost eleven games on the trot.

I couldn't find a football study, but Martha, whom we met earlier, and Harvey investigated the difference between going to the stadium and watching on TV, using basketball fans.

UConn Huskies fans inside the arena in Connecticut were fitted with heart monitors, as were fans watching remotely. The findings were not encouraging for me.

The heartbeats of fused fans in the stadium lined up with each other and stayed that way throughout the game – even during half-time. Those watching remotely were out of sync.

My solitary rants at the television were not binding me to a larger organism. They were not elevating my nervous system into some collective rhythm. They were merely alarming the dog, unsettling the family and dysregulating me.

I was doing football wrong.

* * *

As well as the emotional regulation of the ritual, Les believes football provides much-needed structure in an uncertain world. This is also a form of regulation.

The social spaces that provided structure in the past – churches, the workplace, even pubs – are thinning out. The rhythms that used to organise our weeks have loosened. Humans dislike uncertainty. We crave pattern. Football with its weekly fixture list, pre-match rituals, familiar faces and venues provides anchoring.

The same need for structure shows up constantly in my clinical work. Obsessive-compulsive disorder (OCD) is characterised by intrusive thoughts – often violent, sexual or catastrophic – and the urge to perform highly ritualised actions to neutralise the anxiety they provoke. Washing, checking, counting, repeating phrases silently. The behaviours are rigid, repetitive and redundant. And yet, if someone with OCD is prevented from performing them, anxiety can spike to unbearable levels. Football players do the same thing; the former Chelsea keeper Thibaut Courtois was reported to perform pre-match rituals which included texting his girlfriend to say he was going to get changed, removing his shoe and left sock first, sending a selfie of him on the toilet to four friends, wetting the tip of his goalkeeping glove, and kicking the right post, then the left.

Personally, I'd be too knackered to play after all that. But it seemed to work for him.

'Afterwards,' he said, 'I'm in a trance and nobody can destabilise me.'

* * *

Les disagrees with the Screamers Jenny, Becky and Ian – that football crowds are unruly mobs. In his view, crowds operate with subtle, unwritten rules – a form of self-policing about what is acceptable. We talk about where those lines sit. About what can and can't be said. I tell him about conversations I've had with people who were shamed out of the game, like Alfie Perkins and Dale.

Football fandom, Les argues, opens up an alternative public world where ordinary social protocols fall away. As Kallum Nix said, fans chant things they would never say elsewhere. That permission – to offend, to provoke, to ignore polite norms – generates a charge that is both exhilarating and dangerous.

Like comedy, the power lies in flirting with a line between what is acceptable and what is transgressional. Comedians – like football fans – are rewarded for pushing the line and punished for crossing it. Ricky Gervais is an example of someone who creates the tension by standing on the line, pointing at it, ridiculing it and jumping back and forth. He tells jokes about trans people, disability, religion, fat people and childhood cancer. His comedy thrives on suspended norms and shared transgression. Like for football fans, comedians face a fine line. Gervais survives, while Frankie Boyle telling a joke about Katie Price's disabled son gets him into trouble. Jo Brand faced backlash (and a police complaint) after joking about throwing battery acid at politicians. What about football chants? When do they go too far? Is chanting about Phil Foden's mother acceptable in this alternative world? What about chanting about stadium disasters like Hillsborough? Sectarian chants in Scotland? Songs celebrating stabbings, assaults or the physical harm of rivals? When does collective effervescence tip into sadistic dehumanisation – when empathy is overridden and we become unconsciously unhinged?

In 2023, the Crown Prosecution Service updated its prosecution guidance on football-related offences confirming that tragedy-related abuse can be prosecuted as a public order offence. In 2024, an Everton supporter was arrested and banned from games for three years for making gestures at Manchester United fans, mocking the Munich air disaster in 1958.

Les believes there's a danger that we project our own capacity for cruelty on to convenient 'folk devils' like Alfie and Dale, without properly examining ourselves. He reminds me of what Paul Gilbert says about having tricky brains with the potential for the nastiest cruelty of any species on the planet.

'Those extreme cases often contain things that are familiar,' Les thinks. 'Ordinary. That's the unsettling part. It's easy to say these people are monsters. But when you look closely, there's often a great deal of ordinary life in the hinterlands of that extreme moment.'

46

Roxy the Brat

It's five in the morning and I'm trying to set up a profile on a sadomasochistic fetish website called FetLife.

After chatting with Les, I'd had a brief exchange with a Millwall fan called Paul Bleakley. Paul is a criminologist and the author of one of my favourite research paper titles of all time: 'Football hooliganism, the death drive and Millwall fandom as symbolic masochism'. We'd been talking about how football fans sometimes form a kind of masochistic identity around being hated by others – or around being perpetually rubbish. Millwall are an obvious case (known of course for their iconic chant, 'No One Likes Us, We Don't Care'), San Marino another.

Masochism, broadly defined, is pleasure – often sexual, but not always – derived from pain, humiliation or submission, whether inflicted by oneself or another. People who practise BDSM often describe it as cathartic and meaningful: a way of feeling something intensely and on purpose. The pain is real, but it's contained and often ritualised. There is an emotional cathartic release that comes from stepping into suffering in a contained space.

I remembered one of Peter Cook's football-manager characters, Alan Latchley, who once described football as 'a cruel mistress', who could leave you bloodied and in tears. Cook, a tormented Leeds fan, was speaking in character, but the line fitted neatly with his wider comic worldview. He was fascinated by the absurd, often painful contracts people enter into willingly – marriages, institutions, patriotism and football clubs. Football was a cruel mistress because it could give you ecstatic pleasure and make you suffer in equal measure.

Part of the appeal of entering into such a contract with a football team, I began to suspect, and as Adam Alter pointed out, is precisely that suffering isn't meaningless. It's a consensual relationship with pain. You know it will hurt you but you enter anyway. That was when I came across a blog by someone calling herself Roxy the Brat.

'What's the difference between a masochist and a football fan?' Roxy asks.

'Isn't watching any sporting event the same as locking yourself into a cage? You're stuck, adhered to the screen, you can't turn away no matter how bad it gets and there's no getting out until the final second has ticked off the clock. And don't get me started about stress positions.' The only problem was that in order to get hold of her I had to join the FetLife community. So I'm sitting in my dressing gown, tapping away, trying to make myself a profile. I need to upload an avatar and I Google 'middle-aged 50s cartoon of football fan' but I'm presented with men who appear rested and youthful. At the same time I don't want to come across as some ancient Daddy Dom figure, looming in the digital dark like a leather-clad Gandalf. Roxy might take one look and scroll past.

Eventually I settle on a cartoon of an older-looking Wolves player mid-celebration. Too young still, but just about passable.

The homepage flashes up: 'Stay True to Yourself. Go at Your Own Pace. Consent Matters.' I nod gravely and add the website to my bookmarks bar, next to HMRC and BBC Sport.

The sexual orientations I need to select from are punishing, especially this early. I've had all the diversity training but the field seems to evolve faster than I can track and deciding one sends me into a brief ontological panic.

- Noetisexual
- Benignosexual
- Fraysexual
- Aceflux
- Graysexual
- Reciprosexual
- Aegosexual
- Autochorisexual

To name but a few. I find myself hovering over reciprosexual. Someone who only feels sexual attraction after learning the other person is attracted to them.

My wife pops her head in. We're selling the house and she wants to print a utility bill.

'What are you looking at?' she asks.

'Nothing,' I say, defensively. 'I'm on a fetish website.'

It goes silent.

'I'll explain later,' I add. 'It's research.'

As soon as the word 'research' leaves my mouth I regret it. I've worked with sexual offenders and 'research' is what child molesters say in court when caught with something unspeakable on their hard drive.

She drops the bill on the desk and backs out of the room slowly, still peering over my shoulder.

I track Roxy down. There are dozens of pictures of her in sexual poses. In some, she looks utterly at peace. In others the gear is gone and she's lounging in sports kit in salubrious bars, sipping malt whisky. Then there's one where she's towering over a grey-haired man – taped mouth, knees bent, tiny black pants – while she poses, confident and dominant, draped in a football shirt. Is that a Man City top?

I send her a message and she agrees to meet with me online before my dinner that evening.

She has long brown hair pulled back into a ponytail, carefully manicured eyebrows and big attentive brown eyes. She's wearing a black hoodie and has white AirPods in. I was right about her being a Man City fan. She watches games on TV from her home in Nevada. A few feet away from her is a steel cage.

Until relatively recently, Roxy was a business analytics consultant for one of America's top five corporations. She majored in psychology and anthropology; subjects she was drawn to after surviving a difficult childhood. It was the kind of trauma that left her disconnected from her body.

Her talent for analytics was spotted early. During an internship in her twenties, the CEO of a leading company noticed her, fast-tracked her, and before long she was earning serious money. The apartment she shared in New York, though, was small. The space was so compact she had to conduct and lead high-powered meetings by resting her laptop on the steel cage. Anywhere else and the metal bars would creep into frame. She was brilliant at the job and hated it. It was mortifyingly dull. Roxy met her partner five years ago and calls him dad. She's in her thirties now; he's eleven years older. From a young age, she'd been aware that what she went through in childhood left her feeling numb. But numbness, she learned, isn't emptiness. Underneath it sat sadness. And a deep, restless rage.

Until she found BDSM, Roxy used cocaine to feel something intense enough to cut through the numbness. Alongside a sadomasochistic relationship with her partner, she now earns her living selling clips and working as a domme voice for a BDSM phone sex operator.

'Is it better than the corporate job?' I ask.

'Oh, God, yes,' she says. 'Anything is better than that.'

She admits she sometimes wishes she had more vanilla sexual tastes.

'Normal people just check they've got condoms. We have to ask: where are the keys? Are we using ball gags?'

I nod meekly.

She barrels on with her list. 'Can you breathe? How many chains? How hard are we going? There's a lot to keep track of.'

Roxy's dog, Skylar, makes an appearance and curls up on her lap. She loves dogs. Apart from BDSM and football, rescue dog videos are the one thing guaranteed to make her cry.

For Roxy, the central similarity between BDSM and watching football is that you are consenting to feel emotions deeply and violently inside a highly structured, ritualised space. You're locked in, she says, but crucially, you still have a choice. You can always walk away – use the safe word, turn the TV off, get up, leave. But most of the time you don't. Something pulls you deeper. You're absorbed, suspended, 'trapped and not trapped', willingly putting yourself through a roller coaster that includes real discomfort, even pain.

She's spent a long time asking herself why that kind of intensity feels necessary. The answer, she thinks, is that in most areas of life – especially at work and in social relationships – we're expected to stay within a narrow emotional bandwidth. You can't be wildly manic or devastatingly low. You have to keep yourself functional and socially acceptable. Football and BDSM are two places where that rule collapses. Like Les, Robin and Mark, she agrees they are alternative worlds, where it's OK to feel and scream.

The intensity of football and BDSM also gives participants rare moments of total presence. They are meditative in that sense, utterly absorbing. 'Somebody slaps you in the face,' she says, 'and your brain is like, oh – I'm right here.'

For Roxy, the cage is not only a place to feel intensely, like a stadium – it's a place to surrender control. Just as she willingly hands control to her Master, football fans hand control to the referee and the players, to the Cruel Mistress herself. It's a voluntary surrender, tightly contained – a way of giving yourself over to something else for a fixed stretch of time, because you're tired of holding yourself together.

Roxy reminded me of the phrases used by sports psychologist Eric Dunning, who said football can be understood as a site of 'the controlled decontrolling of emotions', a paradoxical process in which feelings that are usually suppressed – rage, fear, tribal hatred, ecstatic joy – are temporarily loosened but never fully unleashed. Football crowds may appear wild and uncontained, yet this apparent loss of control is held in place by ritual, rules and collective understanding, allowing intensity without anarchy. What looks like chaos is therefore carefully engineered release.

Roxy's seen the same impulse among high-powered businessmen. 'Lord knows I've met them,' she says. 'They've got the plastic bag over their head, and some girl's pissing on their face, and blah blah blah.' People who spend their lives tightly bound – constantly reining themselves in – sometimes crave the opposite. 'It sounds horrible,' she adds, 'but sometimes it's nice having your control taken away.' There's a *mindful mindlessness* to it.

47

I'm Not OK

It's half-time at the Amex where Brighton are hosting Spurs on Saturday, 20 September 2025. Brighton are leading 2-1. Normally, fans would drift off into the concourse or start dissecting the game, arguing over who was at fault for a goal or slagging off the ref.

But right now, they are in a trance.

Nearly everyone is staring at a short film playing on the giant screens. The noise has fallen away. It's eerily quiet, as if the crowd's collective consciousness has been intercepted. It's like a scene from a sci-fi film where the signal cuts through and everyone suddenly listens.

On the screen, two young men are heading to a football match. They're joking, laughing, trading bits of banter on the train, walking into the stadium. But you can tell, somehow, that something isn't right with one of them. There's a slight delay in his smile, a heaviness in his eyes.

The action unfolds as the real stadium stays silent. No one's actually been told to hush, something invisible just keeps them in sync.

Now, on the screen, one of the friends is chanting in the stands. He's chanting, 'I'm not coping. No one sees me.' Tears well up in his eyes. He looks wrecked.

After the game, the two men leave the stadium. Just before they part ways, one asks the other if he's okay. 'I'm fine,' he says, but his friend can see he isn't. He puts an arm around him. 'Come on, you can tell me,' he insists. They walk off together.

In the real stadium, the crowd are still quiet. Then they burst into applause.

I wasn't there, but my friend Jesse from six-a-side on a Thursday was.

'It was one of the weirdest experiences I've ever had,' Jesse tells me before we kick off. I watch the film, made by the Samaritans, and it gives me goosebumps.

48

Football Saved My Life

Richard Perkins, forty-seven, sits with his arms tucked low beneath his desk. I'm speaking with him because he posted on Facebook about the pilgrimages he makes to away games each week. Richard runs Tatter Travels, organising coaches for fellow Wolves fans – routes mapped out, pub stops planned. Sometimes he gets former players on board: Steve Bull, Kenny Hibbitt – dozens over the years.

After Wolves were drubbed 3-0 at Chelsea, he posted a selfie from the coach, fans clustered behind him, with the caption: 'Good day out – the match itself was the only negative.'

Today he looks tired and subdued. Sitting beside him is his Staffordshire Bull Terrier, Indiana. He's telling me about 22 December 2024 – a coachload of familiar faces heading to the King Power Stadium for the Leicester game.

Richard was adopted at birth, taken from parents on a Wolverhampton council estate to one of the grander stately homes in the region. The house came with a helicopter pad, stables, electronic gates, a long gravel driveway and forty-eight acres of land – a world away from the life of his biological parents. His adoptive parents moved in rarefied circles: friends of Sir Jack Hayward, who would later become Wolves owner, and Rachael Heyhoe Flint, then the club's vice-president and captain of England's women's cricket team.

His father, George, took him to his first game at Molineux – Wolves versus Derby, 5 December 1993. Steve Bull scored the opener before going off injured. Wolves were 2-1 down with seconds remaining when David Kelly bundled in a last-gasp equaliser. I watch a short clip of the match on YouTube. Tackles are flying in everywhere. God knows how many players would have been sent off by VAR in the four minutes I saw alone. Richard says he was fused from that moment – one of the most intense memories of his life. He became a season ticket holder at sixteen and never looked back, going to games with his father whenever he could. More recently, he fulfilled his father's ambition to watch Wolves at Old Trafford. Sir Jack once told Richard that if he was ever unhappy with anything at the club, he should do something about it. Richard took him at his word. After Sir Jack sold Wolves in 2007, Richard launched a fan newspaper called *The Tatter*. The aim was to give supporters a voice. He printed it himself and gave it away free from makeshift booths outside the stadium, tethered with gold and black balloons. At first, he sold all the advertising personally, cold-calling local businesses to see if they wanted space. He hated it. So he put the costs on a credit card instead. By the time he stopped, he'd printed 750,000 copies and was £17,000 in debt. He wound the paper down after the club was bought by its current Chinese owners, Fosun, hoping Wolves were now in safe hands – and that he'd kept his side of the bargain with Sir Jack.

Then he set up Tatter Travels, ferrying fans to away games. Sometimes he'd lay on seventeen coaches at once. It never made him a fortune. Any profits went to the local hospice where his mother died at the end of the pandemic. By the time Richard travelled towards the King Power to watch the game with

Leicester, his father was stricken with dementia. As the coach headed along the motorway he took a call on his mobile. He went quiet. He tried to keep it together, but by the pub stop in Ashby-de-la-Zouch he was breaking down.

Wolves won 3-0 that day – the same match that led to my testosterone-fuelled status parade through the church with the dog – and Richard did his best to keep smiling for his customers. But as the coach pulled back into Wolverhampton, he couldn't hold it in any longer. He was in floods of tears. Eventually, he picked up the coach microphone.

'Sorry for being upset today,' he said. 'But if you've seen me cry, it's because my dad passed away this morning on the way to the match.'

The coach stood and applauded. Others hugged him.

Richard says the ritual of going to the football has always given his life structure, but particularly since the death of his parents, when everything felt it was falling apart. He goes because he feels programmed to go.

'We'll moan all through the game, moan all the way back, sing stupid songs about the owners. We actually pay stupid amounts of money to be miserable – but we feel the need to do it.'

He says if it wasn't for the football, he'd be feeling sorry for himself.

He pauses, searching for the right words.

'Everyone's carrying something. And for that day – just that one day – it doesn't matter. It gets put on hold.'

He tells me he's cried and shared more at football than he ever has with friends outside it.

'I don't really understand why,' he says. 'Maybe it's because you all love the same team. Maybe it's because you spend hours together, every other week, going up and down the country. But

I've told things to people I barely know that I've never said to close friends.'

He shakes his head slightly, as if surprised by himself.

'I feel embarrassed crying in front of people who really know me,' he says. 'But there – it's different. It's easier. It's like the football gives you permission.'

* * *

I tell Richard that I'm writing about Paul Mitchell. He remembers him instantly. Then I tell him how it ended.

He goes very still.

For a few seconds, nothing happens. Indiana, his Staffie, shifts at his feet.

'Let me be honest with you,' he says eventually. 'I've been suicidal.'

'Since your dad?'

'Yeah.' He glances down. 'That's why I keep my arms down here.'

He doesn't show me. He doesn't need to.

'It's embarrassing,' he says, almost apologetically. 'But if I didn't have the football, I genuinely don't think I'd be here.'

He nods to himself, as if checking the thought.

'When you said Paul got depressed after he couldn't go to the games any more – after he did bad things – I get that. Completely. Take the football away . . .'

He trails off.

'I wouldn't be here either.'

'Really?' I ask. 'You think it's kept you alive?'

'Yeah,' he says.

He talks about the coaches with the same faces and voices every other week.

'They're my family now,' he says. 'Mum and Dad are gone. So this – this means everything.'

'Well,' I say, 'I'm really glad you're still here, Richard. I really am.'

'It's been close,' he replies. 'Really close.'

EPILOGUE

Harry's Story

Alexandra Park in Hastings is a splendid area spanning over 100 acres unfurling for two and a half miles through the town, and home to some of Britain's most unusual trees. It boasts nine 'champion trees', the largest of their kind in the UK: giant silver-leaved ashes, cypresses, horse chestnuts and weeping American limes, scattered between lakes, tennis courts and winding paths.

Standing beneath a champion horse chestnut tree is Maria. I spot her after parking by the five-a-side pitch where I play football on Thursday nights with a bunch of middle-aged men whose bodies are betraying them. She sees me crossing the lawns with the dog and lifts a hand in greeting. We've never met before. We go to the nearby café.

Maria's son, Harry Dennis, is the eleven-year-old boy whose grave I noticed on my walk near the Saxon church, just as I was embarking on this project. Two weeping girls had arrived before me and placed sports drinks beside the footballs, the Manchester United memorabilia and the small trophies arranged on the stone.

Harry got his first football shirt aged six and turned out to be a gifted player. By seven he was playing central midfield for Hastings Athletic, and by ten he was doing front flips when he scored, his curly blond hair braided like Beckham's or Paul Pogba's. Hastings Athletic played on fields close to the Saxon church, and the family walked the surrounding woods too

– Harry leaping into the stream, swinging from the ropes in Guestling Wood. He loved it there.

He almost never took his football shirts off. He even wore them under his smart clothes at weddings, so he could peel off the formality the moment the speeches were done.

And though he was probably the best player on the pitch, Maria tells me one of his teachers once said the thing that stood out most about Harry was his humility and kindness. When he played for the school team, he always crossed the line to shake hands with the opposition first. He seemed to understand, instinctively, that football was an opportunity for connection.

On 14 December 2022, Harry stayed up late to watch his hero, Kylian Mbappé – a fellow number ten – playing for France in the World Cup semi-final against Morocco. France won 2-0.

Harry loved watching football, but he had 'ants in his pants' and found it hard to sit still. Sometimes he watched matches upside down, balanced on his head.

On the morning of 15 December, he was still asleep when Maria left for work. She hadn't wanted to wake him after his late-night viewing of the World Cup game.

She left a note on the kitchen table: 'Morning, mate. I've gone to work. I didn't want to wake you because you had a late night watching the football. I'll see you after work. Love you best in the whole world, Mum.'

Harry's dad, Lee, was taking their daughter to a hospital appointment that day, and Harry went along for the ride. Snow had fallen overnight. Lee drove the VW Passat along the country lanes towards Eastbourne, Harry in the front seat, 'jabbering away' about the snow.

Coming around a bend, there was a terrible impact. A flatbed truck was approaching from the other direction, driven by a scaffolder. One of the wooden boards had not been properly secured. It came loose, smashed through the windscreen and struck Harry in the neck.

He was flown to King's College Hospital by air ambulance. Two days later, he died. The scaffolder driving the lorry was later jailed for four years for causing death by dangerous driving.

Maria and Lee absorbed the catastrophe differently. Lee wept. Maria went numb. One night in January she found herself on Hastings beach, the sea sliding over her ankles in the dark, the cold working its way up her legs. Friends found her there and wrapped her in warm clothes and took her home.

The football community gathered around them. Gifts and flowers appeared on their doorstep. Matches were dedicated to Harry. His number 10 shirt was retired. Young players wore black armbands stitched with HD10.

When the team won the league a year after his death, the title was dedicated to him too. Children and parents cried together on the pitch.

It was the love of that football family – and the love for the family she still had – that kept Maria going.

She tells me something strange happened a week before he died. For reasons she can't remember, the subject of death came up. They began talking about organ donation and Harry looked repulsed by the idea, as any child might. Maria explained that many children could not play or even watch football like he did because they were too sick or too badly injured. Harry changed his mind and his organs have since saved the lives of five people.

Maria has gone on to campaign successfully for changes in the law around awareness and training for drivers carrying loads in smaller lorries.

She wanted Harry buried somewhere he belonged. The family lived outside the church parish and they were not observant. Still, she begged the vicar to let Harry be buried in the graveyard, close enough to the pitches that you can hear the children playing. The parish held a vote and agreed unanimously. He was buried with a football and his boots.

It has taken me a few years to write this book, and I walk past Harry's grave at least twice a week. I have watched it change with the seasons: Manchester United-coloured bouquets in spring; ribbons and scarves in summer; pumpkins painted like footballs in autumn; a Christmas tree hung with tiny footballs in winter.

And always the Prime drinks he loved so much, appearing again and again, set down beside him to keep him refreshed.

'It's just so peaceful down there,' Maria says, as we reach the end of our conversation. 'If you ever want to chat with him about football, he's there.'

That afternoon, I go back to the church for my walk. Beneath the tree by Harry's grave is a new bench with his name engraved. I sit on it and reflect upon this strange, magnificent game.

Acknowledgements

Many thanks to all the friends, family and colleagues who have tolerated me and encouraged me to keep going with this project. I'd especially like to thank my brilliant agent Rob Dudley and my fabulous editor at Oneworld, Cecilia Stein. I roped in nearly all of my friends to read through bits of the manuscript but some took the hit more than others. So a special thank you to Dan Britcher, John Hodgson, Neil Johnston, Mark Mukerji, my sister Fiona, Mum, Dad and brother Ben. Thanks to Anna Dudley – my other lovely sister-in-law – who provided so much calming hospitality throughout this process and to Mark Sheerin for preventing me from completely flipping out one day, as did Dan Hind, Rob Blyth and Rob Blayney. Without my friend Alex Watts, I would not have started and he came up with the name for the first section: 'The Man Who Punched Jack Grealish'. Thanks also to Andrew Rees for his creative and technical brilliance and support. Thanks to Sam J, who has been bugging me to write this book for years (I told you I'd get round to it).

I took a while trying to find a football widow in this book, but one thing I definitely did create was a book widow. Thank you to Harriet, my wife, for tolerating my absence for so long, for all the scones, and reassurance, and love.

References and Further Reading

Introduction: The Unravelling of a Grown Man

For those looking to steady their nervous systems through breathing, the Balanced Minds website offers some very good Soothing Rhythm Breathing scripts.

PART I: The Man Who Punched Jack Grealish

Chapter 1: Anyone Out There?

I'd like to thank the fans on Facebook – and the long-suffering wife of one of them – who inspired me to write this book, especially Andrew Caddick (watching from Detroit) and John Wilson (who travels from Cardiff and once moved higher up in the stadium to stop himself behaving like a 'dipstick').

Chapter 2: The Punch

Footage of the punch and Grealish's interview can be viewed on YouTube.

I am grateful to Debbie for her hospitality and honesty during such a difficult time, and to Hayley as well. I hope I have done justice to Paul's complexity and humanity.

Chapter 3: Face Slashed

For a fuller court report of the incident, you can read the online BBC report: 'Jack Grealish: Birmingham City fan jailed for pitch attack' (11 March 2019).

The *Sun*'s full online story is headlined: *HOOLIGAN IN HIDING: Jack Grealish thug Paul Mitchell goes to ground after sick knife attack image goes viral on Twitter – but he still 'won't say sorry'* (18 April 2019).

Chapter 4: He Gets Hit Again

Several newspaper articles cover the game and the slap. Pep's 'lack of class' comment can be read on the *Guardian* website under the headline: '"Lack of class": Guardiola hits out at United fans' chant about Foden's mother' (6 April 2025).

Information about Phil Foden's mum comes from various sources, including a profile featured in an online version of the *Sun*, headlined: 'Protective parent: Who is Phil Foden's mum Claire Rowlands?' (7 April 2025).

PART II: Us

Chapter 5: My Brother, the Liverpool Fan

Thank you to my sister-in-law Alice for her amazing cooking and gentleness, and to all of my wife's family for tolerating my football meltdowns over the years. For the record, I love my brother – I'm just not a fan of his football allegiance.

Chapter 6: Children and Chimpanzees

The chimp study can be accessed here: Horner, V., & Whiten, A. (2005). 'Causal knowledge and imitation/emulation switching in chimpanzees (*Pan troglodytes*) and children (*Homo sapiens*)', *Animal Cognition*, 8, 164–81.

I learned about CREDs from the anthropologist Joseph Henrich, particularly through his book: *The Secret of Our Success* (Princeton University Press, 2016).

Sports psychology professor Dan Wann was extremely helpful during this section. I can recommend his 'bible' on sports psychology: *Sport Fans: The Psychology and Social Impact of Fandom* (Routledge, 2025). The stages of attachment to teams have also been researched by Daniel Funk and Jeff James, who introduced the term the *Psychological Continuum Model (PCM)* in 2008.

The information on children choosing teams through video games came from a survey by the European Football Clubs (EFC), titled *The Future of Fandom.* It contains many other interesting facts and figures about the changing face of football fandom and can be accessed online.

Chapter 7: When the Team Becomes Me

For more information on identity fusion there is no better book than Harvey Whitehouse's *Inheritance: The Evolutionary Origins of the Modern World* (Hutchinson Heinemann, 2024). Thanks also to Harvey for sending me a helpful email when I had to cancel our meeting because I had flu and explaining I was pretty much doomed to support Wolves for evermore.

I learned more about Jim Jones and the massacre in Guyana from the Stanley Nelson-directed documentary *Jonestown: The Life and Death of Peoples Temple* (2006).

Gary Neville reflects on Sir Alex Ferguson in the MUTV interview 'Gary Neville: Seven things that made Ferguson great' (4 June 2024).

Chapter 8: Flirting at a Carol Service

Thanks to Martha Newson, one of the first academics I consulted on this project, whose early encouragement inspired me to continue. She hosts a webpage showcasing her publications, and her compelling Nudgestock talk on belonging, 'The Power of "Us"', can be found on YouTube.

Chapter 9: The Man in the Stetson

A special thanks to Holly Baker and Guy Butters for setting this up, and to Chris and Jenny for keeping us entertained. Thanks to the fans with dementia who allowed me to be there. You can read more about Albion Memories on the Brighton & Hove Albion Foundation website.

The Alzheimer's Society has more information on reminiscence therapy on its website. If you're worried about dementia – for yourself or someone else – the charity can be contacted on 0333 150 3456. To fundraise or for general enquiries, call 0330 333 0804.

Chapter 10: Back in the Dock

More details of the court case can be read on the *Birmingham Mail* website under the headline: 'Birmingham City fan Paul

Mitchell who punched Jack Grealish jailed again for breaching football ban' (6 September 2022).

Chapter 11: The Blue Girl

Huge thanks to the Iranian activist Sara and psychologist Dr Fahimeh Mianji for filling me in on the background to this story. As of writing in May 2026, Sara and her family are safe in Iran. Additional information was sourced from online articles written by Amnesty International, the BBC and the *Guardian*. Thank you to podcaster Adele Jackson-Gibson for helping me connect with Sara.

Chapter 12: Cup Upset at Blundell Park

It was a pleasure to speak with Bill Brewster, who offered a wealth of engaging reflections. I was particularly interested in his anecdote about visiting a nightclub after a match some years ago and seeing a Grimsby player on the podium, clearly high on MDMA.

Thanks also to Peder Clark, who spoke to me about his book chapter 'The "Love Thugs": Ecstasy, Homosociality, and the Decline of Football-Related Violence in 1990s England', which appears in *Pop Cultures and Ecstatic States of the Body Since World War II* (Palgrave Macmillan, 2025). Peder was careful to stress that rave culture was only part of the story. The decline in hooliganism was also shaped by forces such as the move to all-seat stadiums, increased CCTV surveillance, and changes in policing and crowd control.

There is free access to the classic paper investigating oxytocin's dark side: De Dreu, C. K. W., Greer, L. L., Van Kleef, G. A.,

Handgraaf, M. J. J., & Shalvi, S. (2011). 'Oxytocin promotes human ethnocentrism', *Proceedings of the National Academy of Sciences of the United States of America*, 108(4), 1262–66.

The MDMA and oxytocin paper can be read here: Dumont, G. J. H., Sweep, F. C. G. J., van der Steen, R., Hermsen, R., Donders, A. R. T., Touw, D. J., van Gerven, J. M. A., Buitelaar, J. K., & Verkes, R. J. (2009). 'Fusion: Increased oxytocin concentrations and prosocial feelings in humans after ecstasy (3,4-methylene-dioxymethamphetamine) administration', *Social Neuroscience*, 4(4), 359–66.

PART III: Them

Chapter 13: The Delicious Downfall of Bruno Fernandes

Apologies to my mum, sister and nephew for revealing their dark sides.

Chapter 14: Tall Poppies

Thanks to Tiffany for indulging my requests to talk about football when she was very busy moving house. Her book on schadenfreude is hilarious: *Schadenfreude: The Joy of Another's Misfortune* (Little, Brown Spark, 2018).

The puppet theatre study: Mendes, N., Steinbeis, N., Bueno-Guerra, N., et al. (2018). 'Preschool children and chimpanzees incur costs to watch punishment of antisocial others', *Nature Human Behaviour*, 2, 45–51.

I found the information about Grealish being fouled more than anyone else on a website called StatMuse.

The Grealish interview with EA Sports can be found on YouTube, posted by *Soccer AM*, titled 'Does Jack Grealish mind being called a "diver"?'

Chapter 16: The Darker Side of Schadenfreude

Lots more research on schadenfreude can be read in Wilco's book: *Schadenfreude: Understanding Pleasure at the Misfortune of Others* (Cambridge University Press, 2014).

Fans smiling at missed penalties: Boecker, L., Likowski, K. U., Pauli, P., & Weyers, P. (2015). 'The face of schadenfreude: Differentiation of joy and schadenfreude by electromyography', *Cognition and Emotion*, 29(6), 1117–25.

The electric shocks football fans study can be read here: Hein, G., Silani, G., Preuschoff, K., Batson, C. D., & Singer, T. (2010). 'Neural responses to ingroup and outgroup members' suffering predict individual differences in costly helping', *Neuron*, 68(1), 149–60.

Mina Cikara has lots of additional reading and resources on tribalism on her Harvard Intergroup Neuroscience Lab website. She also has a great TEDx talk called 'When "I" Becomes "We"', which can be found on YouTube.

William James quote from: *The Principles of Psychology* (Macmillan, 1891).

Chapter 17: Robbers Cave

The original paper can be read here: Sherif, M. (1956), 'Experiments in group conflict', *Scientific American*, 195(5), 54–9. There is a very interesting take on the experiment in the

Guardian headlined 'A real-life Lord of the Flies: the troubling legacy of the Robbers Cave experiment', published in April 2018.

I was also guided in my thinking about football and perceptual bias by Liverpool supporter Rupert Brown, Emeritus Professor of Psychology at the University of Sussex. Rupert was enormously generous with his time, and his work on Henri Tajfel – a pioneer of intergroup psychology – was invaluable, particularly *Henri Tajfel: Explorer of Identity and Difference* (Routledge, 2019).

Chapter 18: Condolence Page Vigilantes

Thanks to Dr Chrissy Cook for helping me to see the difference between keyboard vigilantes and trolls, among other types of social media aggressors. There was so much more to our conversation I wish I could have included. For more on the links between online trolling and football hooliganism, see Cook, Karhulahti, Harrison, & Bowman (2023), 'Trolligans: Conceptual Links Between Trolling and Hooliganism in Sports and Esports', *Communication & Sport,* 12(1).

Chapter 19: When Hate Finds a Target

Thanks to Alfie Perkins for having the courage to talk with me. Background to the story came from various online news reports at the time.

JCB Story: I still yearn to tell this story – and place the blame squarely on my good friend David Lloyd (who made me do it) – but it was edited out in the last round of cuts.

Troy Deeney's moving life story can be read in *Redemption: My Story* (Cassell, 2022).

Much of the information on Barrington Patterson came from *One-Eyed Baz: The Story of Barrington 'Zulu' Patterson, One of Britain's Deadliest Men* (John Blake Publishing, 2013).

Chapter 20: Deluded by Design

Examples of such studies include: Dunham, Y., Baron, A. S., & Carey, S. (2011). 'Consequences of "minimal" group affiliations in children,' *Child Development*, 82(3), 793–811.

PART IV: Revenge Junkies

Chapter 21: Hunted

A special thanks to everyone who spoke to me in this chapter – Gemma Lowery, Kallum Nix and Dale Houghton. See notes on Chapter 24: Bradley's Legacy for how to donate to the Bradley Lowery Foundation.

Chapter 22: Revenge at the Farmhouse

James Kimmel Jr.'s fascinating book is *The Science of Revenge: Understanding the World's Deadliest Addiction – and How to Overcome It* (Harmony, 2024). James has an accompanying website with lots of resources on it, including links to Revenge Anonymous.

To read more about the role of oxytocin and revenge, you can read: Han, X., Gelfand, M. J., Wu, B., Zhang, T., Li, W., Gao, T., Pang, C., Wu, T., Zhou, Y., Zhou, S., Wu, X., & Han, S. (2021), 'A neurobiological association of revenge propensity during intergroup conflict', *eLife*, 10, e66696.

Chapter 23: Finding a Way Back

Thanks to Dale for talking to me when he could easily have chosen to remain in obscurity.

Chapter 24: Bradley's Legacy

Jack Grealish making Finlay Fisher's dream come true can be seen on a Sky Sports YouTube video, titled '"I call it the Finlay" – The inspiration behind Jack Grealish's World Cup celebration.'

To donate to the Bradley Lowery Foundation to support children and families fundraising for medical treatment or equipment, go to their website. The charity's site also shows pictures of the new holiday home for kids, called 'Super Brad's Pad'.

Thanks to Ben Bird for sharing his powerful story about his conversion to Islam after witnessing the love Liverpool fans showed for Mo Salah and learning about the reported drop in hate crime in Liverpool following the Egyptian's arrival. You can read more about Ben's story on his British Muslim Gentlemen website. I loved our conversation. Up The Saddlers.

PART V: Nightmares in Nairobi

Chapter 25: The Terrible Tale of Suleiman Omondi

A massive thank you to the photojournalist Peterson Githaiga for arranging my security, the reassuring presence of Pineas Mokhara, and the visit into the Pipeline Estate.

Meeting Peterson and Stephen, the taxi driver, were highlights of this project. This part of the book would not have existed without their help. I hope Stephen and Ernesto meet up one day.

Chapter 26: Asunta's Story

I am grateful to Asunta for allowing me into her home and telling her harrowing story. There are several domestic abuse organisations in the UK, including Refuge, whose helpline number is 0808 2000 247.

Chapter 27: Life and Death in Sunderland

Bill Kirkup's paper was a real inspiration for this book. Football being a matter of life and death felt like a solid premise. He also normalised my meltdowns. His paper can be read here: Kirkup, W., & Merrick, D. W. (2003). 'A matter of life and death: Population mortality and football results', *Journal of Epidemiology and Community Health*, 57(6), 429–32.

To read about anger and heart attacks: Buckley, T., Hoo, S. Y. S., Fethney, J., Shaw, E., Hanson, P. S., & Tofler, G. H. (2015). 'Triggering of acute coronary occlusion by episodes of anger', *European Heart Journal: Acute Cardiovascular Care*, 4(6), 493–98.

More can be read about the Wearmouth Colliery on the Durham Mining Museum website, and miners' recollections can be found in an article by Liam Caffry, titled 'Ex-Miners reflect on the miners' strikes in Sunderland 40 years later', on the University of Sunderland's Spark radio station website, dated 8 March 2024.

Chapter 28: 'Real Fans'

A massive thanks to John Price, aka Jack Sparra, who helped me navigate the world of Facebook groups for football fans. John has appeared in a moving short documentary film about men's mental health, produced by Graham Everitt. The video can be seen on Graham's Gap in the Mind website and has been posted by @gapinthemind on the MENTALk YouTube channel. MENTALk runs free meetings for men who are struggling with their mental health – see their website for more information.

Thanks also to Ian Davis, the admin of a separate Wolves Facebook group. He was responsible for kicking Steve out and restoring some self-worth in me for a while. I find that Ian offers a sage perspective on Wolves.

Chapter 29: A Narcissist, Moi?

Cialdini's original study can be found here: Cialdini, R. B., Borden, R. J., Thorne, A., Walker, M. R., Freeman, S., & Sloan, L. R. (1976). 'Basking in reflected glory: Three (football) field studies', *Journal of Personality and Social Psychology,* 34(3), 366–75.

To read the World Cup study involving England fans BIRGing and CORFing: Fan, M., Billings, A. C., Zhu, X., & Yu, P. (2020). 'Twitter-based BIRGing: Big data analysis of English national team fans during the 2018 FIFA World Cup', *Communication & Sport,* 8(3), 317–45.

The obituary study can be read here: Campbell, J., Dandignac, M., Bankert, C., Hall, C., McArthur, K., Sessions, B., & Young, C. (2021). 'Die-hard fans: Selective self-presentation in newspaper obituaries', *Mortality,* 26(1), 112–23.

Ben Larkin's study on narcissism and fair-weather fans can be read here: Larkin, B., Fink, J. S., & Delia, E. (2022). 'Toward a better understanding of fair-weather fandom: Exploring the role of collective narcissism in basking in reflected glory and cutting off reflected failure', *Journal of Sport Management,* 36(6), 575–86.

Chapter 30: Emmanuel's Story

Thank you to Emmanuel for agreeing to speak with me. Also, thanks to the Nairobi-based researcher Mario Schmidt, who spoke to me about football betting in Kenya and masculinity more generally. You can read more about masculinity and 'the pressure of being a man in an African city' in his book *Migrants and Masculinity in High-Rise Nairobi* (Boydell & Brewer, 2024), which features a brilliant picture of the Pipeline Estate on the front.

Michael Kimmel – described by the *Guardian* as 'the world's most prominent male feminist' – was helpful to sanity-check my understanding of masculinity. I enjoyed his book *Angry White Men: American Masculinity at the End of an Era* (Nation Books, 2015).

PART VI: Why Does Football Affect My Mood So Badly?

Chapter 31: Tricky Brain

Paul Gilbert was as close as it gets to being a mentor for me on this project. He kindly met with me twice before breakfast, and his understanding of rank and status provided a backbone for this book. He has written several books on the cultivation of compassion and how it relates to our 'tricky' human brains; they are available on Amazon. He has also delivered many fascinating talks on compassion, which can be found on YouTube. You can find out more about his work on cultivating compassion on the Compassionate Mind Foundation website.

You can read an entertaining account of the blue-balled vervet monkeys by typing 'John Scott Price Biography' into Google.

The testosterone study involving crestfallen Italians can be found here: Bernhardt, P. C., Dabbs, J. M., Jr., Fielden, J. A., & Lutter, C. D. (1998). 'Testosterone changes during vicarious experiences of winning and losing among fans at sporting events', *Physiology & Behavior*, 65(1), 59–62.

For Christian Burk's study referencing female testosterone levels see: Burk, C. L., Mayer, A., & Wiese, B. S. (2019). 'Nail-biters and thrashing wins: Testosterone responses of football fans during World Cup matches', *Physiology & Behavior*, 209: 112596.

The study in Brazil can be read here: Newson, M., Shiramizu, V., Buhrmester, M., Hattori, W., Jong, J., Yamamoto, E., & Whitehouse, H. (2020). 'Devoted fans release more cortisol when watching live soccer matches', *Stress and Health*, 36(1), 108–19.

For the full Obama-masturbation crossover episode, see: Markey, P. M., & Markey, C. N. (2011). 'Changes in pornography-seeking behaviors following political elections: An examination of the challenge hypothesis', *Evolution and Human Behavior*, 32(6), 442–46.

Chapter 32: The Scientist Who Lost His Mojo

Thank you to Alex Jordan for being so candid about his post-football testosterone collapse. More fascinating work on animal behaviour – including studies involving aquatic species and field research in marine and freshwater environments – can be found on his website, The Behavioural Evolution Lab: Max Planck Institute of Animal Behavior (thejordanlab.com).

For the full account of Barcelona's alleged baby boom, see: Montesinos, J., Cortés, J., Arnau, A., Sánchez, J. A., Elmore, M., Macià, N., González, J. A., Santisteve, R., Cobo, E., & Bosch, J.

(2013). 'Barcelona baby boom: Does sporting success affect birth rate?', *BMJ*, 347, f7387.

For the psychological science behind post-defeat comfort eating, see: Cornil, Y., & Chandon, P. (2013). 'From fan to fat? Vicarious losing increases unhealthy eating, but self-affirmation is an effective remedy', *Psychological Science*, 24(10), 1936–46.

Chapter 33: The Bipolar Mind of a Football Fan

Special thanks to Tim McGeever, a lifelong Chelsea supporter with a bipolar diagnosis, who spoke openly about living with the highs and lows of the condition and did not hold back in explaining his feelings about Tottenham fans.

Chapter 34: Bicycle Locks and Broadmoor

Gwen's Reith lectures can be accessed through the BBC website. Her brilliant book *The Devil You Know*, also written by Eileen Horne, is published by Faber & Faber (2022). I first read Gwen's anecdote about Peter Sutcliffe in a *Guardian* article on 19 August 2021, headlined: 'I was a therapist to killers in Broadmoor – and felt "radical empathy" for them.'

The original domestic violence study Gwen cites is here: Kirby, S., Francis, B., & O'Flaherty, R. (2014). 'Can the FIFA World Cup football (soccer) tournament be associated with an increase in domestic abuse?', *Journal of Research in Crime and Delinquency*, 51(3), 259–76. It also features on the Women's Aid website. More analysis from the study's authors can be read on The Conversation website in an article headlined '"If England gets beaten, so will she" – the link between World Cup and violence explained', published 11 July 2018.

Chapter 35: Confessions of a Nine-Year-Old Loser

Many thanks to Derek Farrell for helping me understand the origins of my less-than-graceful losing. His articles are available online, and interviews with him can be found on YouTube.

For more information on EMDR, you can visit the EMDR Association website. Another valuable resource is Mark Brayne's EMDR Focus page.

Apologies to my dad. He has been a model parent in almost every domain. It is only under conditions of competitive stimulus – especially sport and card games (especially 'Slap, Bang, Slosh') – that his character alters.

PART VII: Addicted

Chapter 36: I'm Never Ever Watching Again

Thank you to Dave, Harry, Liam (and Nathan Judah) for keeping me sane – especially Harry Mansell, who appears as prone as me to having meltdowns. You make me feel seen! Their shows can all be found on YouTube.

Chapter 37: The Most Compulsive Sport in the World

It was brilliant to meet Adam, a Liverpool fan, who has to watch football on TV all the time. His book on behavioural addictions is excellent: *Irresistible: The Rise of Addictive Technology and the Business of Keeping Us Hooked* (Penguin, 2017). Thanks also to Paul, the cameraman, for a memorable coffee.

Dr Lanzaro's thoughts are articulated here: Lanzaro, M. (2017). 'A new syndrome? The sport identification addiction and the case of Italian football ultra-fanatical support', *European Psychiatry*, 41(S1), S461.

The following paper was particularly helpful in clarifying some of the evolutionary and neuroscientific threads running through the book, especially those relating to football's unique power as a fan experience: Butler, M., Brar, G., Abed, R., & O'Connell, H. (2025). 'The people's game: Evolutionary perspectives on the behavioural neuroscience of football fandom', *Frontiers in Psychology,* 15: 1517295.

For a fuller account of the juice study, see: Berns, G. S., McClure, S. M., Pagnoni, G., & Montague, P. R. (2001). 'Predictability modulates human brain response to reward', *The Journal of Neuroscience,* 21(8), 2793–8.

You can read more about Rangers fans in brain scanners here: McLean, J., Brennan, D., Wyper, D. J., Condon, B., Hadley, D. M., & Cavanagh, J. (2009). 'Localisation of regions of intense pleasure response evoked by soccer goals', *Psychiatry Research: Neuroimaging,* 171(1), 33–43.

For a thoughtful challenge to the disease model of addiction – and a clearer explanation of dopamine than I could manage – see Marc Lewis's *The Biology of Desire* (PublicAffairs, 2016).

Thanks to David Goldblatt for being a sanity check when Donald Trump hijacked the FIFA Club World Cup. For a sweeping global history of the game, see his book *The Ball Is Round: A Global History of Soccer* (Penguin, 2006). His new book, *Injury Time: Football in a State of Emergency* (HarperCollins Publishers, 2025), is recognised as a *Telegraph* Best Book of 2025.

The cookie jar study can be read here: Worchel, S., Lee, J., & Adewole, A. (1975). 'Effects of supply and demand on ratings of object value', *Journal of Personality and Social Psychology,* 32(5), 906–14.

To read about the role of dopamine in novelty see: Morrens, J., Aydin, C., Janse van Rensburg, A., Esquivelzeta Rabell, J., &

Haesler, S. (2020). 'Cue-evoked dopamine promotes conditioned responding during learning', *Neuron*, 106(1), 142–53.

Chapter 39: Man Seeking Football Widow

Many thanks to Mumsnet founder Justine Roberts for speaking to me about her experience as a football fan. I was particularly taken with her story about telling people she had received a blood transfusion of Kevin Keegan's blood as a baby – hence her lifelong allegiance to Liverpool. She also made me reconsider the tired idea of the 'football widow', which feels increasingly out of date in a game followed by millions of women.

Among other things, Ernesto helped me shed some lingering shame about how bad I was at playing the recorder (it turns out it's a harder instrument than it looks). Thank you for your patience – and for making me laugh.

PART VIII: Let It All Out

Chapter 42: From Cradle to Grave

The full version of Matthew's great blog can be found by searching for an article titled '"Ridiculous Excess": The Emergence of Football Mania' on the *History of Emotions Blog*.

Chapter 43: The Opera Singer Who Tried to Mow Down Forest Fans

Lunch with Mark Glanville was a highlight of this project. I regret not being able to include more of our conversation. His remarkable life is explored in his book *The Goldberg Variations*

(Flamingo, 2016). Thanks to Millwall fan Andy Mulvoy for connecting me with Mark and for his helpful research throughout the project.

Information about the Atlantis Commune and Primal Scream Therapy came from various online sources and the book *They Call Us the Screamers* (Caliban Books, 1980). Well worth a listen is Garrett Carr's documentary *The Silence and the Scream,* which can be found on BBC Sounds.

Chapter 44: Robin the Screamer

Many thanks to Robin de Brea for sending me a copy of *They Call Us the Screamers* and for our enlightening conversation. We've agreed to meet at a Wolves game soon – I hope we do.

For an excellent article on Kingsley Hall and some of its residents, see Sean O'Hagan's article in the *Guardian,* headlined: 'Kingsley Hall: RD Laing's experiment in anti-psychiatry' (2 September 2012).

Brad Bushman's study on catharsis is here: Bushman, B. J. (2002). 'Does venting anger feed or extinguish the flame? Catharsis, rumination, distraction, anger, and aggressive responding', *Personality and Social Psychology Bulletin,* 28(6), 724–31. His excellent TEDx talk on the dangers of getting hangry, *Don't Get Hangry: Feed Your Brain Healthy Food,* is available on YouTube.

To read about how we like to stick pins in voodoo dolls representing our partners, you can read the original study here: Bushman, B. J., DeWall, C. N., Pond, R. S., Jr., & Hanus, M. D. (2014). 'Low glucose relates to greater aggression in married couples', *Proceedings of the National Academy of Sciences of the United States of America,* 111(17), 6254–7.

Chapter 45: Synchrony

Les Back's illuminating podcast on football chanting can be heard on BBC Archive. It is called: *Here We Go! The Art of the Football Chant.*

The original referee study demonstrating how they are swayed by home crowd noise can be read here: Nevill, A. M., Balmer, N. J., & Williams, A. M. (2002). 'The influence of crowd noise and experience upon refereeing decisions in football', *Psychology of Sport and Exercise,* 3(4), 261–72.

For the full review of the impact of Covid-era ghost games on referees, see: Leitner, M. C., Daumann, F., Follert, F. et al. (2023). 'The cauldron has cooled down: A systematic literature review on home advantage in football during the COVID-19 pandemic from a socio-economic and psychological perspective', *Management Review Quarterly,* 73, 605–33.

For those interested in the brain mechanisms behind home advantage, see: Zhang, L., Zhang, H., Li, S., Ding, J., Peng, Y., & Huang, Z. (2022). 'Influence mechanism of the home advantage on referees' decision-making in modern football field: A study from sports neuro-decision science', *Frontiers in Psychology,* 13: 873184.

To read more about why Sunderland's goalkeeper has more testosterone than anyone else, see: Neave, N., & Wolfson, S. (2003). 'Testosterone, territoriality, and the "home advantage"', *Physiology & Behavior,* 78(2), 269–75.

Thank you to Nikita Rathod at Brentford for connecting me with Andy Godfrey. Andy speaks about his experiences on the club's 'Thousands of Stories' page in a piece titled *The Sound.*

You can read more about the fire walk and other rituals in *Ritual: How Seemingly Senseless Acts Make Life Worth Living* (Profile Books, 2022).

For the science behind why shouting at your television is not the same as being in the stands, see: Baranowski-Pinto, G., Profeta, V. L. S., Newson, M., Whitehouse, H., & Xygalatas, D. (2022). 'Being in a crowd bonds people via physiological synchrony', *Scientific Reports*, 12, 613.

For more details about the CPS's position on football-related abuse, you can visit their website and read the article 'CPS cracks down on football tragedy abuse'.

Thanks to the comedian Henning Wehn, with whom I had an enjoyable lunch, and who led me to think about the connection between comedy and football fan behaviour, as well as tribalism. Thanks to Casper Cummins for setting up this lunch.

Chapter 46: Roxy the Brat

Paul's wonderfully titled paper can be read here: Bleakley, P. (2018). 'Football hooliganism, the death drive and Millwall fandom as symbolic masochism', *The Journal of Fandom Studies*, 6(3), 225–41.

My thanks to Roxy for our conversation. If you'd like to read her full essay on football and BDSM, you'll have to venture on to FetLife – as, for research purposes, I did.

You can see Peter Cook, aka Alan Latchley, speaking with Clive Anderson about football as a cruel mistress on YouTube.

Chapter 47: I'm Not OK

The Samaritans video can be found on the Samaritans website. It is called *Together Against Suicide.* The Samaritans number is 116 123.

Chapter 48: Football Saved My Life

Thanks to Richard for his candour and his positive message about the profound impact of football. Tatter Travels has a website.

I'd also like to acknowledge Forest Green Rovers Football Club – especially Dale Vince – for providing free tickets to a match and a lovely lunch and introducing me to MP Dr Simon Opher, who is prescribing football tickets instead of anti-depressants, and Niels Beier, who also spoke to me about his experience of depression and how football has helped, as did Sally Hayward.

Epilogue: Harry's Story

Since speaking with her, Maria's campaign to improve safety standards on trucks and small lorries has achieved remarkable results. It has led to the Driver and Vehicle Standards Agency (DVSA) updating its load security guidance, and she has met with senior politicians and police officers to prevent similar tragedies. She has gone out with police officers to speak directly to drivers with unsecured loads, telling them her story – some were reduced to tears. It is hard to ignore a mother standing in front of you explaining exactly what an unsecured load can do.

Note on Jack Grealish

I made several attempts to speak with Jack Grealish, including through his agent and his clubs at the time of writing, but I imagine he receives thousands of requests. I hope that, despite my own tribal allegiances, I have portrayed him in a fair and positive light.